Amish Life through a Child's Eyes

Best Wishes
Alma Hershberger
7-10-90

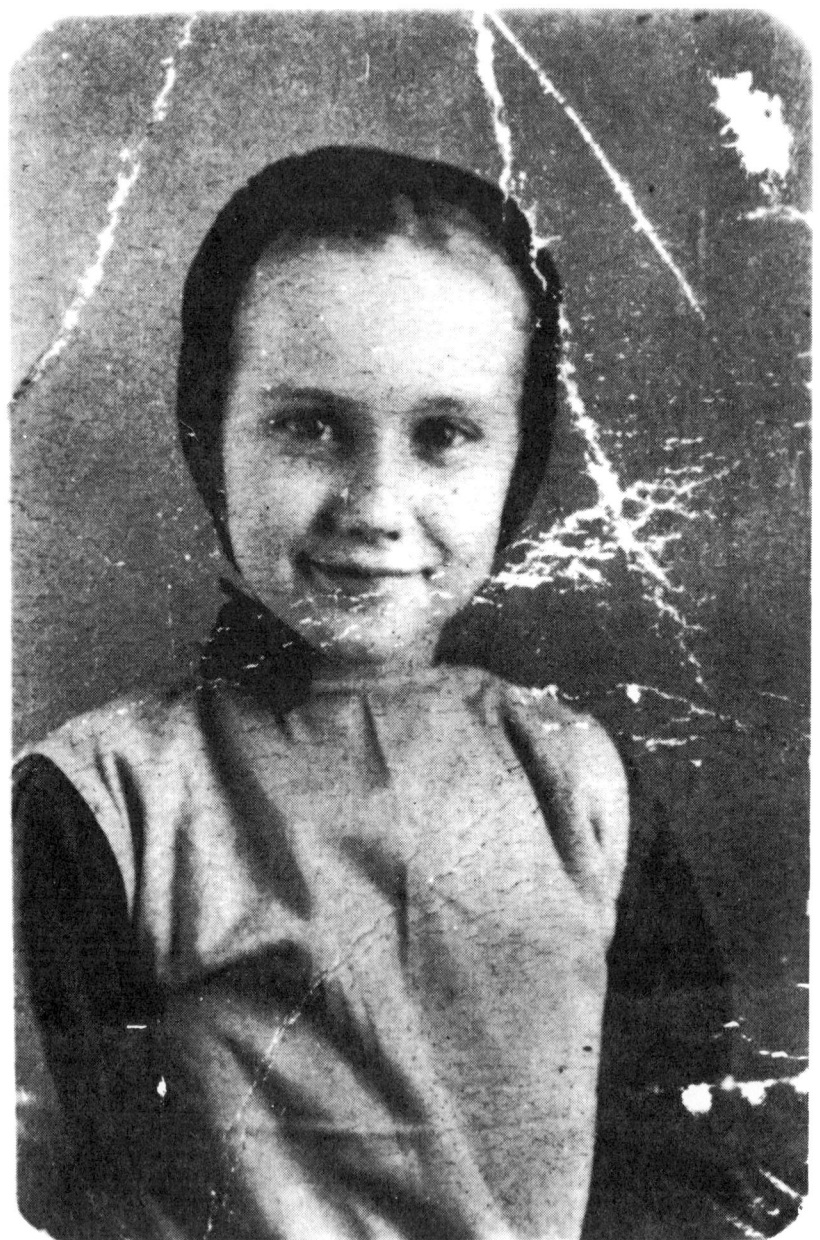

Amish Life through a Child's Eyes

A Unique Experience in Amish Life

Alma Hershberger

Illustrated by Joe Rush

VANTAGE PRESS
New York / Atlanta
Los Angeles / Chicago

FIRST EDITION

All rights reserved, including the right of reproduction in whole or in part in any form.

Copyright © 1987 by Alma Hershberger

Published by Vantage Press, Inc.
516 West 34th Street, New York, New York 10001

Manufactured in the United States of America
ISBN: 0-533-07310-3

Library of Congress Catalog Card No.: 86-91787

To my dear mother
and my oldest brother

Amish Life through a Child's Eyes is based on true journals and family histories passed down through the years. This is my journal of events in the Amish tradition.

A.T.H.

Contents

Introduction xi

The Move to Iowa 1
Father's Accident 5
Visitation 14
Uncle Judas's Influence 23
The Farm 31
Planting and Harvesting 37
School Days 47
The Stranger 55
Junior: All Boy! 59
Stories at the Dinner Table 67
Lizbet and I in Foster Homes 73
Sickness Strikes 77
Where There Is a Will There Is a Way 81
Electrical Storm 87
Billy Goat Rough 93
Bottomless Hole 99
Mischief 107
Hunting Season 113
The Missing Dresses 119
Old-fashioned Winter 125
Eli's Disappearance 133
Shunning 139
Leaving Iowa 145
Epilogue 150

Introduction

The Amish are people who take pride in their country and their freedom and take great interest in their farmland. The Amish lead a very plain life and live quietly in their own community. They believe in God. However, their religion is based on their tradition. They believe you are to be different from the world. Tradition is handed down from the past. You should do as your forefathers did. My mother always said, "Love your enemies" (Luke 6:35) and "Judge not others; then you won't be judged" (Luke 6:37).

My family takes great interest in their heritage. They compiled a book going from our ancestors of 1763 to 1979.

My mother's last family book was compiled by Laura (Stutzman) Gingerich in 1979 and titled *Stutzman History Steps from Switzerland*.

My father's family book was compiled by Mr. and Mrs. Eli Mast in May 1975. In the beginning it gave a little history.

The stars fell in 1833. My father's family book explained how the men and women awoke about at eleven o'clock one night. They awoke their children to see a display that alarmed them. They thought the whole atmosphere was burning. The children were too young to understand and weren't afraid.

The night was as quiet as death. There wasn't a breath of wind. The stars fell in the manner of a heavy snow falling. Every star, large and small, was falling straight down. They couldn't see any of them hit the earth. The believers and nonbelievers thought this was the end of the world. They all got down on their knees and prayed. The display lasted for two hours.

History is passed on from our ancestors to families of today. My uncles compiled a book titled *The Troyer Team*. This book tells how their family moved to Oklahoma when they were young boys. In the depression, Grandpa lost their farm. The boys built a wagon, and Grandpa made a map of the way to Oklahoma. The boys each had a wagon with a team of horses. Since there was no money to move, they followed each other, like a wagon train. One wagon hauled the hay for the boys to feed the horses every night. Another hauled grain. One had the household goods, and another wagon had the wagon wheel grease, the blankets, and the food that Grandma had made for them to eat on the eight-day trip. This trip was made from Kansas to Oklahoma.

The largest Amish settlements are in Indiana, Ohio, Illinois, and Pennsylvania. Due to the overcrowding of settlements and the mixed feelings toward their tradition, the Amish have moved to other states. To my knowledge there are settlements in every state except Alaska and Hawaii. There are two settlements in Canada. These two settlements are thirty-five miles apart. However, there is a settlement in South America, too.

My family decided to move to Iowa in the winter, January of 1943. The story of *Amish Life through a Child's Eyes* is the history of my Amish family's experience from 1943 through 1951. My family didn't realize that their trials and tribulations were just beginning for the entire family when they made the move to Iowa. In 1951 my family decided to leave the hard life in Iowa. This was Mother's way to keep the family together.

When I was an eleven-year-old Amish girl, a vision flashed through my head. It was as if a voice was saying, *Write a book about your life in Iowa.* I asked, "Write a book about Iowa? But how? I don't even know how to begin." As the time went by, I could never forget that moment.

Some years later, I talked to my family about the book and asked them what they thought of the idea. They didn't say too much at first. Later, my oldest sister asked me not to write about our life. I asked her why. She said, "You still have brothers with the Amish, and it may make hard feelings. You would't want to do that, would you?" She didn't understand that this idea had nothing to do with my family still being Amish.

I want everyone who reads this book to realize that I love my brothers and sisters dearly and I'm proud of each and every one of them. Remember, the Amish community of Buchanan County was unique. And this famiy was a unique one among the Amish. Once you start to read the story, you'll see what I mean.

I kept asking myself, *Why do I feel that I am supposed to write this book? Why me? I must write it even if it's against my family's wishes.* My book began to be an obsession with me.

This is a true story. Some names have been changed to protect my family's privacy.

You may find that my writing is a little backward, as I am an Amish woman. But really it's correct; it's just that you English people are a little backward with your language.

Amish Life through a Child's Eyes

The Move to Iowa

About the first thing I remember was the move from Oklahoma to Iowa. I was three years old and had six brothers and sisters when we packed up and moved. I was the sixth child born to my mother, and I was named after my aunt, Alma Hershberger. At that time, our family consisted of: Jonas, age 11, born November 23, 1932; Eli, age 9, born January 9, 1934; Sarah, age 8, born August 18, 1935; Enos, age 5, born August 14, 1938; Alma, age 3, born February 25, 1940; Lizbet, age 2, born April 6, 1941; and Junior, age 6 months, born July 30, 1942.

We moved in the winter, after the crops had been harvested in the fall. We moved by train. At the time, my older brother Jonas was eleven years old. He was an ambitious boy with light brown hair and blue eyes. He and my father herded the livestock into cattle cars. All our household goods and personal belongings were crated and moved in boxcars. Mother, the girls, and the younger children rode in the coach while Father and the older brothers rode in the cattle car.

I can't remember much about that trip, only that the train went very fast and a man in a blue suit with a funny cap checked with Mom to make sure everything was all right. Mom's brother, Uncle Judas, and her sister, Aunt Pauline, both farmers, had come, along with Uncle Henry, to meet us at the train station. Uncle Henry was Mom's brother, too, and he was a minister in the Amish church.

According to our family history book, my father's Amish ancestor Samuel Mueller arrived in America, from Canton Berns, Switzerland, in a ship with Capt. Charles

Smith. The ship landed in Philadelphia on November 1, 1763, with 193 passengers.

My mother's ancestor Jacob Ammann came to America from Switzerland in 1749. Jacob Ammann was known to be one of the founders of the Amish settlement in Hertzel, Pennsylvania.

The Amish families that left Switzerland were looking for a free country where they might live and worship according to their own beliefs, without restrictions.

However, at that time none of the Amish men were bishops. Through mail, Mr. Jacob Ammann, from the Old Country, was nominated as their first bishop. Traditionally, when the Amish need a preacher, the Amish members nominate several men from the congregation on one Sunday and then in two weeks they take the same number of songbooks and place a piece of paper in one of them. Whoever receives the book with the paper is the chosen one.

The Amish hold church service in their homes. When the congregation grows too large for their houses, they divide the congregation. They pinpoint the center of the Amish community and draw a line from west to east and south to north. The ones who live in the western section belong to the West Church, those in the east belong to the East Church, and so on. This rule is used all over the United States. In some communities you may find a Middle Church necessary when the four "directional" congregations grow too large.

In Buchanan County, Iowa, we had three churches. My family belonged to the West Church. Church services started at nine o'clock and lasted until one in the afternoon. Dinner was served after the service and consisted of peanut butter and jelly on bread, with pickles and red beets placed on a large platter, so everyone could reach and help themselves. The people in our new church were all very nice to us, but their ways were different from what we were used to.

In Iowa, the men's church shirts were made of all-white cotton material. The style was open just enough to get the head through, with long sleeves and about three hooks and eyes sewed on instead of buttons to close it. The white shirt was worn with a black suit and vest. The boys' hats were made out of black wool with extra wide brims. The watergate of the pants had buttons instead of a zipper. (Watergate is a nickname for the slacks opening, what the English call the fly.)

The Oklahoma clothes didn't fit into the Iowa style because they were made to conform to the body. Iowans' clothes are looser. To the Iowa Amish eyes, Oklahoma clothes were immodest.

The church people told Mom and Dad they could change their clothing style as we wore our clothes out and then replace the Oklahoma style with Iowa style. Six months after we moved to Iowa, we were told we would have to get rid of our Oklahoma clothes and dress as the Iowans did. The material was to be a solid dark color and made of cotton.

Father was able to rent a vacant farm about four miles from the one we bought. The farm we bought needed some work to get it ready for us to move in, so we lived on a rented farm temporarily. Dad wanted our new home done in time for us before it was time to work in the fields.

When we pulled up to the new house, everything felt so strange. I wished Mom could have told Dad to turn around and take us back home. The vacant farmhouse had a big front porch with lots of glass windows, and if I stood on my tippy-toes, I could just about see out. On our first day at the new house, many Amish people came to help Mom unpack. They stayed until it was time to do their evening chores. So we made a lot of friends that day.

There are no other denominations in Buchanan except for the English people. According to the Amish, the English people in Buchanan were the only people who don't speak the Amish language.

I slept with my two other sisters. Lizbet, who is fourteen months younger than I, was a slender girl with black hair. Sarah, who was eight, has blond hair and a fair complexion, with blue eyes. She thought she should have her own bed. Mom said sleeping together was a good way of keeping warm, so we didn't really mind it so much.

There was a lot of work to be done at the new farm, so I came to miss my father and brothers very much. They were gone before I woke up in the morning, and we didn't get to see them until suppertime. Stories at the supper table were always fun, because the boys would tell us how things were coming on the new farm. We were also looking forward to moving in, not realizing that the trials and tribulations were just beginning for the family.

Father's Accident

The Wapsipinicon River, with woods on both sides, ran across Buchanan County from the southeast to the northwest, through our ninety-four-acre farm. It ran along the far south side of our land, running east and west and making a turn at the far west end, running north. The river was about a quarter-mile from the house and outbuildings.

Behind the outbuildings we had a natural running creek traveling southeast like a snake through the barnyard and woods, emptying into the river. The river and the creek had its low and high banks.

Dad and the boys had about four miles to go back and forth from the new farm. On the first day of March 1944, the ground was still covered with snow. Dad hitched a team of horses to the old box bobsled and loaded the two-man timber saw and ax. He left with my brothers to go to the new farm to cut firewood, using methods that had not changed since the days of the early American settlers.

While Dad and my brothers were cutting firewood, the sun came out and the snow disappeared, leaving the roads covered with patches of ice. When Dad and the boys had the sled loaded and came out of the shaded woods and into the sun, the snow was too far gone to try to take the heavily loaded sled over the melted roads. They parked the loaded sled and unhitched the team of draft horses.

Dad lifted the two boys, age ten and eleven, up on one horse and jumped on the other horse. They started back home with the team, riding by holding onto the har-

ness. They had traveled for two miles when they came to a farm at a curve. Father's horse slipped on the ice-covered road and fell on top of my father. Father's horse tried to get up but slipped again. With Father still astride, the horse went back down again, falling on Father's leg and thumping Father's head down on the icy road. The boys immediately jumped off their horse and ran to the house for assistance. They helped Father to the house and called the doctor. Father was the type that didn't believe in X rays or hospitals. He was just too stubborn to go.

By the first of April, we were able to move to our new farm, but Father's leg continued to give him trouble. His phsyical problems seemed to be changing his mental attitude. He went into a depressed state of mind. He claimed there were men in the woods coming after him. Then he began showing suicidal tendencies.

One day my brother Jonas was on his horse ready to go after the cows when Dad stopped him and said, "I'll go." My brother gave him the horse, and Dad went to the woods. However, he didn't come back. Finally, Mom decided to send the boys down into the woods to see if they could find him. Soon the boys came running back and reported, "Dad's sitting down on the riverbank with his shoes off, hanging his feet in the river. He's looking into the water and saying, 'Look at the little devils in there. Little devils are all over. It's full of little devils.' " Later Dad came back without the cows. Then Brother went after the cows. Another day, Sister Sarah was standing at the windmill when she saw Father walking toward her from the barn. Unaware of our father's disturbed state of mind, she walked over and hugged his leg and started to say something. "Shh," he said. "Everybody will hear you."

"Who will hear me?"

"Everyone in the world will hear you."

She looked around, but didn't see anyone. As a nine-year-old child, she couldn't understand that statement and was silent. Soon she left in silence.

Mother knew she had to do something, but what and how was a problem. She tried to cope with Dad and wouldn't say anything to anyone about what was happening until one Sunday when our entire family was humiliated by Father's strange behavior.

Typically, on Sunday morning, our family had a brief devotion and prayer meeting at home before leaving for church. This one Sunday morning when it was time to have prayer, Dad started from the beginning of the prayer book that he used. The book was in German, and we were on our knees for an hour. Our time was running out, and we were going to be late for church services.

Mom realized what was happening, so she interfered. "Glen, you can't go through that whole book; we'll be late." He wouldn't stop. Soon Mom got to her feet and said, "Come, children, eat your breakfast." We all followed Mom quietly to the kitchen, leaving Dad still on his knees. Soon he followed.

After breakfast, Mom suggested, "We are an hour late; why don't we skip church today?"

"No, we're going to church," Dad replied.

We went to church, and how embarrassed the family was to arrive at midmorning. Church started at 9:00 A.M. and was over at 1:00 P.M. After service, Mom tried to explain and had a long talk with her brother, Uncle Judas, about Dad's attitude.

Uncle Judas went to Independence to see what could be done. Independence was the closest city, about fifteen miles from the farm. When Uncle Judas returned, my mother was faced with some very difficult decisions to make. She began to realize that if she hoped to find help for my father, she would be forced to seek this help outside our Amish community. Amish people value their independence and do not believe in involving governmental agencies in their lives. My mother also knew she was three months pregnant. How could she manage her family without the help of her husband if he was not at home?

Time passed for a while without any major incidents. My sister Annie was born and was still a tiny infant when a terrifying event occurred in my mother's life. One night after she went to bed, she sensed something coming toward her and ducked her head. She felt my father's fist going into the pillow, hitting the headboard and barely missing her head.

Another day, Father hitched the horse to the buggy and said, "I have to go to Joe Miller's." Joe lived across the river and was the bishop of our church. When Father arrived there, he didn't know what he wanted anymore.

Uncle Paul and Aunt Pauline's farm was on the east side of our farm. We were next-door neighbors about one fourth-mile away. They began to realize that something was wrong with my father. Sometimes Dad would take off running into the woods and then he would be on Aunt Pauline's doorstep. They would ask him, "What are you doing?" He wouldn't know what he was doing there or what he wanted.

Uncle Judas and Aunt Pauline wanted Mom to take Dad to a doctor, but there was no way Dad would go. As I said before, he was too stubborn. However, Uncle Judas heard about a special doctor in Waterloo, Iowa. So he came to see Mom. He asked, "Would you be interested in taking Glen to see a special doctor?"

"Ja."

"But how are you going to get him to go?"

"I don't know."

"Why don't we ask Sister Pauline and her husband Paul if they would go and the three couples would go together? Pretend that everyone needs a check-up?"

"I'll go see if they agree."

"All right."

Soon Uncle Judas came back and told Mom that the others would go. They made arrangements for the three couples to go see the doctor. When they arrived, Uncle Judas and his wife Tilly went in first. This gave Uncle Judas the opportunity to explain Glen's ways to the doctor before Dad and Mom went in. Then Paul and Pauline were called in. When it was time for Mom and Dad, the doctor wanted to examine Dad.

Dad said, "She's the one that's sick; nothing's wrong with me. You check her."

They all left disappointed. Uncle Paul was still afraid of his mentally disturbed brother-in-law living on a farm next to his. Now what could they do?

By now, Mom had the new baby, Annie. Mom knew she had to watch Dad to make sure he didn't hurt one of the children or even himself. Tension grew very strong in our home. Sometimes my father would get up throughout the night and Mom would have to check him. The guns were put away, along with the sharp knives.

More and more, my father was losing touch with reality. In Iowa, we had red fox season and the men would get together during this time for fox hunting in the evening. Out of season, Dad sent Brother Eli to the neighbors and to Uncle Judas, to tell them that he wanted them to come over to go fox hunting. Everyone but Dad, of course, realized it was not red fox season.

Uncle Judas went again to call the doctor to plead with him to come out and check Glen.

"Is he sick in bed?" the doctor asked, knowing about Dad's condition.

"No."

"Well, if you can't make him come in and if he's not sick in bed, there is nothing I can do for him."

Uncle Judas had to go to the police about the problem. They said they would pick Dad up at the house.

The neighbors came over that night, and Uncle Judas notified the church congregation that Glen would be picked up that night. The neighbor men were out fox hunting, and they were called in. We had company. Uncle Judas informed Mom of what he had done. The church members and family came to lend their moral support.

After supper, as the women were doing the dishes, I saw a car coming down the road. I watched the car until it passed the house. The car pulled up in the driveway, turned around, and stopped.

Two men in plainclothes stepped out of the vehicle and asked the boys in the yard, "Is this where Glen Hershberger lives?"

"*Ja*," was the reply from the group.

The men came to the house, and someone opened the door for them to step inside.

"Mom, two guys are here," I said.

"Is Glen Hershberger here?" one man asked.

"Yes," Mother answered.

"Where is he?"

"He's in the living room."

The man looked in and asked, "Which one is he?"

"The one with the little one sleeping on his lap."

The men went to the door and asked, "Is Glen here?"

"Yeah," he answered, standing up to place the baby on the daybed and walking toward them.

"We came to pick you up; will you go with us?"

"Yeah," he answered and led the way to their car without saying anything to anyone as he left.

The gentleman asked Mom if she had a way to get to Independence in the morning. If she didn't, they would come and pick her up and bring her back again. She had to go in to sign some papers to transfer Dad to the state hospital in the morning. She thanked the gentleman and told them that she would be there. They asked her not to visit my father at the new hospital until they notified her that it would be all right. The gentleman left the house to join his friend, who was waiting in the car with Dad.

The room was silent after the man left. I think everyone was surprised that my father left voluntarily. None of the guests seemed to know what to say.

Then one of the Amish men broke the silence in the quiet room. "Well, we'd better head for home. Katie, if you need help, let us know."

Uncle Judas spoke. "I'll have my boys help you with the farm," he said.

When all the guests had gone, Mother said, "We'd better go to bed so we can get up in the morning."

We children were sad that Father had to leave. We all obeyed in silence, hoping there would be help for Father in Independence. We all thought he would be well and back home again soon.

Visitation

Three months dragged by. Mother was finally permitted to visit the hospital to see Dad and check on his progress. His condition would vary from visit to visit. Sometimes he was quite rational, and other times he wasn't too good.

As time passed, the little ones wouldn't eat their food. Mother tried to coax, but they would only sit at their place crying, asking for their father. The older ones had to brace themselves and looked at us younger ones with courage to be strong. At times likes this, it was always silent, except for the one that cried. Our wordless eye contacts did most of our talking across the table for us. Sometimes we had to swallow twice to stay in control. It was hard to explain to the ones who were too young to understand. We all longed for our father to be home.

Mother contacted the hospital and made arrangements to bring the little ones in for visitation. Since all the children were minors, she had to get permission from the hospital before bringing them in to visit.

On the Saturday morning of the first scheduled visit, Mother told the older boys to get the family team and buggy ready for the trip to the state hospital. "We are going to see your father today," she said. It was the first trip to Independence for the young ones. We were in store for a new adventure.

We had traveled about ten miles when Mother pulled into a farmer's yard. A friendly middle-aged farmer's wife, with brown hair and a bib apron, walked out to greet us. Mother stepped from the buggy and met her halfway. Mother asked, "May we give our horses some water, please?"

"Sure! Just pull over there to the windmill by the water tank."

Mother thanked her, and we watered our horses and continued on toward Independence.

We came to a racetrack with rows of bleachers. There were men exercising horses pulling two-wheeled carts around the track. We children really admired the beaufiful sight. After we passed the track, we came to our first paved street as we entered the city limits. With two horses pulling the rig, we passed along Main Street. The children's eyes were open wide. The city and its sights were a novel experience for young Amish children.

Past the center of town, Mother turned left onto a side street. We noticed a large building high on a hilltop.

I said, "Oh! Mom, look at the big beautiful place up there."

"*Ja*, that's where your father's at."

"Oh! Really? It's beautiful!"

"*Ja*, it is."

She turned onto the paved drive that cut through a huge yard surrounded by beautiful trees on either side. When we reached the building at the end of the drive, a gentleman came out to meet us. He reached to clutch the horses by the reins while we stepped out of the buggy. Mother thanked him and found a spot to tie the horses to a fence post. Like a mother hen with her baby chicks behind her, my mother led us into the building.

Oh, how excited we were to see Father again! I remember, when we went inside, how I admired those large hallways with the open stairways to the second floor.

Mother stopped at the desk. "We are here to see Glen Hershberger," she said.

They sent us to the second floor. As we went upstairs, I noticed the beautiful chandeliers hanging from the ceiling. To a young Amish girl, this was a most beautiful sight. At the top of the stairs, we turned left through double doors to the first room on the right. In the small room was a large window, a bed, a dresser, and a chair. This was Dad's room. Someone went to the recreation room to fetch him as we waited with excitement. Soon Dad came in and took a chair across from Mother while we children sat on his bed opposite them.

We visited for a while, and, of course, Junior, who was a toddler, became restless. He climbed up on the bed and walked to the window to look outside. Father stood up and quickly grabbed him off the bed and spanked him. Junior cried. Mother took him in her arms and sat him on her lap. Soon Mother said, "We have to go." She feared we were upsetting Father.

On our way home, we stopped at the same farm to give our horses some water. No one had much to say all the way home.

A couple of weeks later, Mother received word that Dad had left the hospital on his own. They had found him downtown. When they picked him up, he had bought a poison of some kind. Since then, they were keeping him locked up for a while in a ward. Later we received word he was doing better again and was able to move around the hospital grounds.

We visited him several more times at the hospital. One time he was sitting out in the yard on a bench under a shade tree while most of the others were inside watching television. Another time when we arrived they said he wasn't in.

Mother asked, "Where is he?"

"He's out helping make hay."

They called him in from the field on a radio. We walked to the barnyard fence. We could see Dad coming toward us in good spirits. We visited for a while and left.

The visits with Dad helped Mother cope with the pressure when the children missed their father and wanted him home.

One summer day we received word that Dad was released from the hospital for two weeks for a vacation at home. When we received word, Mother directed, "Jonas and Eli, you hide the gun."

"Where do you want us to hide it?" Jonas asked. Eli listened attentively.

"Where do you think would be a good place?" she asked.

Eli suggested, "In the haymow."

"No, it has to be where he won't go. He may help throw hay down and find it there."

"Should we put it upstairs under our bed?"

"No, he surely would find it in the house. It can't be in the house or barn."

Everybody was nervous and started to think hard. Hiding the gun in the buggy shed or at the blacksmith's wasn't a good idea.

Someone suggested, "How about the ditch across the road?" Everybody agreed.

Someone asked, "What if he goes after the mail?"

"We'll put it in the deep part where the weeds are, and we'll have to make sure we go after the mail before he does."

When we picked up Dad, they told Mom, "Now if you have any trouble, you may bring him back before his two weeks are up." We were happy that Dad was coming home, but we were all nervous, not knowing how he really was going to be for two weeks. We had already had him home several times just for the weekend, and he was always ready to go back to his second home at the end of the weekend. We had to watch him very closely, and it was a strain on all of us.

On the first day, Dad was glad to be home. He was in good spirits. The second day, he walked to the kerosene barrel and saw the lock on it. He started to talk to himself and giggle. He walked to the blacksmith shop to get the hammer and came back and knocked the lock off with one strike. Then he picked up a tin can and filled it with kerosene.

Mom and we children were standing inside the house watching Dad. We were astonished to see him break the lock so easily, and we were all concerned. He destroyed it as fast as a blink of an eye.

Mom expressed, "Oh, na!"

One of the children asked, "What is he going to do with the kerosene?"

Then there was dead silence. Dad started to walk toward the barn.

Mom said, "Stay here," and she followed him. When she caught up with him, he was out behind the barn.

She asked, "What are you going to do, Glen?"

Dad looked at her and brought the can up to his mouth to take a drink. Mom quickly reached out and knocked it out of his hand, spilling it to the ground. He started back to get more, talking and laughing to himself. He filled the can and went to the house.

Mom stated firmly, "If you don't put that down, I'll take you back where I picked you up at." He looked at her and she commanded him, "Give the can to me." He handed it to her peacefully. We all were silent and scared for what might happen. We all knew he had more strength than we all had put together. After this incident, he was quiet again for that day.

Several days later, Dad asked, "Where is the gun?"

"The gun isn't here," Mom answered.

Dad walked out to the road toward the mailbox. We all watched in silence and fear.

Eli went outside quickly and said, "Dad, I got the mail already."

Dad didn't say anything.

Eli repeated, "Dad, I got the mail."

Dad stopped and looked at him, then answered, "Oh, you got the mail already."

"*Ja.*"

Then Dad started to talk again and walked in the road, looking across the fields. We didn't dare say any more, for Father might suspect something. We could relax again when Father walked away without seeing the gun.

When my mother was only thirty-two years old, I noticed her hair was almost all white.

One afternoon it was quiet around the house. Mom checked to see where Dad and we children were. She saw Dad standing at the northeast corner of the barn with a long lead pipe in his hand. He was beating at something, but she couldn't see what. She looked to see where we children were, but couldn't see any of us around. She was breathless. I can only imagine what horrid thoughts went through her head. She quickly walked around the northwest side of the barn to see what Dad was beating at. She saw we were standing in fear by the creek behind the barn watching him beating the corner post.

With relief, she said softly, "*Kinder*" (children), getting our attention. We looked. She said, "Come this way." We all went to her while keeping an eye on Dad.

Mom decided she couldn't keep an eye on Dad for two weeks. The horse and buggy was hitched up to take Dad back to his second home.

This was hard on Mom, as well as for the rest of the

family. We felt guilty taking my dad back early. We also hated being without a man in charge in our family. It was up to us all to do the farming and keep us in food and clothes.

Two years later, the doctors asked Mother to transfer my father to Davenport State Hospital for testing. Davenport was much farther from our home, but the doctors thought Dad would get better treatment there. They wanted to see what was causing his condition, because they still didn't know. They had given him as much treatment as they were able to with the knowledge they had.

Mother made arrangements to have Dad transferred. Two weeks after he was transferred, we received word that the doctors wanted to talk to Mother. They thought they might have found what was causing the problem.

Mother state, "Good! Maybe we can get this problem solved."

We couldn't believe the doctors knew already what was wrong. We were excited. Mother left early in the morning, and all the children stayed at home, anxiously awaiting word of what the problem was and what could be done.

Chores were done and supper was on the table, but Mother wasn't home yet. We didn't wait on her, because we didn't know what time she would be home. While we were at the table, she opened the door. She gave us her friendly smile and came inside.

"What did they have to say about Dad?" Jonas asked.

"Well, they claim he received a pinched nerve in his lower back, a nerve that is connected to his spinal cord. This was caused from the accident he had."

"Will they be able to correct it?"

"Well, they are going to try."

While my father was in Davenport Iowa State Hospital

for two years, Mother made arrangements to take the children to visit him only once. It was so far away, we couldn't make the trip to see him very often. We had to get someone with an automobile to take us to Davenport, and that cost money that we just didn't have.

Arrangements were made to visit Dad in Davenport. We all went and we were taken on a tour through the hospital. It was a fascinating experience for us. They had a large room with every part of the human body on display. The skulls lined up on shelves and the skeletons in rows made a gruesome sight. However, the cadavers that still grew hair and nails were so grotesque that it left an indelible impression on our minds. This array of horror would leave any child with a chilling memory, but especially for young Amish children, who normally lead such sheltered lives, this experience was unforgettable.

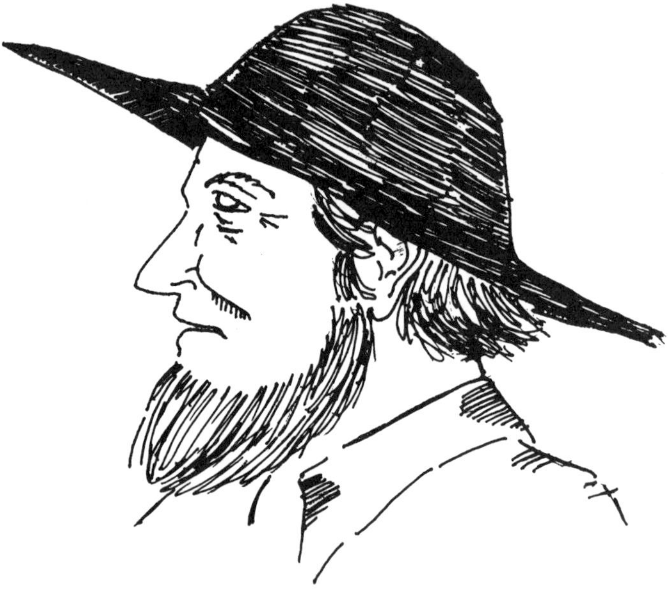

Uncle Judas's Influence

A father with seven children under twelve years plus a wife with a newborn has a lot of responsibility. However, our father had been admitted to the hospital and all his responsibility now fell onto our mother. She had her hands doubly full with the farm, children, and her own duties.

Mom would get up at 4:30 A.M. to build a fire in the old iron cooking stove. Then she would get the boys up to get the cows ready for milking. While the boys got the cows ready and did the other chores, she placed the iron skillet on the stove, and sliced and placed the cooked cornmeal in the pan to fry while she went to the barn to milk a cow by hand. After one cow was done, she ran to the house to turn her mush over to fry the opposite side and called the girls to get up. Then she went back to milk another cow. The boys continued their milking until all the cows were done.

The milk was carried to the house to be separated. A separator is a machine that separates the cream from the milk. The cream would run into a five-gallon can to be shipped away. A milk truck would pick it up. The milk would run into a five-gallon bucket and then be carried to the pigs. A dish for the dog and cats would be filled as well. While the milk was being separated, the smaller children would get an empty glass and run to fill it with warm, fresh milk and drink it.

After all the chores were done, we had breakfast at 7:15 A.M. On school days we left the house at 8:00 A.M. In the evening the younger children helped to milk in Mom's place.

However, our daily duties weren't Mother's only problems. She received a letter from state authorities saying that they wanted to see her concerning Father's expenses and who was to take care of them.

Mom and Dad didn't have any insurance because the Amish people did not believe in having insurance with insurance companies, as most people do today. The Amish believe in taking care of their own.

Mom learned that she had a bigger problem yet. She and Dad didn't have a will made. Since there was no will made out, it was necessary to appoint a guardian to take care of Dad's money. Mom couldn't use his money for the family. The family was to stay on the farm. That was in our favor. The state agreed to take care of part of the expenses, and the Amish congregation picked up the remainder.

Mom's brother, Uncle Judas, was a tall man with dark eyes and hair, who lived one mile across the field. He tried to help her make decisions in respect to her husband's finances. Eventually she gave this responsibility entirely to him. In retrospect, I still don't understand why my uncle did the things he did in his role as family advisor. When the money was turned over to him, he not only took Father's share, he took Mother's also. He told Mom he would get our groceries as we needed them.

Father had had the outbuildings remodeled and painted before we moved to the farm. Father's dream was to do the house at a later date. But he was hospitalized before he was able to complete this.

The first year that Father was hospitalized, the Amish community helped Mom and the boys farm. After the first year, it began to be old hat and help came more and more seldom. However, Mom and the boys continued the farming on their own.

My oldest brother, Jonas, was in fourth grade when Mother took him out of school to help her on the farm. The second boy was Eli, and he went through the fifth grade before Mom took him out to help Jonas. They had to grow up fast and work extra hard for young boys their age.

When Uncle Judas was appointed Father's guardian, he volunteered to take Mom's share of the money along with Dad's. When we needed groceries, Uncle Judas took it upon himself to buy flour, sugar, yeast, Karo syrup, baking powder, soda, salt, oatmeal, and cornmeal. Anything else we had to raise and cold pack and then store away for the winter season. Sometimes his calculations were off and we ended up with too much or too little of important staples.

One family in Indiana heard of our plight and offered to help. They wrote to the Amish newspaper *The Budget*, printed in Sugarcreek, Ohio. It circulated among the Amish communities in the country. They started a money shower, asking people to send some money to help the family.

However, Uncle Judas saw this plea for help in the paper. He began coming over to the house every day when it was time for the mailman. He even had the nerve to meet the mailman at his mailbox and asked him if he wouldn't leave my mother's mail at his box. The mailman, of course, refused.

Uncle Judas came over regularily to check with Mother to see if she received any money from the shower. One day for instance, she had received three letters. He asked her for them. She turned them over to him like a little girl obeying her father. My mother didn't say much at first. However, when she needed money and Uncle Judas refused, then she really was upset and complained. She told us children what he was doing. She was upset because she couldn't even get Jell-O or a box of tapioca for a special dish once in a while. She couldn't understand what the shower money had to do with Dad's money. Why was Uncle Judas doing this to us?

Uncle Judas carefully confiscated all the envelopes that contained money for the family. Mother didn't get one cent from that shower! She never did know how much was sent to her or where it came from.

In the spring of that year, some cows and heifers had calves. One calf grew up to be a grade-A bull. Uncle Judas offered Mother twenty-five dollars for the bull. This upset Mother because she knew he was worth more than that. Another farmer had offered her eighty-five dollars. She told Uncle Judas she wasn't interested in selling it.

Mother had to buy eye blinders for the bull, because he was dangerous. When we were told to go after the cows, we were afraid of him. He would charge us girls if we weren't careful. We always tried to sneak up behind the herd and get the cows moving before he spotted us. Sometimes he would lift his head up to try to look under his blinders to see who or what was coming toward him. Then we would run with everything that was in us.

The bull was such a danger to us that Mother decided to sell him for the best offer. Two weeks after she sold him, Uncle Judas found out about it. He came over and asked Mother for the money from the sale of the bull.

"I don't have any money," she told him.

"What did you do with it?"

"I can take care of my own business."

He couldn't understand what she did with it and left. Mother wasn't the kind of woman that would argue. However, she had decided it just wasn't any of his business.

What my mother wanted to do was finish Father's

dream. It was always Father's dream to have a porch built onto the southeast end of the house. When Mother decided she was going to complete his dream, she ran into trouble. She still blames our Uncle Judas.

Following the sale of the bull, my mother went to Independence and deposited the money from the sale in a bank, even though it was against the Amish tradition. Our Amish community didn't believe that you should collect interest on money, because you didn't earn it from labor. But in our case, this was a last resort, since Mother was determined to keep the family together and complete Father's dream. We lived by the axiom, "Where there is a will, there is a way." Mother had the will to keep the family together, and she decided to do it any way she could.

The Amish in our settlement were only allowed to earn up to as much money as would not obligate them to pay federal income taxes. Now that Mother had deposited the money in the bank, she would not have it readily available to give to her brother in case he should ask for it, and she didn't have to lie about it either. This was the easiest way, since he was constantly overstepping the boundaries of his authority.

Mother ordered the porch materials from a lumberyard in Independence. She said she would pay for it when she picked it up. The day she was supposed to pick up the material, she couldn't get to town. She asked her modern friend from Littleton if she would pick it up for her. Her friend said she would be more than happy to pick it up.

Mother paid for the material on her next trip to Independence. Soon after, Mother realized she had forgotten to order the entrance door. She asked her friend if she would order the door for her when she went to town. A few days later, the lady stopped over and said the man at the lumberyard claimed they were not allowed to extend credit to Katie Hershberger.

Mother's friend asked her, "When you went to town, you paid for the other material, didn't you?"

"Yes, I did."

It was then that Mother realized her brother had probably said something. She needed the door, so she hitched up the horse and buggy and drove into Independence to get the door and pay for it. When she arrived home, she stated, "Judas probably couldn't figure out how I was able to get the material. Well, where there is a will there is a way."

Mother and the two eldest brothers were planning to add the porch themselves. An Amish man asked her, "What are you going to build with your lumber?"

"I want to tear down the unsafe open porch and build a new enclosed one."

"Who's going to build it?"

"I thought the boys could help me."

"Well, you know it's our tradition to help each other with something like that."

"I don't want to be a burden to anyone."

"When did you plan on building it?"

"Next week."

"I'll have all the men come over Tuesday afternoon. It's a small job and we can have it done in half a day."

"I'll have dinner for you then."

"No, that won't be necessary."

After the neighbor man left, Mother was upset. She said, "It may be their tradition to help each other with something like this, but it is also my duty to serve them a meal in return." Then she did a little more thinking.

My brother Jonas finally commented, "Maybe they don't want to eat here since Dad's not here."

Mother agreed. "They don't want to take food away from the table, so I have more for my children," she added.

Mother never did completely accept the neighbor's refusal and regarded it as a personal affront, not being allowed to furnish their dinner. However, she accepted it because they insisted on having it that way.

Mother was well pleased with the porch when it was completed. She placed her treadle sewing machine on the porch to do her sewing from spring through autumn, then moved it into the living room for the winter. We children enjoyed the new porch as much as she did.

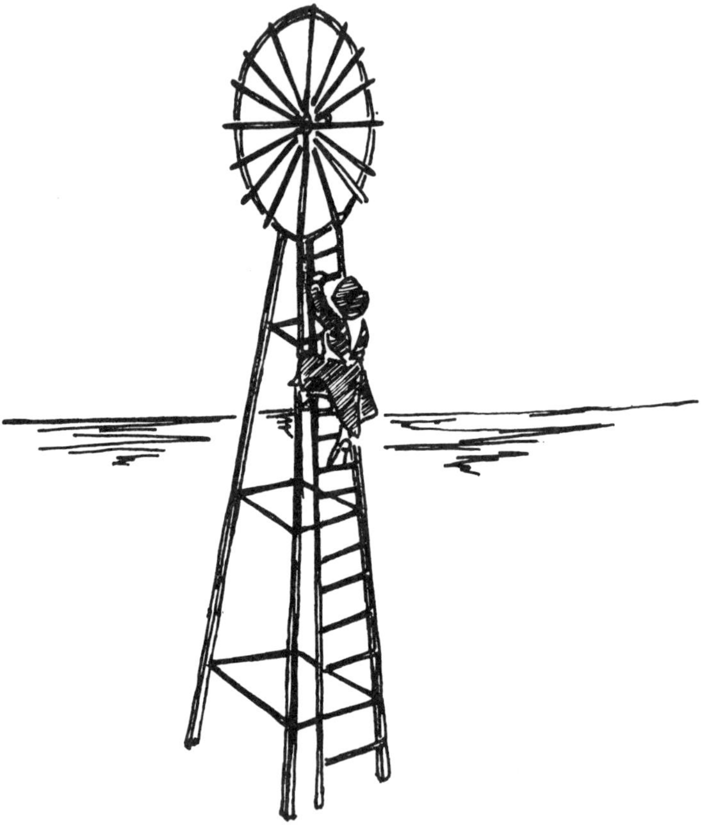

The Farm

Last night I had a dream that I was back on the farm again. In my dream I was instantly that little five-year-old Amish girl with blonde hair and blue eyes, living on a farm in Iowa. All the scenes of my childhood came vividly to my eyes.

When I actually was five years old, I remember I used to step outside the house and see the wind spinning wheel on top of the windmill. The mill was my biggest temptation on the farm; I knew it was a no-no. One day as I watched the wheel rolling, I walked down the hill to the old gray steel-framed mill. I started to climb the windmill feeling guilty and knowing Mother always told us children to stay off it. We might fall and get hurt, she always cautioned. When I came to the top, I clung to the steel frame and looked out into the sky. I watched a bird flying alone and wished I could fly like a bird or a plane. I admired the height of the beautiful clear blue sky. It looked so peaceful.

I stood on top of the mill, looking out over the old homestead. I could see the hand water pump standing underneath the old gray windmill. I could see the flowers in full bloom in the garden. I could see the rows of vegetables outlined, with a row of rhubarb and horseradish. On the opposite side grew a row of fruit trees and a grape arbor. We children had to help hoe the garden, pick vegetables, and clean them for cold-packing for the cold winter season that was only a couple of months away.

The old two-story house we lived in sat on a hill above the old mill. The house was painted white and had a stone foundation that rose to about three feet up from the ground on the west side. On the south side of the house was a cement slab leading to the screened porch, where Mother stored her washer when it was not in use. Every Monday she would pull the old clothes washer out on the slab to do the laundry. At that time, we had a washed with a hand agitator and wringer.

When I was about seven years old, Mother managed to get an automatic agitator and wringer, powered by a noisy gasoline engine. The clothes were rinsed twice and then hung on the clothesline to dry. Doing the laundry for nine people was an all-day job.

The three solid irons were placed on the wood stove to heat. The clothes were ironed as they were brought in from the line. Two irons were put on to heat while the other was being used. It was a continuous walk back and forth to the stove and ironing board until all the clothes were finished.

A young willow tree about the size of a dogwood grew in the southeast side of the yard. Little did we know at the time we moved here that it would be our discipline tree. It didn't take long to find out that when you didn't obey, a soft branch was broken off and cleaned for our discipline. Mother spoke once and we knew we had better listen or else. Sometimes she would order one of us to go and fetch her a switch. With no hesitation, we ran out to get her a willow branch. Whenever Mother had the willow branch lying beside her or in her hand, we knew she wouldn't hesitate to use it with a swish over our little bottoms and legs. It only took one or two strikes to get us in order. The willow branch did the talking for her. It did the job very well. Burn? Wow-wee! We would jump!

Looking down from the windmill, I could see the path leading to the old hand pump where we fetched our buckets of water for household use. We had to carry two buckets in the morning and four in the evening. This doesn't include how many it took on washdays, which was enough for the washer and two rinse tubs. It was easier to carry a bucket in each hand rather than just one. One made you lopsided! It felt better to have both shoulders dragged to the ground. I wonder if this is where I got my long arms?

There weren't any drains in the house. The used water would be poured in five-gallon buckets for slop. The slop was carried from the house down to the pigpen for the hogs to drink. The pigpen was located about five feet to the north side of the windmill, and the chickenhouse was on the south side of the water pump. It was the children's responsibility to feed and water the chickens and gather the eggs twice a day. How we hated to take care of chickens.

Seldom could I walk in the hen house in my bare feet without getting my feet dirty. I never wore shoes in the summer. When I went to gather eggs, I would peer inside to determine whether I could avoid the chicken manure on the floor. On tiptoes I would step in gingerly, but to no avail. "Oh no, not again!" I'd shout. The goo would ooze up between my toes. As I would gather the eggs, I would come upon a biddy that didn't want to be disturbed from sitting on her nest of eggs. When I reached to get the eggs under her, she would peck me with her beak. I would jump with fright and then go back again for the eggs. Some hens pecked much harder than others. You never knew what to expect.

On Saturdays, we children would get the garden hoe to clean the roosting shelves. The chicken droppings were spread evenly on the garden for fertilizer.

There were days when our work was done and the chickens served a different purpose. I would go in the hen house and catch a beautiful banty rooster to pick the prettiest feather that he had. My sister and brother would do the same. The things we did next really stretched the imagination. We pretended these feathers were our horses. Whoever had the prettiest feathers had the best team of horses. We would pretend we were working in the fields or going to see some friends or to town.

Built adjacent to the chicken house was our outhouse. If that little wooden building could have talked, what stories it would tell. I remember scrubbing it out on Saturdays. We used the Sears Roebuck catalogue instead of toilet paper. When I saw the catalogue, I couldn't help but think of a lonely widowed Amish man who lived in our community. He longed so for a wife. One day he saw a woman in the Sears catalogue and placed an order. How astonished he was to receive a dress. "I didn't want the dress; I wanted what was in it," he grumbled. It's a shame that he was so naive.

There was a winding creek running through the barnyard behind the outbuildings, down past the garden, across the boundary line, and through the neighbors' woods. This creek emptied into the river, which wound through the woods about a quarter-mile from the buildings. The creek had several deep holes, where we would pull our ankle-length dresses up over our knees to go wading. This we would do at every opportunity, enjoying the cool water on hot summer days.

Grandpa and Grandma from Oklahoma would visit us for the summer season. When they caught us in the creek, Grandpa would yell at us, "Get out of there and let your dresses down; your legs are showing!"

We weren't the only ones that enjoyed the creek. The ducks enjoyed the water also. The cows and horses would drink from the creek, and I can't forget the watchdogs.

They enjoyed getting in the creek to bathe and cool down on hot days. As they climbed out on the bank, they would shake their whole bodies and get us all wet. With a new dog who wasn't sure about the water, we would throw him in, and before long he was enjoying himself with the rest of the barnyard family.

On the path between the house and the barn we had a natural sandbox, large enough for the younger children to enjoy playing in. Using our foot for a pattern, we would add water to pack the sand, and upon removing the foot, we would have an entrance to the tunnel.

On the southwest side of the creek and barnyard was a tillable field. This field was usually underwater during the spring floods. High water would take the good soil with it and leave the field covered with sand. Where there was sand, there were sandburrs.

Early one evening, Lizbet and I were asked to go after the cows. We ran down and through the barnyard, raising our dresses to cross the creek. "Let's take a short cut through the field," I said. Lizbet agreed as she ran along beside me. About twenty feet into the field, she hollered, "Ouch!" I hollered back "Ouch! Ouch!" There we stopped. We both lamented, "This hurts. Oh! *Nah*, there's no place to step." We tried to clean our feet and give each other support while doing so. It was impossible. We started crying and screaming for help.

Grandpa, hearing us, yelled, "What's wrong?"

"Our feet are covered with sandburrs. The field is covered with them."

Grandpa came to our rescue. He carried us both out of the field. Then he told us to take the pasture path, which we usually did. We didn't disagree.

My brother Enos came along while I was surveying the homestead from the windmill and caught me.

"What are you doing up there?" asked Enos.

"I wish I could fly."

"You'd better get down before Mom sees you."

"All right, but I'm closer to heaven up here." I climbed back down.

"If Mom catches you, you're in trouble."

When I reached the ground, I said, "It's really nice up there."

"Let me go up quickly," he whispered.

"All right."

Enos was climbing up the old mill when Mother walked outside from the house and caught him. Guess who was in trouble?

Planting and Harvesting

There was only one Amish sect or denomination in Buchanan, Iowa. However, in some areas there are many. There are as many as twelve denominations of Amish in Holmes County, Ohio. As an example of types, there are two different denominations of horse-and-buggy Amish. One is named the Behinders, and the other is called the Old Order Amish. Our Buchanan denomination fell somewhere between the Behinders and the Old Order Amish.

One of the more modern sects is the Beachy Amish. They use a black automobile for transportation. The women's and the men's style of dress is different from the traditional Amish style, yet an outsider can't tell that there is a difference. Amishmen probably all look alike to the outsider's eye because the clothing styles are so similar from sect to sect.

The Beachy have many more modern conveniences in their homes, such as electricity, telephones, wall-to-wall carpeting, drapes, and other modern appliances. However, the Old Order Amish use gasoline-powered washers, solid irons, and horses to do their farming and harvesting. Water is drawn from the well by windmill or gas engine. For light, the Old Order use kerosene lamps and gasoline lanterns.

We had a team of draft horses that we used for farming. The boys would hitch the team to a plow to till the ground. It was a continuous back-and-forth pattern, since the plow tilled over one row of ground at a time and had a seat for one driver. Every so often, my brother would stop and let the horses rest.

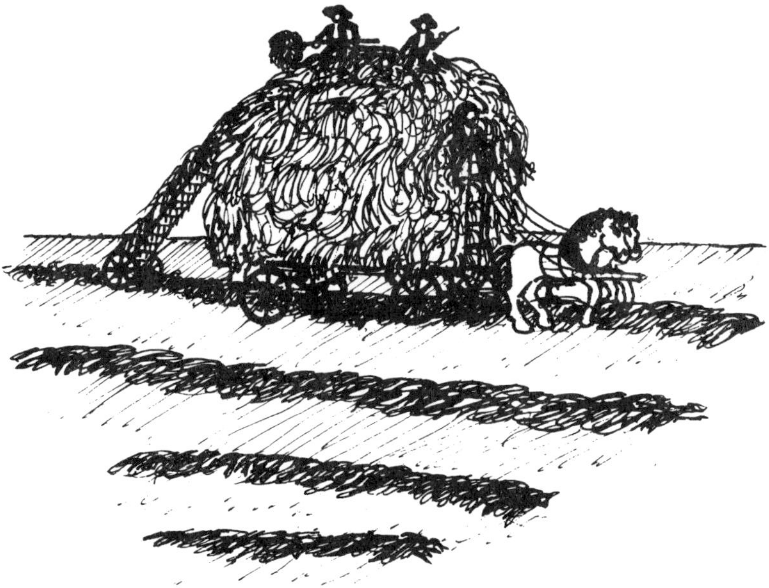

Midmorning and midafternoon, Mom would ask one of us younger ones to carry a jug of water out to the field for our brother. Sometimes we would surprise him with spearmint tea.

It took a whole day for one of my brothers to till an entire field. Although the Amish are allowed to own a pocket watch, wristwatches are not permissible. My brothers didn't have a pocket watch to tell when it was dinnertime, so, like the Indians, they went by the sun. Judging by the sun, they knew when it was 11:30 A.M.. Then they would come in for dinner.

When the plowing was done, they would disc the field. With the driver standing on the rake, a team of horses pulled a large rake across the field to even up the dirt. Finally, the seeds were planted, with a prayer for a good crop according to God's will.

Once, when my brother Enos was quite small, he lost his balance and fell, with the rake being pulled over his legs. Luckily he was all right. However, this incident scared him enough to be more careful afterward.

We had a field that had a good-sized hill. When Dad was hospitalized, Uncle Judas told Mom to farm the dangerous field. Brother Jonas harnessed the team of working horses and hitched them to the one-row plow with a one-man seat. Jonas went out to till the field with Mom and Brother Eli following him on foot. Jonas started out with the reins in his hands, sitting in the seat, and at the age of thirteen had to do a man's job. Mom and Eli stood at the end of the field to watch Jonas to make sure he was all right. He started down to till the first row. His plow promptly turned over. He quickly jumped to safety, losing his straw hat. He picked up his hat and placed it back on his head, covering his blond hair. Mother and Eli ran over to help him set the plow back up on its two wheels.

Jonas made one trip down and back. He turned around and started another row. His plow turned over the second time. Mother feared for his safety. She was angry because she had tried to tell Uncle Judas that it would be better to turn this field into a pasture for the livestock. However, as the boys became older, they could see that we needed more corn and hay for the animals. With Mom's consent, they decided to fence in twenty acres of the pasture at the far northwest end of the other flat fields. The dangerous field was converted to a pasture. There was a piece of ground that was not fenced and was used for pasture alone. Uncle Judas always said, "It is no good." The brothers knew we needed more feed for the animals. Against Uncle Judas's wishes, Mom, Jonas, and Eli loaded the barbed wire, fence posts, post digger, and tools on the hay wagon and headed out to fence in the ground that Uncle Judas always said was no good. They added a field to the third one on the northwest side that couldn't be seen from the house. The field was plowed, disced, and raked, and corn was planted. We hoped the earth was fertile. When it was time to harvest the corn, we had to build an extra corncrib, because the new field brought such an excellent yield of corn.

My brothers were proud of God for making it possible. Despite the negative leadership Uncle Judas had given us, my brothers showed us all that what Mom preached to us was true: "Where there is a will, there is a way."

Our fields were fertilized with natural fertilizer from the barn. When the barn was cleaned out, the manure was spread over the fields. Uncle Judas wouldn't let Mom fertilize the fields except in this way.

We would rotate the crops every year. Mom knew what to plant in each field every year, and she taught the boys what to plant. For example, where there was oats one year, she would plant hay the following year. After hay, she would plant corn and then wheat. She would never plant the same kind of crop twice. She planted peanuts in the sandburrs. When we needed molasses, she would plant sugarcane.

The Amish believe everything should be done manually. When it was time to make hay, the hay was mowed and laid out for a day or two to dry. Then it was raked into a row and laid for a half-day to make sure it wasn't green or wet.

When it was time to bring the hay to the barn, everybody gave a hand. We would hitch working horses to the hay wagon, and we younger children took turns driving the team in the fields. When it was my turn to drive, we hitched the hay loader to the end of the wagon and I had to keep a horse on each side of the row. Two of my brothers, each with a hayfork, were on the wagon. The hay loader picked up the loose hay and dropped it on the wagon. They would take the fork and stack the hay evenly on the wagon. The hay piled up until it finally covered above the ladder where the driver stood. Since this was the first time for me to drive, my attention was on the horses, to make sure they stayed in a row. I ignored what was happening in the wagon behind me. Suddenly I felt the hay moving up my back. I looked around and Brother Eli smiled, noticing I was frightened. He reassured me, "You'll be all right; just climb the wagon ladder, and when we go higher, you stay behind the ladder until we are loaded. The ladder will keep you from falling off."

"Okay," I said.

When the wagon was loaded, my brothers called out, "Whoa!" I stopped the horses and looked up. Then I was really scared. I couldn't see my brothers for the mountain of hay above my head. Soon I felt them moving to the front and they asked, "Want to come up here?"

I didn't know what I wanted at the time, but I answered, "How?"

Eli leaned down and reached out his arm and said, "Give me your hand and I'll pull you up."

"All right." I reached up and he grabbed my hand and pulled me up to the very top. My stomach felt strange. "Oh, we're so high; won't we tip?" I asked.

"*Nah*, just sit down in the middle. I'll drive the horses in." I gave him the reins, and he walked the horses to the barn.

The wagon was parked on the east end outside of the barn to unload the hay. We had a four-tooth fork connected to a rope that ran on a pulley up to the haymow. Then the rope ran out and tied to a horse in the driveway. My two brothers would be in the haymow and one on the hay wagon to load the fork. When it was ready, they would yell at me, "Ready!" I would drive the horse on foot out away from the barn, pulling the load up into the loft. When it arrived in the mow where they wanted it, one of my brothers would yell, "Whoa!"

The brother in the barn would pull on the rope to the fork to release the hay when I stopped the horse. We would repeat this process until the hay was unloaded.

Sometimes we would borrow a neighbor's hay wagon so when one was unloading, the other one was being loaded. Mom would take care of the fork outside the wagon and send one brother up into the haymow. The other two were sent back to the field.

I remember I thought I was really a big girl out there helping my big brothers. I felt I had to act like I was really brave, although inside I was really scared. After a while I became used to it and the job didn't bother me anymore and I enjoyed it.

When it was time to do the wheat, it was combined and shocked. Then all the neighbors got together and helped each other. Every farmer took turns getting the wheat in. We called this "threshing season." The farmer's wife was informed when she was going to have the men, and she would prepare dinner on the day they worked on her farm.

After everybody's wheat was in, we all gathered together and had an ice cream supper. Every family would take a full freezer of ice cream along, so there was a variety of ice cream. It was their way of showing appreciation to the others and a way to get some relaxation after a month of hard work.

In autumn the corn was picked. Mom and my older brothers would put a corn picking glove on and use the box-grain wagon to throw the corn in. The corn was picked and husked by hand. When the wagon was loaded, it was shoveled into the corncrib. This cycle was repeated until all the corn was harvested. When we needed corn for the animals, we had to shell the corn off the cob. We had a corn sheller sitting at the end of the crib. We younger children would shell daily as we needed it. One would feed the machine as the other one would turn the crank.

We pretended it was something wild and hungry. The faster we turned the crank, the angrier the monster would get, until it would eat the corn off in a matter of seconds. The monster would spit the corn into a container and shift the cob out the end. We used the cobs to start the fire in our wood and coal stove.

We would harvest the vegetables and fruit. We had green beans, peas, tomatoes, carrots, red and white radishes, red beets, and corn. We would use field corn when it was new; we had to get it before it hardened. It really was good. I hated green peas. We planted an area of potatoes. Everybody would help with this, because it was a big job. The brothers would get the field ready. Then with a team of horses they would use a plow to make the row. We dropped the eye potatoes in a row a foot apart and covered them up. In the fall, my brothers used the plow again to dig them up. We would all go out and pick the potatoes up. They were stored in the ground basement in a bin for the winter. Everybody enjoyed the potatoes on the table. We cold packed the rhubarb, plums, and apple sauce. This was our fruit on the farm. The grapes were eaten off the arbor. The arbor wasn't very big. Apples that weren't made into apple sauce or pies were wrapped individually and stored in an old milk can in the basement. In January, we could open the can and the apples were just as fresh as the day we picked them. We cold-packed the rhubarb. We ate rhubarb until I learned to hate it. Plums were the same way. I always preferred cooked cornmeal with gravy over it to any of the two fruits. We had a few strawberries. Mother would cold-pack them, too. This ruined them, or maybe I just got tired of them, too. I used to eat strawberries in our cold bread soup for supper. In the summertime, we would break a loaf of bread into bite-size pieces in a big bowl. Next we added one cup of sugar, poured cold milk over it, and mixed it. We placed the big bowl in the center of the table. A bowl of fruit was set on the table, too. Then you dipped a dipperful of bread soup in your soup bowl. Next you added one or two spoonfuls of fruit over your bread soup and ate it. We often had cornbread, milk and sugar. This was good. Brother Eli would sometimes eat leftover cornbread with milk and sugar for his breakfast cereal.

For breakfast we had pancakes with homemade syrup. Syrup consisted of: 2 cups of brown sugar, 2 cups of karo syrup, 2 cups of water, and 1 teaspoon of vanilla. We brought it to a boil and boiled for ten minutes, then served it over hotcakes.

Oatmeal was our favorite cereal. However, we also had fried mush or cooked mush served with brown pan or cream of tomato gravy. Sometimes cooked mush was eaten with sugar and milk over it, like cereal. There were home fries with creamed tomato gravy for breakfast. Creamed tomato gravy was made at least once a day. For breakfast or dinner, a table without a bowl of gravy was unheard of. Sometimes we had gravy over bread. Our main meal was lunch. This meal usually consisted of potatoes, gravy, vegetable, meat, apple sauce, and a pudding or another kind of desert.

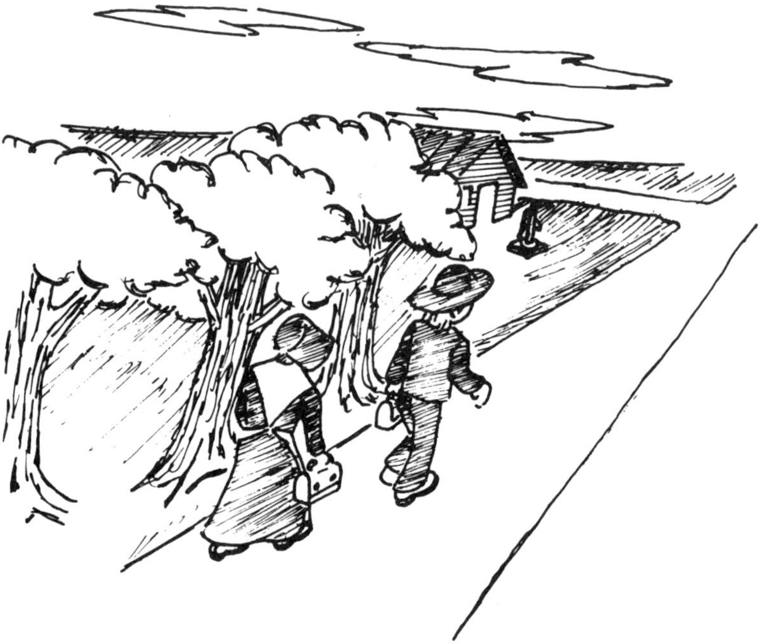

School Days

When we moved to Iowa, the new Amish settlement still didn't have its own school in our district. I went to Fairbank Public School for two years. With the harsh winter, the school bus couldn't make it to the house every day. My older brothers would walk to the neighbors' farm to catch the bus, but seeing me as a sickly little girl, Mother wouldn't let me walk. The snow was usually so deep it came up to the boys' knees and to my hips.

"You can't go, Alma," Mother said. "You're too small."

Not being able to go to school disappointed me very much.

One morning, I was almost left behind accidentally. The bus had stopped with the door closed. I was standing there waiting for the driver to open the door, but he didn't. The bus started to pull away. My eyes welled up with tears. I felt as though my eyes were ready to jump out of my head with disbelief.

I heard the children on the bus yelling. Then the bus stopped. I ran to catch it. "I'm very sorry; I didn't see you," the driver said. "Next time, knock." I thought it was strange he couldn't see me. I thought I was as big as anyone else in my class. I stepped on the bus and didn't say a word all the way to school. He had hurt my feelings. I couldn't believe he didn't see me.

At first, school was strange to me. Dutch was spoken in the home and German in the church. School was my first real experience with the English language. It rather frightened me, and then, too, the Amish children were also set apart because of their style of clothes. I didn't really envy the other students, and I liked school.

My dress was a solid color and came down to my ankles. Over it I wore an apronlike covering. I had two school dresses for the week. Other girls wore pretty outfits, sometimes skirts and jumpers, with blouses or sweaters.

Mother always said, "Don't wish for what somebody else has, and don't be jealous."

Everybody spoke English. That was a strange and foreign language to us Amish-speaking children. The teacher was familiar with the situation, having had Amish-speaking children in her classes before. The teacher and the other students worked with me to help me learn English. But for a long time I would still speak Amish. At recess or as soon as school was dismissed, we Amish children would speak Amish to each other. The teacher would hear us. "You're never going to learn to speak English if you keep on speaking Dutch," she would say, reminding us to speak Engish. That was the hardest thing to remember when I had another Amish friend by my side. It wasn't until halfway through my first year that I began to speak English regularly. I would rather not say anything than speak English.

During my second year, the public school had pictures taken of all the students. This was against the Amish belief. When the pictures were sent home to the parents, the Amish parents decided it was best to buy them and then bury them in the ground.

Mother bought the pictures, but kept two pictures of each of us children and hid them without telling anyone.

During my third year of school, a new school opened in Littleton, Iowa, as a public school of that district. We had to furnish our own transportation. It was about two and a half miles to and from school, which we walked most of the time, Sometimes we were treated to our horse and hack buggy for our trip. A hack buggy is similar to a buckboard with no top and only one seat. The young ones would sit in the buggy box in the rear while my sister Sarah sat in the front with the driver.

The horse and buggy was parked on the school grounds, under the shade trees in the south corner of the two-acre lot. One day, Brother Eli went to get the rig with Sarah, Enos, Alma, Lizbet, and Junior all packed in. When we left the school grounds, they walked the rig, because the children were walking on both sides. Some students made fun of us, and others watched with interest. One kid was as ornery as the day was long. He walked up to another boy, who was walking beside us admiring the horse, and pushed him in the path of the rig's wheel. I saw it happen and screamed, "The front wheel went over that boy!"

The frightened boy jumped to his feet and ran. Before we could ask or even check to see if he was all right, he was gone. The schoolteacher heard the screams and checked to see what had happened. The culprit who did the pushing was punished. He had to stay after school for an hour for two weeks. Pushing someone in front of a buggy was a serious offense.

Even though I had missed so much school the previous year, I was happy to see that I had all Ss on my report card. That was the best you could get in those days. About a month after school started in Littleton, though, I received a setback. I was doing my arithmetic when the teacher came over to me and said, "Alma, I received a report from the state concerning you. Since you missed so many days last year, they want you to take the first grade over again, even though you had passing grades."

In my shyness, I just looked up at her and nodded my head. I was disappointed. I liked what I was doing and didn't want to repeat what I had done last year. I didn't argue the case, but dropped back a year with my sister Lizbet. Later in the year I was bored and started to work out of another book. The teacher told me that I was doing fourth-grade problems.

The Amish decided to open their own school about four miles from Littleton out in the country. They obtained a certified teacher from Oelwein, Iowa.

The school was a one-room building. There was a small shed out back where wood and coal were stored for the winter. The eighth-grade boys had to bring in some coal and wood every afternoon before they went home and bank the fire in the large pot-belly stove for the night.

There were two outhouses close by, one for the girls and one for the boys. The hitching posts for the parents to tie up their horses were on the north side along the school building.

We carried our lunches to school every day. There was no such thing as a cafeteria. When the sun was shining and it was warm outside, we would grab our lunch buckets and run outside to sit under a big shade tree. We had an hour for lunch. Usually after eating we would play. We'd play ball, jump rope, ride the merry-go-round, and swing on the swings. We didn't have modern playground equipment, but we were content with what we had. We also would swing and turn somersaults on the hitching posts. It was fun turning those somersaults, but many times we'd catch the bottom edge of our ankle-length dress on the heel of our shoes and tear out the hem. We sat through school with a torn hem and fixed it when we arrived home.

If the weather was bad, we played inside. The teacher had a handcrank record player she let us use, or we'd write on the blackboard or play jacks. Our teacher wasn't just someone who was there for a paycheck. She was a teacher, friend, and mother and always had her pupils under control. She would explain, "If there isn't order when the people from the state visit our school, it can be closed."

One day you could have heard a pin drop. I looked up from my studies. I had a question and was looking around the room for the teacher. All the other students were busy on their assignments. I started to get up, but then I noticed some strange people in modern clothes in the back of the room. *Oh, the people from the state,* I thought.

So I raised my hand and the teacher, with a smile on her face, nodded to me. I quietly went up to her and asked her the question. I don't think very many students had heard those visitors come in. I hadn't. I was surprised to see them there. They were gone by recess time. It sure was nice that we were all working hard when they arrived. That was a good mark for the teacher. I could tell she was proud of her students.

The school had an old-fashioned hand bell to ring when it was time to start classes, reminiscent of the pioneer days. When we heard that bell, we all ran for the schoolhouse. We had just three minutes to be in our seats. The Amish country school's enrollment for the first year was fourteen, the next eighteen, and the third year twenty-three. One teacher taught all the students from the kindergarten through the eighth grade. She'd spend time with one age group, then give them an assignment, then go on to another group. Sometimes we'd split up into little circles to do our work.

When I was in first grade at Littleton, I realized how I felt about the outside world. One day when I was playing with some non-Amish girls, one of them asked, "Would you spend the night with me?"

Until this moment I had been unaware of the fact that

I was afraid to visit with a "modern" family. I was fully at ease with my friend and liked her as a classmate, but I was afraid to go to her home. I didn't know what to say to her, because I didn't want to hurt her feelings. I could tell the little girl really wanted me to come home with her. Shyly, I shook my head in the negative. I told her, "I will ask my mother."

I was so afraid that I never asked. I just told the girl the next day, "I can't stay over."

I imagined her family would fight. Because all the rest of the world had just completed World War II, I thought all the people who weren't Amish were fighting all the time. The Amish are peace-loving people. They do not believe in violence. Violence was one way we knew that my father was not himself anymore. My father wasn't a violent man before his accident. We knew something was seriously wrong as time went by after his accident. His mental attitude was changing too rapidly, and this wasn't normal.

One sunny morning, we children took the buckboard to our Amish school. On our way home we saw dark clouds approaching fast. We hurried the horse, trying to beat the storm home. As we reached the drive, the wind was gusting with great force. The strong winds lifted one side of the rig, and we came in on two wheels. We all screamed with fright, shifting our weight to bring the rig back down. Enos parked beside the east end of the barn, where the wind wasn't as strong. He was unhitching the horse when the wind slowed up. He yelled, "Run for the house."

We three girls ran for the house, leaving Enos behind. Sarah and Lizbet reached the house, with me right behind them. But before I had a chance to get hold of the door, a strong wind lifted me off my feet, carrying me away from the house.

"Come on, Alma!" Lizbet yelled.

The wind had taken my breath. I looked down and realized I was moving. The wind was carrying me without touching the ground.

This frightened me. With my toes digging down in my shoes, I tried to reach the ground, but to no avail. I started to swing my feet hard under the skirt of my big dress. But that just made me go away from the house faster. I was flying into the yard when I managed to grab a hold of a tree in the yard.

Lizbet yelled again. "Hang on, Alma!" She stood watching from the porch in fear.

I couldn't answer. I hung to the tree for dear life, hoping the wind would ease a little. When it did slow down, I ran to the house to safety.

The next day, we heard a chicken house had been turned over and a barn roof had been blown off. We realized God was with us and knew how lucky we had been.

The Stranger

That particular summer morning was turning into a beautiful sunny day, with the temperature at a pleasant eighty-six degrees. My teenage brothers didn't hesitate in doing the morning chores, happily hitching the team of draft horses that they would need for the day's work. Their younger sisters also busied themselves with their routine.

Sarah, age eleven, mixed the bread dough before breakfast. She added four packages of dry yeast to four and a half cups of warm water in a mixing bowl and let the yeast dissolve. Then she added six tablespoons of sugar, a fourth a cup of melted shortening, two tablespoons of salt, and seven cups of flour. She beat this mixture until smooth, then added more flour (about six cups), a little at a time. She let the dough rise and punched it down. Then Sarah formed four loaves and let them rise. She baked them for about forty-five to sixty minutes at 350 degrees. The dough would rise while they had breakfast. Lizbet fetched the water from the well in the old wooden bucket and provided an armful of wood for the kitchen stove.

As we sat at the breakfast table, Mother directed, "Enos, bring in the buggy horse and hitch it up, because I'm going to Independence today."

"May I go with you?"

"No. I want you boys to help each other repairing the broken fence so the cows won't get out and forage in the neighbors' corn. That fence has to be repaired today for sure."

When Mother journeyed to Independence, it was an all-day trip, easily a two-hour ride each way by buggy.

Mother readied herself and left early in the day. The boys loaded their tools on the hay wagon and set off to mend the fence. Sarah kneaded her bread dough and covered it once again to let it rise. Then she started washing the milking equipment. While washing the separator, the girls heard an automobile pull to a stop out front. Sarah and Lizbet stopped what they were doing and looked through the window. A man was sitting in the vehicle parked out by the road.

He opened his car door, stepped out for a few moments, and just stood there surveying the house. The man appeared well tailored and affluent.

As the man started walking toward the house, Sarah, the elder of the girls, said, "Lizbet, take Annie Baby upstairs and hide under the bed. Be very quiet and don't make any noise. Mother says to always be cautious of strangers when we are by ourselves."

"What about you?" Lizbet whispered back.

"Don't worry about me; just take Annie and go before he gets to the door."

With some concern, Sarah shoved Lizbet into the kitchen and said, "Please! Take the baby upstairs and hide right now so I won't have to worry about you. And remember, no noise! I don't want him to know you are here."

Lizbet promised and Sarah, sighing with relief, whispered, "Good! Go now and shut the upstairs door, too."

Sarah returned to the separator room to lock the outside door, closing the kitchen door behind her. She knew the lock was not too secure, but she locked it anyway and stood on the opposite side of the room, trembling in silence. A knock came on the door. Sarah stood frozen to the spot. A second knock. Still Sarah refused to break her silence, hardly daring to breathe, hoping the man would leave. The third knock came immediately, followed by a harsh voice.

"Open up; I know you are in there!"

Now there was a loud banging on the door.

"Come on, open up or I'll bust it down!"

Sarah moved behind the door and asked timidly, "What do you want?"

She braced her foot against the locked door to help prevent it from breaking. The man shoved on the door until the lock let loose with a loud bang. Sarah couldn't hold the door closed any longer. She started to cry as the man roughly pushed her back against the wall.

The man asked her if anyone else was in the house.

"No, I'm all alone."

Little did Sarah know that her sisters, in their concern for her, were not hiding upstairs as they were told, but were in fact lying on the kitchen floor peering under the door to see if Sarah was in any danger.

The man walked up to her and said, "I just want to talk to you." He grabbed her dress and said, "I won't hurt you."

"Please leave me alone," Sarah pleaded.

With a cruel laugh, he ripped her dress down over her shoulders. "I just want to talk to you. You are a pretty little thing."

He moved closer to her as if he wanted to kiss her.

Sarah struggled with him. She was afraid of him because he was stronger than she was. Fighting him off, she shouted, "I will yell for my brothers if you don't leave me alone!"

"How many brothers do you have, honey?"

"I have four brothers. All I have to do is yell, and they will come running!"

"Where are your brothers?"

"They are working in the barn."

"I just want to talk to you." He moved toward her once more.

"I will yell if you don't leave and leave now. My brothers can take you with no problem."

"You sure about that?"

"Yes! They are strong," she warned him, facing him eye to eye.

He backed off. Sarah pulled her dress back over her shoulder, trying to gather herself together again.

He looked through the window, paled, and hurriedly exited through the door. Sarah walked to the window to make sure the man was really leaving and noticed the boys coming in from fixing the fence. She cried with relief and was still crying when the boys came in to see what the car was doing there. She tried to wipe her tears away, but her brother Eli knew when he saw her that something wasn't right.

"What's wrong?"

She was crying so hard she couldn't answer.

"What happened?"

Lizbet and Annie opened the door and excitedly started to tell him what had happened. Sarah managed to get herself together and told him the story. The brothers were angry and questioned, "What can we do to prevent this from happening again?"

Jonas and Eli continued about their duties around the farm. For the rest of the day the boys stayed close to the house. The evening chores were done early. At the dinner table, Eli announced, "Jonas and I are going to see a friend. We know he had some puppies, and we'll see if we can still get one. We are going to raise it to be a watchdog so what happened today won't ever happen again."

Two hours later they came home with a cute collie puppy. Just like the brothers had said, we trained him to be a watchdog. And an excellent watchdog he was!

Junior: All Boy!

The first boy born after me carries our father's name. He resembled his father, too. He is two and a half years younger than me and was the first sibling I remembered growing up.

There was also Lizbet, evenly spaced between him and me. Our ages were so close that I didn't regard her so much as a sister, but as a playmate and friend.

Junior grew up to be all boy, as they say, full of orneriness. He had the ability to make us laugh and was quite a daredevil and yet quite ambitious.

It seemed this boy was always cutting up, especially around mealtime. Mother would warn him, "Junior, you'd better watch yourself or I'll show you something."

"What will you show me?"

Junior was always ready with a smart and usually funny comeback while keeping a straight and serious innocent look on that oval, fair-complexioned face with brown eyes. The rest of us either broke out laughing or, if we were eating, forced ourselves to stifle our laughter, nearly choking on our food. Even Mother's stern facade broke many times. She had to turn herself around so Junior wouldn't see her laughing.

One beautiful Sunday, our church services were being held at the neighbors' house across the river. We had taken our horse and buggy across the woods and river for a shortcut.

When we were ready to leave, Mother asked, "Enos, where are the boys?"

"They walked with the other boys to the woods."

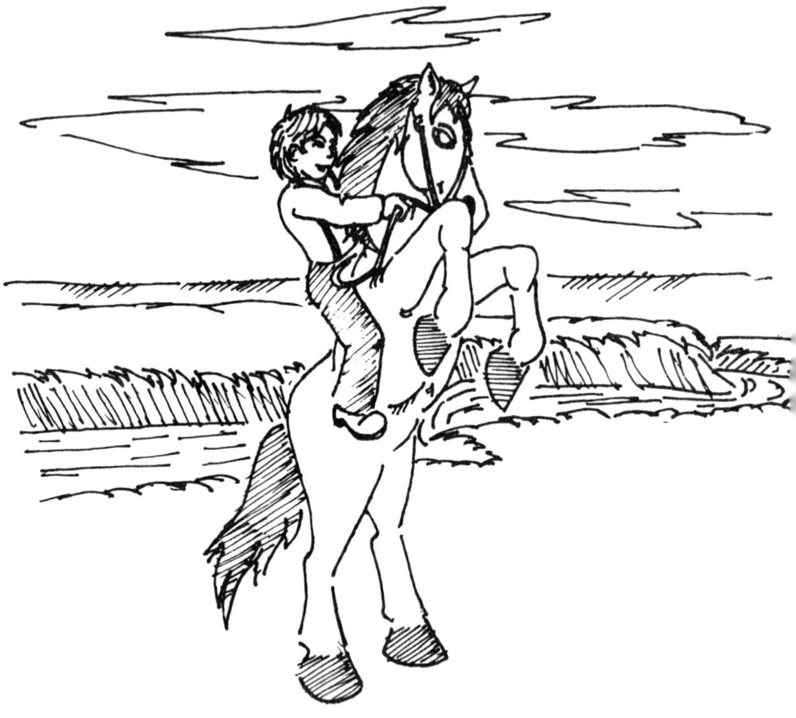

"Get in the buggy; we'll pick them up on our way."

They both sat in the buggy, and we followed our morning path back to the woods, where the boys were watching something.

We stopped and asked, "What are you looking at?"

Jonas walked over and said softly, "There is a beehive in the tree."

After we had stopped and were focusing our attention on the boys, Junior had climbed out and walked around on his own adventure.

Enos yelled, "Junior is walking toward the swarming bee nest."

"Oh, *nah!*" Mother jumped out of the buggy and ran for him.

Jonas ordered, "Stay here! I'll get him."

He ran over and picked Junior up, fighting off the bees. Mother ordered us to get the rig moving away from the trees. She received a couple of stings. Jonas received a couple of stings as well, and Junior, age four, was stung several times. When we arrived on the other side of the river, he became sick to his stomach. He was very ill for the rest of the evening. Mother stayed by his side throughout the night.

One spring evening—he couldn't have been more than three years old—Junior wandered out to the barn, where the older two boys were hauling horse manure. The older boys had been spreading it in the fields in preparation for the next day's plowing.

That evening, Eli had parked the spreader in the barnyard alongside the other pieces of farm machinery. Junior tried to get out of the way, but he fell and one of the heavy steel wheels ran over him. Apparently Eli hadn't seen him. It was evening, with very little light, and Amish children wear dark-colored clothing. The child started to cry, a cry of pain. The oldest brother, who had been directing the parking, ran around the back. The other brother stopped the team of horses, jumped off the spreader, and ran back to see what was wrong.

Mother could hear the child's cry from the house. She stepped outside and yelled toward the barnyard, "What's wrong?"

Jonas shouted in reply, "We backed the manure spreader over Junior!"

Jonas picked Junior up and carried him to the house.

"Did you smash him?"

We girls were in the kitchen helping to prepare supper. We froze when we heard the question and almost dropped the plates. What horrors flashed through our minds. We were relieved when we heard Jonas holler, "No! It just went over his legs."

"Are his legs okay?"

"He's all right; that crying he did was more of fright than pain."

Mother examined his legs under the kitchen kerosene lantern. "Boy! Are we lucky!"

We girls rushed over to check, too. Sarah scooped Junior into her arms and carried him to the living room, where he received a lot of attention that night. That wasn't the first or last time Junior had wandered on the farm and was injured.

When he was four, Junior had gone after the cows with his older brother. Jonas opened the barn door to let the cows in for milking and asked Junior to chase them in the barn. The entrance was about two feet higher than the ground, and the cows had to jump to get through.

My little brother thought he could do what his big brothers could. He was full of ambition and daring. However, he didn't realize the dangers around animals. He was following the cows too closely, and when the last cow came in, he grabbed her ankle and barked like a dog. This surprised the cow, and she jumped and her hind foot came back and hit him in the forehead. He was knocked down and out.

When Jonas locked the cows in their stall, he went to the door to close it. He found Junior lying on the ground. He had to look twice to make sure he was seeing right. He bent down and Junior started to cry. Jonas noticed Junior had a gash and was bleeding from the forehead. He picked him up and carried him to the house. Of course, Mother and Junior's sisters took care of him for the rest of the evening.

Mother commanded, "Don't let him go to sleep for the first several hours."

We girls were surprised with her statement. We asked, "Why?"

Mother answered, "The doctor had told me if at any time anyone gets hit in the head, never let them go into a sound sleep. They may never wake up. So make sure you don't let him go to sleep for the first four hours."

Junior was awakened every two hours throughout the night. This was to make sure he was all right. As of today, he is still wearing the scar, although he outgrew a lot of it.

By the time Junior was seven, he was riding our buggy horse quite a bit. But he wasn't content to keep the horse's four legs on the ground. He would go out behind the barn where he couldn't be seen from the house, and then he would rear the horse up on its hind legs. He would spend a whole afternoon teaching his horse fancy tricks. But before doing so, he would always say, "Don't tell Mom I'm going out behind the barn with the horse."

Several times Junior came to his sisters, saying "Promise not to tell Mom if I tell you something?"

"Ja."

"The horse reared so high he went all the way over."

"Were you on the horse?"

"Yeah." With a daring smile.

"Did you hurt yourself?"

"Nah." He laughed impishly.

We sisters shook our heads unbelievingly. We both agreed, "One of these days you are going to get hurt."

"He isn't afraid of anything," I stated.

Lizbet agreed. "That's for sure."

"Don't tell Mom" became a common phrase around the house when we did something we knew we weren't supposed to.

Many times when this boy was supposed to get the cows we would find him out back of the barn. Oh, how he loved that horse. He had been attracted to the fields early. Perhaps it was his love for horses and watching them work.

As ornery as he was, he decided to play a trick on Annie, who was two years younger than himself. "Annie, there is a rabbit hole out in the field. Want to go see it?"

"Yeah."

"Come on, I'll show you."

Both went trotting out to the field, taking the dog along. When they reached the hole, Junior told Annie, "Where there is an entrance there is an exit, too. You stay here and watch while I go over there to see if I can't find the exit."

"All right," she replied, not knowing any better.

Junior got his dog to start digging for him while Annie stood watch over the hole. The dog dug until he hit the underground rabbit trail and then started barking.

"Can you see a rabbit?"

Annie looked down into the hole and answered, "No! I don't see one."

"Well, you have to get down closer to see."

The dog was still digging away. As she stooped down to look, a rabbit came tearing out right into Annie's face. She jumped with a scream and fell to the ground in terror. Junior burst out laughing.

"Oh! Du dummel ding du." (You dumb thing you.)

She realized the joke was on her and started laughing along with him.

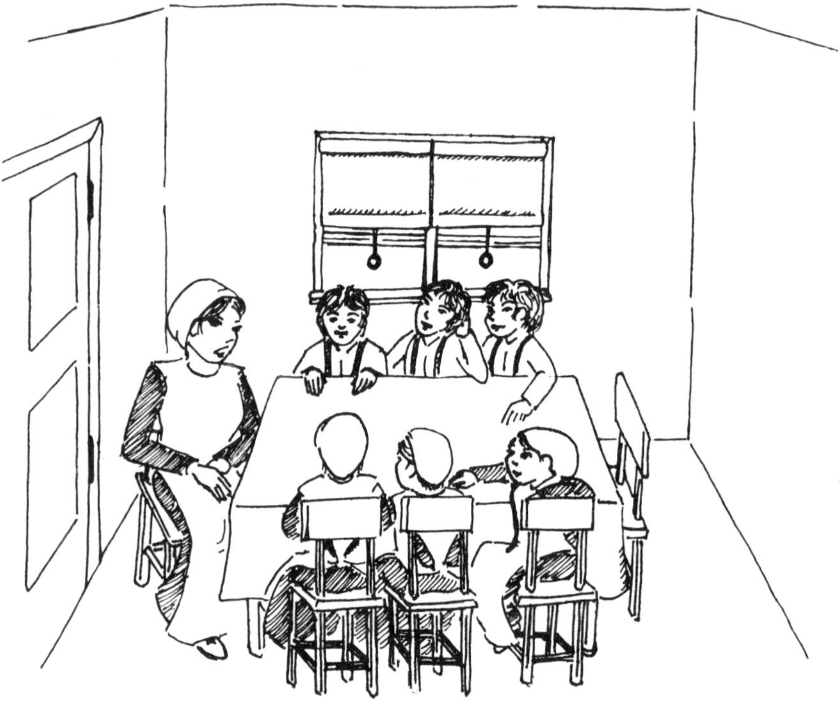

Stories at the Dinner Table

Our dinner table was covered with a plain white oilcloth. The place setting consisted of a variety of dishes. A water glass was placed by each setting.

Water glasses were filled with water from a pitcher before anyone was seated. The food was served in large bowls, and when the food was passed, everyone was to place the amount that they could eat on their plate. Each plate was to be empty when one finished eating. There is no waste allowed in an Amish home. Leftover food was placed in smaller containers and kept in an icebox. This food was always used later in some way.

For good table manners, children were taught at a young age that you chew with your mouth closed and you don't talk with your mouth full.

Only in summer did we have an iceman. He delivered ice twice a week to the Amish homes. On hot summer days we would serve spearmint tea instead of water. The spearmint grew wild on the farm. Spearmint tea was a treat for us, just like soft drinks are for today's families.

When everyone was gathered at the dinner table, the conversation would lead to storytelling.

Mother would tell us about the Oklahoma farm. She and Dad had a farm in Maize County. That's where I was born, at home, in 1940.

Mom would start the story by saying, "Your father was one of the best farmers in the area. He lived on his father's farm. They operated the farm while his aging parents lived in the grandfather's house."

This practice is common among the Amish as the

parents get up in years. Although the children take over the main work of the farm, the older folks still help out.

"We had eleven hired hands on the three-hundred-acre farm. Your father worked it in the traditional Amish way. We didn't have any modern conveniences, so he used horses instead of tractors. I always saw to it that the hired help were fed their breakfast and dinner."

"You cooked for all those men?" I asked.

"*Ja*, everyday. Three times a day.

"We had nine white fellows, one Indian, and one black. On the first day that the black man came to work, I noticed that he wasn't getting ready for breakfast with the others.

"I asked, 'Where is the new man at?'

" 'Don't know,' was the reply.

"I went out to look for him and found him on the porch.

" 'Why aren't you inside getting ready to eat?' I asked.

"He told me he didn't know if he should come inside because he was black.

" 'What?' I said. 'When you work for us, you eat with everybody else. In our house, regardless of what color you are, nobody is any better than the other.'

"I led him into the kitchen and told the other hired men that the black man worked here just like they did and he ate there at the table, too. Just like they did. Everyone agreed with me. And you know what?"

"No! What?" I questioned.

"He turned out to be one of our best workers, too."

"Really?"

"Yeah. Your father needed all the help he could get on the farm, because he baled hay and sold it. The hay was shipped to other states, and he had a deadline to meet. That was hard to do sometimes.

"We had a large number of hogs, but one year they contracted a disease known as black feet and we lost them."

"What's black feet, Mom?" Enos asked.

"Black feet is a fatal poison, and when you cut a dead animal open, it had black under the skin.

"Black feet disease is caused by a bacteria called clostridium noryi. It produces a fatal toxin or poison. Noryi also causes gas gangrene infections in humans or animals. Some people call it swell head or big head.

"One year we planted a huge field of potatoes and used the crop to feed the hired men and the family. We harvested forty bushels, thinking it was an excellent yield. However, they were all gone by next season. We used them all for the employees and family.

"There were also honeybees on the farm, and the family had a good supply of honey."

"How many horses did you have?" one child asked.

"We had several working horses and a pair of jackasses to work in the fields."

"*What* did you have?" I asked.

"A jackass is a donkey."

"Really?"

"*Ja*, and that's just what they were too. They were contrary. Sometimes when you wanted them to move, it would sit on its ass."

We all had to laugh and Mother would laugh with us.

Eli said, "That's why they call them jackasses, right, Mom?"

"*Ja*."

"They have the right name." Jonas started laughing at his own joke.

"What kind of weather did you have?" I asked, changing the subject and hoping to keep the stories going.

69

Mother looked at the clock and said, "Oh my, it's going on two o'clock and we are still at the dinner table. We'll have to tell that one another time."

"Oh! Come on, we could listen to your stories all afternoon," we all cried.

"Oh! All right."

So another story was told about the weather in Oklahoma. We were all ears, because we enjoyed listening to Mother's stories.

"Well, it was hot in the summer, but we would sometimes have tornadoes. More than what we have here in Iowa. In fact, one day black clouds were rolling in and when I noticed them I thought I'd better go get Jonas and get ready in case a tornado came. I looked for him through the house and outside in the yard, but I couldn't find him. Keeping my eye on the clouds, I could see a black funnel forming.

"I had started out to the barn to look for your father when I noticed the baby out by the windmill. I ran after him and picked him up and ran for the basement. A little later, I heard emergency vehicles on the roads.

(According to the newspaper article that I consulted as an adult, on April 27, 1942, one hundred people were killed and five hundred injured. A freak tornado struck on that Monday afternoon in the small town of Pryor, not far from our farm. The tornado traveled with gun-barrel straightness down Main Street for a six-block stretch. The power lines were downed; two out of the three hospitals were damaged. Hospitals in neighboring towns were filled with the injured!)

"By daybreak, three hundred construction workers moved in to help clear the debris. The local Amish men helped look for bodies all through the night and also helped clean up and rebuild the town again."

We children marveled at this story of faraway destruction and felt lucky not to be living in Oklahama. Looking back, I think part of my mother's intent must have been to make us feel this way. And it worked!

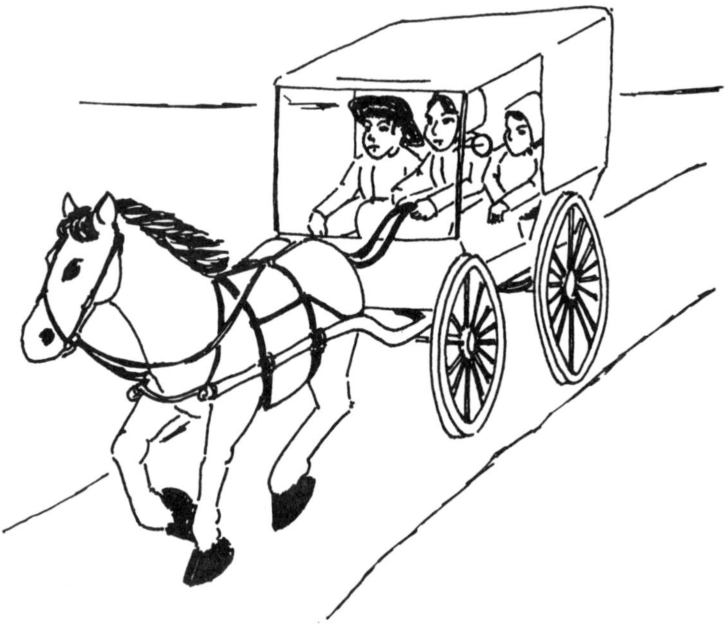

Lizbet and I In Foster Homes

Times were so hard after school was out one summer that Mother asked Lizbet and me if we would go to Aunt Hattie's to stay. We would get room and board in exchange for the chores, including gardening, that we did.

At age six, I agreed to this arrangement, leaving on a Monday and coming home on Saturday. Mother wanted her children home on weekends. It was her way of trying to keep the family together. We girls didn't like going to Aunt Hattie's house, so we agreed to switch off every other week.

The next summer was the same except for one special weekend that I remember. On that weekend, I stayed with Aunt Hattie and Uncle Henry and went to church with them on Sunday. On their way home, they stopped at Mother's house.

Aunt Hattie asked Mother, "Should Alma come along home with us?"

"Do you want to go with them?" Mother asked me.

I nodded my head yes even though I didn't really care to do so. I volunteered to go because I knew my sister Lizbet would have to go if I didn't. I knew my sister didn't like to go either. So they left, taking me for another week. When we arrived at their homestead, everybody went to do their chores.

I had to clean the eggs, and while I was doing the eggs, I started thinking about home. I longed to be there. Tears began to roll down my cheeks. Suddenly I heard steps entering the room. I tried to wipe my tears so Aunt Hattie wouldn't see that I was crying. She walked over in front of me and asked, "Do you have something in your eye?"

"*Ja*," I lied, trying to give her a smile.

Aunt Hattie left the room. Soon she came back and in an exasperated tone of voice demanded, "Why didn't you say you wanted to stay at home?"

I didn't say a word. I didn't know what to say. All I could do was continue my egg cleaning. I knew the situation at home. What's more, I was a shy and introverted little girl. I never said any more than I had to. Hattie finally left the room when I wouldn't answer her.

Oh, how I longed to be at home whenever I was at Aunt Hattie's house! There were times I wanted to run home, but I knew there were wildcats in the woods. Besides that, I would have to cross the river. I didn't know how to swim, and I was afraid I might fall into the deep part. I was afraid to take the road, because one farmer had several vicious dogs. I also knew Aunt Hattie would really make trouble for me and my mother if I ran away. My fears kept me there, but they didn't stop my tears.

While Lizbet was taking her turn boarding at Aunt Hattie's, she also had the same emotions. One day, she just couldn't contain her feelings any longer. She saw a horse and buggy coming down the road. She looked and noticed it was one of Mother's lady friends. Lizbet couldn't resist the opportunity and ran to flag her down.

"May I get a ride home with you?" she begged.

Aunt Hattie saw her and went out to see what Lizbet was doing by the road.

"Go get in the house, Lizbet," she ordered.

Lizbet went to the house, disappointed. She knew she was in trouble. The two ladies visited for about an hour. Then Aunt Hattie came in to see Lizbet. After their conversation, Lizbet realized she could never try to leave again. Aunt Hattie just wasn't the understanding type.

The third summer, Mother didn't ask us to go to Aunt Hattie's. Although we didn't complain, she must have seen how we felt. However, our economic situation was still grim, so my mother was always looking for ways to manage with so many children. One day, she came into the house and announced, "Your cousins Enos Miller and Jonas Williams would like to have two of you children come and stay with them. Enos, would you like to go to Cousin Miller's, and, Alma, would you like to go to Cousin Jonas Williams's house?"

"*Ja,*" I answered too quickly.

I thought about my experience at Aunt Hattie's, and tears came to my eyes. Enos nodded his silent approval.

Mother realized we weren't very happy about it and said, "Neither family has any children, and they really would like to have you."

"All right," I agreed again and felt my heart sinking.

The next day, Jonas and Eli had the horse and buggy ready for us. Mother took Enos and me to our cousins' houses for a week. Mother stopped at Cousin Jonas Williams's home first and left me there. Then she went to Cousin Enos Miller's to leave Brother Enos at their place. Jonas Williams and Enos Miller were neighbors and lived about one mile from our farm.

Cousin Bertha was Jonas's wife. She was a petite young woman, about five-five, with black hair and brown eyes. She was much more sensitive than Aunt Hattie and realized that I was sad and depressed. The third day, she stated, "We'll take a walk over to Cousin Enos's to see your brother. Would you like that?"

"Oh! *Ja!*" I said. My eyes brightened with surprise, and I gave her a smile.

"All right! Let's go now," she replied, returning my

smile. Cousin Bertha had hit the nail on the head. I realized then that Bertha was going to be all right to live with. I stayed for the summer without wanting to run away.

When school started, I returned home. About a month later, Bertha asked Mother, "Could Alma come over every day after school and help me? We are adopting a new baby from Indiana. Since Jonas is building a new farmhouse and will be working late in the evenings, I could use Alma to baby-sit while I'm doing the evening chores."

At the age of nine I would be allowed to baby-sit for a newborn! I was overjoyed to go help Bertha and stay overnight. Their house was closer to my school, and Bertha would pack my lunch every day. Cousin Bertha had taken to me as if I were her own daughter. She taught me how to sew with the foot-pedal sewing machine and also how to care for a newborn.

Each evening before Bertha went to the barn, she would tell me what to cook for supper and I would have it ready when she finished the chores. I stayed until they moved to their new farm. I couldn't go with them, however, because they had moved into a different school district.

Sickness Strikes

In every Amish home, like any other home, sickness strikes at one time or another. The second year after Father was hospitalized, illness struck our home in the springtime. The old-fashioned measles started with my oldest brother, Jonas, then moved on to Enos, Junior, Sarah, Lizbet, and myself. Mother pulled all the blinds to keep out the light to protect the children's eyes. It was up to Eli and Mother to maintain the chores for the next several weeks.

Several months later, Enos awoke complaining of pains in his stomach and side. Mother watched over him all day. In the evening after chores, he said he still didn't feel good but the pain had left. Early the next morning, Mother checked him. She found he had a high fever. His body was becoming green.

According to the Amish religion, no modern conveniences are allowed. No automobiles and, of course, no telephones are permitted. However, my mother knew she had to get help quick for Enos. She asked Jonas to hop on his horse and hurry over to the modern farmer's house and ask him if he would rush them to the hospital. In the emergency room, Enos was examined. He was immediately wheeled away, a very sick boy. A nurse came out to get Mother's permission to perform surgery at once.

"What is the problem?" Mother asked.

"It appears to be his appendix; we will have to operate right way," she replied.

Four hours later, the doctor came out to see Mother.
"How is he?" she asked.

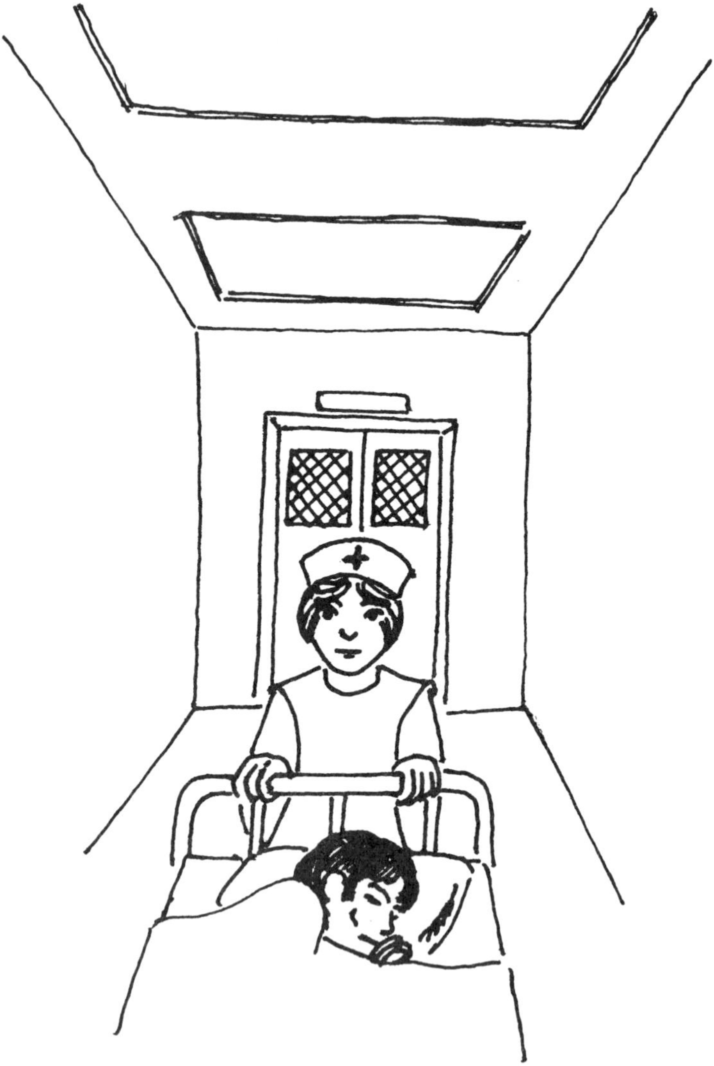

"He had a ruptured appendix, and his condition is critical. We did everything we could. Now it's all up to him, but, frankly, it doesn't look good."

"God, he's in your hands now. Please help him. Whatever your will, let it be so," Mother prayed.

Our neighbor, the modern farmer, left the hospital. On his way home, he stopped at the house to inform us other children of our brother's condition. Mother remained at the hospital until Enos was ready to come home. Due to his youth and strength, he was able to make a rapid recovery. While our mother was away, we children managed the farm unsupervised.

Some years later, both Sarah and Jonas also had their appendix removed. However, their operations were more routine and not as critical as in Enos's case. Sarah also had her tonsils removed while she was there.

Amish mothers always breast-feed their babies, if possible. My mother fed her babies this natural way, too. In 1940, I was her sixth newborn baby girl. Mother tried to breast-feed me, but I was a baby who wouldn't take any kind of milk. I cried a lot and Mother didn't know what was wrong with me. Out of her eight babies, she considered me to be the sickliest child of them all. As a child, on many occasions I complained of my ears hurting.

One evening when I was five or six years old, the family had supper at Uncle Judas's home. As usual, I had an earache. Uncle Judas smoked an old pipe. He volunteered to get his pipe hot, and when it was hot, he carefully blew warm smoke into my ears. Next he placed cotton balls in them in an attempt to relieve the pain. This remedy seemed to help temporarily.

One cold winter day, I stayed home from school with a throbbing earache. It was very painful, but I didn't want to complain to Mother. I went upstairs and climbed onto my feather mattress bed. I huddled under the comforter, hiding my pain in tears. Soon Mother discovered I was missing and came upstairs and found me in the unheated room. Mother picked me up and carried me downstairs, sitting me in a living room chair beside the old potbellied stove. She placed a couple of towels to heat on the wood stove and pressed them to my ears. To help relieve the pain, she put a couple of drops of oil in each ear. That Saturday we visited the doctor in Independence.

For years I lived with a constant earache, day in and day out. In the summer of 1950, when I was ten years of age, I was stricken with pneumonia. My illness had affected my hearing also. My brothers and sisters had to shout for me to be able to hear them. In February 1951, I was admitted to the hospital to have my tonsils removed. I was to be released three or four days after surgery. Just prior to the day I was to go home, a tremendous snowstorm raged through the area. Due to road conditions, I was forced to spend another week at the hospital. Before I left, one of the nurses entered my room carrying a newspaper.

"Did you know your name is in the paper?" she asked.

"No, why?"

"The doctor had it put in to let you know what a good patient you have been."

I thought that was really something. It made me happy and I asked in surprise, "Was I?"

"You certainly were!" she answered with a smile.

Where There Is a Will There Is a Way

One day we younger children were in the kitchen. Mother asked, "Where is Eli?"

"He is outside, in front of the house," I answered.

Mother went outside in front of the house to talk to Eli. Soon he came inside and stated, "I'll see if we don't have some meat for the dinner table." He picked up the gun hanging over the door and walked out.

"Hunting season isn't on," Mother called.

"I'm going to hunt on our farm."

Some hours later, Eli came home with a rabbit to be cooked for dinner.

Most times the cows would come home on their own when it was milking time. One summer evening the cows didn't come, so Eli decided he would go after them on horseback. He rode back through the woods but couldn't locate them.

Soon he came back home whistling and smiling as if he were the king of the cowboys.

"What's he so happy for without the cows?" Sarah asked.

Sitting high on his horse, Eli walked his steed home through the barnyard up to the house.

"What are you so happy for without the cows?" we asked, watching him.

He dropped something on the front cement slab and smiled. We went over to see what he had.

"Here's something for dinner," he gloated.

"Wow! What a big fish," I remarked.

"How did you get that?" Sarah asked.

"I caught it. Will you fix it for supper?"

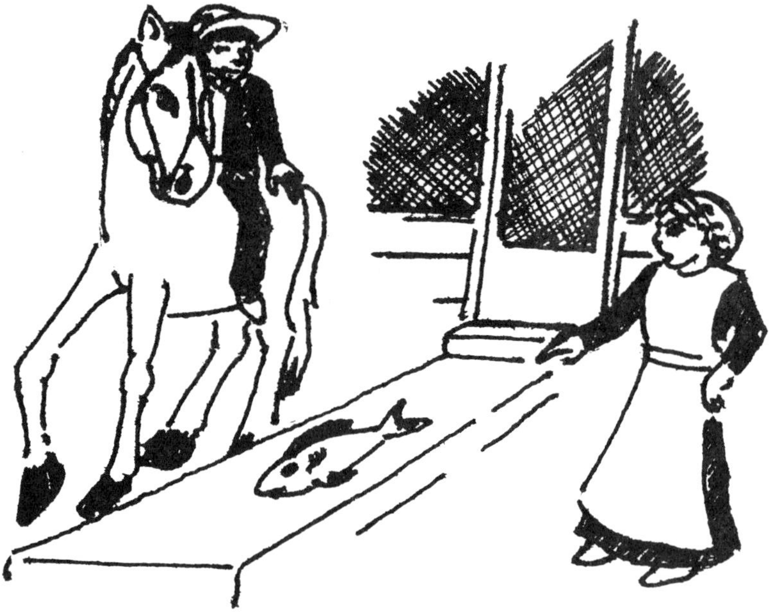

"Ja," Sarah answered with surprise.

"The cows are on the other side of the river, so I have to go get them."

He went after the cows, and Sarah and Mother cleaned the thirteen-pound fish for dinner. At the supper table, we all wondered how this had come about. How had Eli caught a fish without a fishing pole?

"How did you catch the fish, Eli?" Mother questioned.

"While I let the horse take a drink, I looked down the river and saw two fish coming toward me. I quickly took my shoes off, but I didn't have time to throw my clothes off, so I dived in with my clothes on. I tried to catch both, but one got away. They were very slippery to try to catch with bare hands."

"Boy, it's good fish," Enos commented.

"It sure is," everybody agreed.

Everyone was proud of their brother.

"Well, where there is a will there is a way," Eli said.

Uncle Judas wouldn't give Mother money for anything. She had to ask him, and then he would turn her down. The boys managed to get two tame rabbits and started to raise them. They had eight rabbit hutches. When they were full, they would turn the rabbits loose on the farm. We had rabbits under the blacksmith shop, corn crib, and buggy shop, and running free all over the yard. It was a pretty sight to see them hippity-hopping from one building to another or just sitting in the driveway or the yard eating grass.

The boys trained the watchdogs to leave the rabbits alone. When the dogs weren't with the boys, they would sit and watch the rabbits hippity-hopping here and there over the homestead. The boys counted eighty rabbits at one time.

When the boys started their rabbit farm, Mother

started to raise ducks, too. She started with six ducklings. When the boys had eighty rabbits, she had sixty ducks.

The ducks would waddle down to the creek to swim. It was fascinating to watch them. If they saw something moving under the water as they were swimming, they'd dive down head first and all you could see sticking up was their webbed feet and a perfect curled tail. After a while, some of them would come up on the bank and sun themselves.

It was up to us girls to feed the ducks for Mother. One night, Lizbet and I were mixing their feed with water at the pump. As we were mixing the meal, the baby ducklings were running under and around our feet. Lizbet accidentally stepped on one baby duckling, and its eye popped out of its head.

Enos was walking our way when we saw him and yelled, "Enos, come quickly!"

He came over and we showed him what had happened. We were afraid Mother would get angry with us. He picked it up, twisted the duck's head off to make sure it wouldn't suffer anymore, and threw it to the pigs. We were upset about it, but he remained calm and said, "Don't worry about it; just try and be more careful."

"All right."

When the feed was ready for the ducks, we would yell out the duck call: "Duckie, Duckie, Duckie, Duck!"

If that wasn't a noisy group coming to the feed trough! Every duck had its own tone, anywhere from high notes to low. I called it a barnyard concert. Fascinated, we'd stand back watching, but sometimes we had to laugh. They'd get up on the tips of their webbed feet, spread their wings out and up, their bodies expanding with air, and then they'd do a ballet dance to their food. It was beautiful but noisy.

When Mother needed money, she would take dressed rabbit, duck, and sometimes chicken to market. This was her way of working around her brother to get cash for what we needed.

The first time we had to dress rabbits, Eli said, "Alma, come help me."

I went outside to help. He caught a rabbit and tied the hind feet up on the fence. "Hold the rabbit's ears," he told me.

"Oh, no!" I gasped.

The rabbit looked me in the eye, and I looked back in his. It was just like the rabbit was begging me, "Don't do it; save me!"

"I feel sorry for it," I said.

"Oh, the rabbit won't know what happened. It will be quick," Eli promised me, and before I knew it, the rabbit was dead. We dressed three rabbits for Mother to take to market.

We girls had to dress the chickens for her, too. Mother would tell us to go dress three chickens for market. We had a log sitting on its end with two nails on it. I would lay the chicken's head in between the two nails so the head wouldn't move. Then I would take the old ax and cut the head off quickly. I would throw the chicken down on the ground to bleed until it stopped jumping.

The dead chicken was dipped in a bucket of boiling water so I could pluck the feathers.

Sarah always held the chickens over flaming papers to burn off the tiny pinfeathers.

One day, Mother said, "Alma, go catch the chickens to dress." Mother was outside and in a hurry.

"Never mind, I'll do it for you," Mother volunteered.

I handed her a chicken. Mother took the chicken's head in her hand and gave it a couple of twists. After the chicken fell to the ground, she threw the severed head into the pigpen.

I was amazed when I realized it was so easy that way. I wouldn't have to look the chicken in the eye when I laid its head on the log. So I tried it and discovered it was easier to do it Mother's way.

When it was time to butcher the ducks, it took more time than the rabbits or chickens. The ducks were beheaded to bleed, and the fine feathers were plucked and saved for pillows and mattresses before dipping the duck into a bucket of boiling water.

One year at Thanksgiving, Mother said, "Dress an extra duck for our Thanksgiving dinner."

"For our Thanksgiving dinner?" I repeated.

"*Jah*. They are quite good to eat."

I was surprised, because whenever we dressed a tame rabbit or a duck it was always for market.

We thought it was a treat to have a duck on our Thanksgiving table.

The rabbit skin was also sold for extra cash. So you see it's true—despite Uncle Judas. "Where there is a will there is a way."

Electrical Storm

On a calm but hot summer evening, the children had gone upstairs for a good night's sleep.

At 1:00 A.M. my mother laid her hand on one of the boy's shoulders. She said, "Jonas, Eli, Enos, and Junior, wake up. Get up and get dressed."

The boys questioned, "Why?"

"It's storming; we are having an electrical storm," Mom replied.

They didn't argue. When they opened their eyes, the dark night was bright with lightning. Then it would thunder with a loud crack.

Mother went to the girls' room. She shook us awake, mentioning each name.

I pulled the covers up over myself, stating, "I don't want to get up. I want to sleep."

Mother came back and shook me again. "Get up."

"Why? I'm tired."

At that moment, it cracked hard. I jumped out of bed, put my dress on, and ran downstairs to the living room. When I entered the room, the boys were sitting on the davenport. Enos was wide awake with fear, and Eli was nodding his head with his eyelids too heavy to keep them open. Since Jonas was the oldest, he was awake, waiting in case he had to help Mother with the responsibilities. Sarah and Lizbet were asleep on the daybed, and Mother was sitting in a kitchen chair in the living room facing the window. She said, "Come sit down."

"Why do we always have to get up when it storms?"

I sat beside Mother where I could watch the storm.

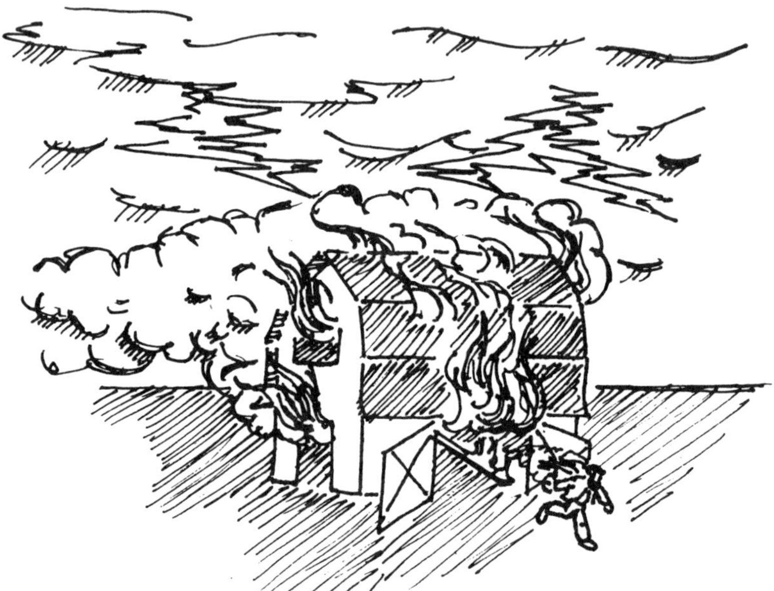

The outside was as dark as the ace of spades. You couldn't even see the building twenty feet away from the house. The next minute lightning would flash and the lightning would be so bright you could see the neighbors' homestead a mile across the field.

Each time it thundered extra hard, we would jump. Mother would get up from her chair, walk to the window, and check every building on the farm, and the neighbors' buildings within sight. Then she would sit back with relief.

Mother wanted us to understand why we had to get up every time there was a storm. She sat up in her chair at attention and proceeded to tell us how they had had a storm in Kansas.

"When my folks lived in Kansas, we had all gone to bed on a hot summer night. No indication of a storm was in sight. During the night an electrical storm appeared. Grandpa awoke about 2:00 A.M. He noticed a continuous flickering of light outside. He got up to check it and went to the window. Without hesitation he grabbed his pants and yelled at the boys upstairs, 'William, Al, Dan, Henry, the barn is on fire!'

"Hastily the boys grabbed their pants and in their bare feet ran to help save the animals. Their sisters hurried to help pump water at the hand pump.

"The window along the stairway had broken from the heat of hot flames, and glass had fallen over the stairs. The boys ran heedlessly through the broken glass lying on the stairway.

"The cows, calves, horses, and a couple of sows with piglets had been left in the barn for the night. The boys ran into the burning barn to get the cows and horses out. They had to lead them out one by one. The barn was so hot they had to fight the last couple of cows to get them out to safety. They led them to a corral away from the barn.

"Grandpa was trying to get the calves out. Burning pieces of ceiling started to drop here and there. They turned the horses loose. When they thought they had everything out, someone said, 'We forgot one cow and calf in a stall.'

" 'Oh, no!' Grandpa ran for the barn once more.

"Neighbors started arriving. They had seen the flames from miles away and were coming over to help. Everyone yelled, 'Don't go back in; that barn's going to collapse!'

"It was too late; Grandpa had disappeared back into the flames.

"The cows were wild. The boys were still struggling to get them into a corral. The cows wanted to run back into the burning barn.

"Grandpa had to struggle with the cow to get it out. He had to leave the calf behind, because he couldn't get to it. He emerged from the barn beating the flames from his shoulders as he narrowly missed being struck by a falling beam.

"Everybody was relieved to see him safe. The neighbors and friends were pumping water into buckets and passing them down a line hand to hand. The water was poured over the buildings close to the barn. Every time they threw water on the building, it would sizzle, with steam rolling into the sky. They all worked hard trying to save the other buildings.

"The cow Grandpa saved had received third degree burns on her back. Before they had her in the corral, she started to run for the barn—back into the burning inferno. They couldn't stop her. She burned with the barn.

"Grandpa was sick at heart to see the animal burn alive. The sows with piglets and a calf were trapped inside and burned to ashes."

I asked, "Did they get everything else out of the barn?"

"No, all the equipment in the barn plus the hay went up in flames. By 7:00 A.M. the barn was completely destroyed. Nothing but hot coals remained, and these smoked for days and days. Friends and neighbors left around 7:00 A.M., when they weren't needed to pour any more water.

"Grandpa and the boys returned to the house exhausted. They washed their feet on the porch. A couple of the boys complained that their feet hurt. When they washed them, they noticed they were cut."

"How did they get cut?" I asked.

"When they ran over the broken glass on the stairway," Mom replied.

"Did they rebuild the barn?"

"Of course. Before all the friends left, they asked Grandpa to get the estimate together to rebuild the barn. Amish don't have insurance on their buildings with an insurance company like a lot of people do today.

"The Amish don't subscribe to insurance through a regular insurance company. It is not in accordance with their beliefs. Therefore, they have their own private insurance.

"If a barn is destroyed by fire or other means, they get an estimate for material needed to replace it and then everyone gets together and in one day they rebuild it. The other families furnish three-fourths of the expenses for the material, and the women bring food along to feed the seventy-five to one hundred men needed for the one-day job."

"What did they do when it was time to milk the cows?"

"After breakfast the boys went out to the workshop and made themselves a one-footed milking stool. Then they milked the cows out in the open of the corral until the barn was rebuilt, rain or shine."

"They really milked the cows out in the open?" I asked.

"*Ja*. There was no barn; where else would they milk?"

"Oh! *Ja*."

"The storm has calmed down, so why don't you all go back to bed now 'til morning?"

"*Ja*." Everybody agreed and was ready to go back to bed again.

After morning chores were done, it was daylight. Enos had walked in from the barn and noticed a split in the house foundation. He entered the house, saying, "Mom! Remember last night we thought it sounded like the house got hit?"

"*Ja*."

"Well, there's a split in the foundation. Lightning must have hit it."

We all had to go out and investigate.

"That was a close one, wasn't it, Mom?" Enos asked.

"It sure was and a noisy one, too."

We were thankful to God for keeping us in his hands throughout the night.

Billy Goat Rough

As per the slogan of the postal service, through rain or sleet the mailman always got through and arrived at our house, usually at the dinner hour. This day he blew his horn several times.

"Go see what the mailman wants, Jonas," Mother called.

Soon Jonas came in and told Mother, "The mailman has a billy goat and wonders if we want it. He can't keep it in town where he lives. We can have the goat if we give him a good home."

"A billy goat," she gasped.

"*Ja!* May we have it?"

"Oh, I don't think so."

"Please, Mom. Let us have it, please. We have enough room here on the farm," Jonas begged.

All the children were surprised and helped him, begging Mother to please let us have the goat.

"How would we get it here?" Mom asked.

"I'll go ask," Jonas replied.

Jonas went out and asked the mailman. He came back to the house and said, "He will bring it out tomorrow afternoon."

"All right," Mother replied.

We were all very excited at the prospect of having a new pet, and it seemed we discussed it every waking moment until the next day.

The next day, at about 1:00 P.M., the mailman honked his horn again and we ran to see who it was. There was Billy in the backseat of the mailman's car. The mailman

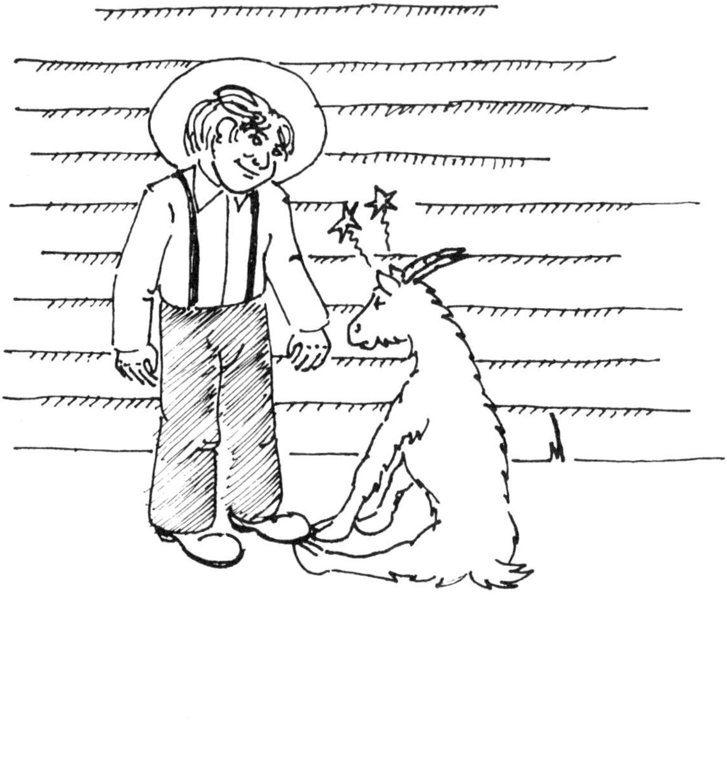

got out of the car, opened the back door, and pulled Billy from the car.

There he was, our new pet, horns and all. He was a buff-colored goat with eight-inch horns.

The mailman expressed his appreciation to us for taking Billy and giving him a good home. Then he departed down the dusty road.

As the dust cleared, we stood there inspecting our new pet, who looked like he had just lost his best friend. This depression didn't last long for Billy, though. He was soon keeping us all alarmed and entertained with his devilish ways.

Sarah always disappeared after dinner. She tried to get out of doing dishes. After dinner, she would take off for the outhouse. She would sit there for an hour or two looking through the wish book (the Sears catalog), wishing.

One day I decided to go with her. As we were walking to the outhouse, Sarah noticed the billy goat and shouted, "Run, Alma, the billy goat's coming toward us!" We took off running as fast as our feet could carry us. Sarah had a couple of crackers in her hand. The crackers flew up in the air and down on the ground. The goat saw them and stopped to check and eat them while we scrambled to the outhouse.

"Boy, that was close," I stated with relief.

"It's a good thing I had those crackers in my hand. But how are we going to get back to the house? I don't have any more crackers to give him."

"I don't know, but he's a mean one." My sisters and I were all secretly afraid of Billy.

We waited and waited for the goat to leave the area. We watched him through a crack in the door. Then we looked through the wish book, hoping he would leave. After an hour, the goat started out toward the barn.

"Oh, he's going for the barn," Sarah whispered.

I looked out to see if he was far enough away so we could make a run for the house. Then the stupid animal stopped and gazed back at the outhouse, looking for us. We waited a little longer as the goat turned toward the barn, walking like he had given us up.

"Run, Alma, as fast as you can go," Sarah ordered.

"All right."

We both took off running as fast as we could, up the hill to the house.

"Here he comes," I yelled.

"Run! Run!" Sarah yelled as she gasped for breath.

Sarah opened the door to run inside and tripped over the steps and fell on her stomach on the porch floor. I saw the goat behind me and jumped over her. Still lying on the floor, Sarah pulled up her knees so I could slam the door. After we were safe, we both started laughing. We laughed so hard that Mother heard us. She came to the door and questioned, "What's going on out here?"

Sarah picked herself up off the floor, and we both explained what had happened. Mother laughed at us.

As we walked into the kitchen, all the dirty dishes were still waiting to be washed. It never failed; the dishes were always there for us girls to do no matter how long we were gone.

One day, Brother Enos was walking to the barn to do his evening chores. When he was close to the barn, he turned around and saw the billy goat. Enos stood there, eye to eye with the goat, watching him to see what he was going to do. As he stood there, the billy goat came running toward him. Enos kept his brown eyes on him and stood still. Just before the goat was going to ram him, he put his head down and closed his eyes to let Enos have it. Enos stepped to his right, and the goat ran into the barn head-on. The goat was surprised and shook his head with pain.

But that wasn't enough; he started after Enos again.

Enos ran and leaped inside the barn and closed the door, causing Billy to crash against it. Enos had to laugh, because the joke was on Billy again.

One spring morning, the brothers came in for breakfast after chores were all done. Jonas and Enos were washing their face and hands in the separator room. Eli was walking into the kitchen, where Mom was trying to get the pancakes done. The sisters were setting the table and trying to have everything ready for breakfast.

Eli asked, "Mother, may I make a harness for the goat?"

"Are there enough scraps of leather in the blacksmith shop to make one?"

"I have to check but I think so."

"If you can find enough, go ahead."

A week later, Eli had a harness made and Jonas had the little red wagon ready. They hitched the goat to the wagon and gave rides to the little ones.

Eli was the master of the goat. He wasn't afraid of it, and the goat knew it, too.

"May I have a ride, Eli?" I asked.

"Sure! Come and get in the wagon."

I was all excited and climbed on the wagon to go for the ride. During the ride, I asked, "May I drive him?"

"Sure, if you want to," he said and handed me the reins. I took the reins and when they were in my hands, the goat immediately stopped. Billy turned his head back and looked at me, and I looked at Billy. I ordered him to go, but he just stood there looking at me. This scared me, so I said, "Here, take the reins; he knows that it's not you." I handed Eli the reins.

Eli took the reins, laughing while he drove me back to the house.

"That's fun, but I don't think Billy likes me," I commented.

"He knows who is boss."

Eli enjoyed his new pet, but it didn't take us long to discover why the mailman didn't want Billy. Billy brought plenty of excitement to the farm.

Bottomless Hole

The Amish tradition is to welcome a new family when they move in from another settlement. Word was passed on in church on Sunday that a new family had bought a local farm about four and a half miles from our farm.

This family had moved to our dry state of Iowa in the spring. The Amish try to move either after crops had been harvested or before fields were planted.

At the dinner table, Mother stated, "I want to go to welcome the Amish family that moved in from Ohio. Too much time has passed already, and I must do it today before we make our second hay for the season. The hay is cut already, and when I get back we'll make hay."

Eli asked, "May I go along, because I heard they have a boy my age?"

"*Ja!* That would be a good idea."

It was on a hot summer day in August that Mother and son arrived at the new family's homestead. Mother introduced Eli and herself, and the newcomers did the same. Mother visited with the folks while Eli visited with their son, Abe.

Through their conversation, Abe learned that Eli lived on a farm with a river running across and through the woods a quarter-mile from his house.

Abe asked, "Are there any deep spots where you can go swimming?"

"Yeah! A couple of deep spots. In fact, one day we were making fences and we wanted to go across this one place, so I dived in to see how tall a fence post we would need. I couldn't find bottom. We had to change our fence line."

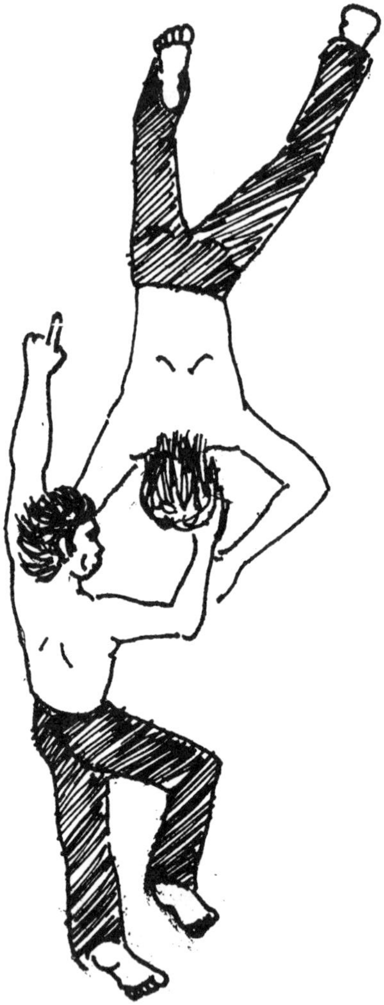

"Do you have to make a fence across that river?"

"Why, sure! If we want to keep the cows from going onto our neighbors' land. When the season is dry, like right now, the river is low and calm, and we can wade across with a horse and buggy in some places. The water is so clear, we can see bottom all the way across it, except for the deep part. The deep part makes good fishing."

"Boy, you are lucky. This farm is dry, no ponds or nothing. Just a water well."

"But it's good for farming."

Abe had to agree. "Do you think we could go swimming tonight after hay making and the other chores are done?" he asked.

"Do you know how to swim?"

"Oh, *ja!* I sure would like to wash the hay dirt and sweat off after this hot sun goes down."

"I agree. We swim almost every day in the summer. We don't care if you come over, as long as you know how to swim. Come on over; it will be refreshing."

Mother called, "Eli, it is time to go now."

Eli was excited. He had found a new friend and was going swimming. Abe came over in the evening, after his work was done.

Since the Amish family was new, they didn't know all the traditions yet. Iowa was different from other Amish settlements.

As Abe walked with my brothers to the river, they began to inform Abe what the local Amish attitudes were. "The Amish here don't want us to go swimming. Let us tell you something that happened with the church about a year ago. We always went swimming, either in the river or the creek behind the barn. One day, at 105 degrees, it was so hot we decided to take a swim in the creek to cool off. We threw our clothes on shore and dived in, in our birthday suits. We never had a swimming suit. To own a swimming suit is against the Amish religion here. It's not considered modest.

"While we were swimming we heard a horse and buggy cross the little wooden bridge. It was about fifty feet from the water hole where we were swimming. Trees and high weeds grew between us. We swam to the far north side so we wouldn't be seen. As the buggy followed the curve in the road, they could look down on the south side of the creek and see our clothes, lying in the open on the shore.

"Next Sunday we had church. We all went to church unaware of any trouble. When we got there, it was announced that there was a meeting being held for the members after service. After service, all the children were excused. Now was the time for all the busybodies that liked to make rules to get busy. Our mother was not aware the meeting was for her benefit.

"The meeting started with, 'One of the members saw Katie's boys' clothes laying on the creek bank.' Some parents started to whisper with astonished expressions. A voice came from the crowd and said, 'Katie, do you have anything to say to this?'

" 'No.' She sat thinking, it was hard to believe this meeting was because her boys went swimming in their own farm's creek.

" 'Do you realize those boys didn't have any clothes on? That is a sin.'

" 'Boys will be boys.'

" 'They are your boys and you are responsible for them.'

" 'I agree.'

" 'Well, what are you going to do about it?'

" 'What do you want me to do about it?'

" 'You should confess your sins.'

" 'I didn't do it.'

" 'They are your boys.'

" 'I can't keep my eyes on them every minute.' Again she sat thinking, *They didn't hurt anybody; they minded their own business. This is ridiculous. The boys work hard to help me farm. They work like men instead of boys. Why did I ever agree to move to Iowa six years ago? Nothing but problems from several nosy women who like to pick, pick, pick.*

"Forty-five minutes passed. Our mother finally made a confession just to keep peace with them, so they wouldn't throw her out of the church. She also wanted to be a good example to us. After the meeting, dinner was served and we left. On the way home, Mother told the story about the meeting. After this public chastisement, Mother made sure that any swimming we did was kept a secret among our family members."

As the boys walked toward the swimming hole, Eli cautioned, "So, Abe, you make sure you don't tell anyone about going swimming."

"Oh! I won't."

When they arrived at the river, Abe said, "Where is the bottomless hole?"

"Right over there!" The boys started taking their heavy, homemade clothes off.

"You have never hit bottom here?"

"Nah! Never."

"That's hard to believe—never hit bottom!" He jumped in with excitement and the boys followed. A little later, they came up to surface.

"Boy, this is great!" Abe said.

Eli and Jonas had to agree. They swam like a couple of fish in the sea for a while.

One by one they all climbed out and sat on the bank.

Relaxed, Abe exclaimed, "It really feels good to be clean!"

They all had to agree on this ninety-seven-degree evening. Abe was on cloud nine. He really was enjoying himself. Eli and Jonas noticed that he didn't swim as well as they did, but he was having a good time.

Abe requested, "I'm going to try to hit bottom. Do you care?"

Jonas and Eli agreed to stay out on the bank with Abe's pocket watch.

Abe dove down and disappeared. Eli and Jonas waited and waited, keeping their eyes on the pocket watch and the bottomless hole.

Eli asked, "Jonas, what do you think? Several minutes have passed."

"Give him a little more time."

However, when a minute passed, Eli stated, "I'm going after him. I just know he's having trouble. You stay here, Jonas, because I'm a faster swimmer."

He dove in and was gone for a while. A little later he came back up to check and asked, "Did he come back up?"

"Nah."

Eli dived back down. Farther and farther he went. He couldn't find Abe! Eli came up to check for the second time to see if he missed Abe. When Eli came to the surface, he looked at Jonas worriedly.

Jonas volunteered, "He hasn't come back up yet."

Eli took a quick dive back down. He continued searching the water, looking for Abe for a third time. He knew he had to keep his cool, for he couldn't panic or they all would be in real trouble. He continued down, hoping to find Abe. Eli knew Abe hadn't floated up, so he had to be somewhere down deeper. He continued to go down even faster. His eyes were wide open so he wouldn't miss

Abe along the way. Eli was getting worried, knowing Abe was in real trouble. He swam straight down, feeling like a fish and knowing he had no time to waste. Every second was crucial for Abe as well as himself. He was getting more and more worried. "A little deeper," he coaxed himself, swimming faster.

"Come on, Abe, where are you?" he said to himself. "I have to find you!"

Eli began to worry about how deep he was going, but his worry for Abe kept him swimming downward. He started to plead with himself, "Don't give up; you just can't give up." Continuing down, he felt himself desperate for air.

However, as Eli swam down farther, he spotted a body and swam over to it. Abe saw Eli and, desparate for help, grabbed him and started to pull Eli down with him. Eli struggled with the drowning Abe.

Abe was gasping for air as they struggled. Eli tried to pull him up, but Abe wanted to go the wrong way. Eli tried to pull him up toward the surface. Abe pulled him under again. They struggled violently. Eli was gasping for air. He was determined and strong, continuing to struggle to pull Abe to the surface.

From the bank, Jonas kept his eyes open and looked for any signs of them in the water. He could see deep into the river, for the water was very clear. He was getting nervous, waiting and thinking, *Where are they both? Come on, you guys.* He knew they both had to be desperate for air at that point. Time passed. However, he couldn't wait any longer. Panic-stricken, he dived into the bottomless hole and went down swimming like a fish. Anxiously, he scanned the water to find his brother and friend. Eyes wide open, he swam farther down. He saw them struggling. He swam over to help Eli. Abe grabbed Jonas, too, pulling him under. Jonas broke loose, swam behind Abe, and knocked Abe out cold. Jonas and Eli both grabbed an arm and swam to the surface. Dragging Abe onto the bank, Eli fell exhausted to the ground and inhaled fresh air with relief.

Jonas worked on Abe, pushing on his body to get the water out of him. Then they all rested in silence.

Eli broke the silence. "Abe, what happened?"

"I lost my sense of direction. I thought Eli was taking me the wrong way."

"Do you realize that I almost drowned down there trying to help you? You pulled me under and put up a fight like that. We are both very lucky that I was a better swimmer and stronger than you. I should have knocked you out."

"You are supposed to knock out the person that you are trying to save so he can't fight back," interrupted Jonas. "They will pull you under if you don't."

"Boy! We are both lucky. Thanks, Jonas, for coming to help me. I don't think I could have made it without you."

Abe was very apologetic and thanked them both. "I will never try to find the bottom of this hole again, because it doesn't have one."

They all dressed and went home with memories of an experience they would never forget.

Mischief

My mother made frequent trips to Independence. Mother probably made more trips than the average parent because our father was hospitalized in Independence.

When Mother went to town on errands and left us children behind unattended, it gave us the opportunity to be mischievous. Mother always said, "What one child doesn't think of the other one will." How right she was on that!

Saturday was usually a day for cleaning and baking. It was also the day when Mother made her trip to town. One Saturday after dinner, Eli was riding his horse around the farm. We didn't have saddles, so the boys always rode bareback.

Eli rode his horse up to the house, and one of us children said, "Do you think a horse could walk up the stairway?"

"Don't know."

"Want to try it?"

"Yeah."

"Does everybody agree not to tell Mom?" Eli asked.

"*Ja!* We agree."

"Okay, but you make sure you don't say a word to Mom."

We placed a younger child at the window to watch for Mother in case she should come home before we managed to get the horse back out.

The horse was brought in through the porch, the separator room, and through the kitchen to the stairway. As he started into the stairway, the horse lifted his tail.

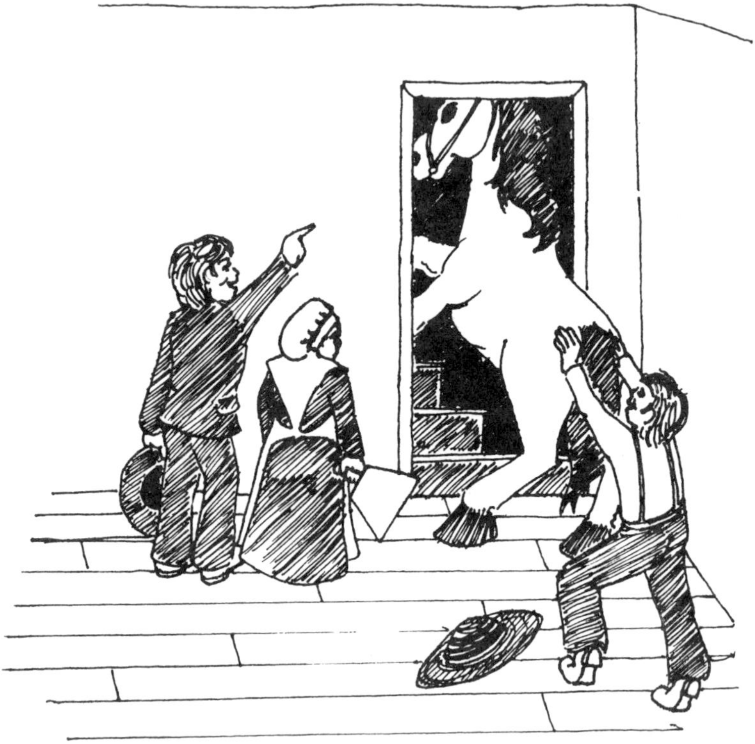

"Oh! He's going to go in the house," Sarah gasped.
"Get the dustpan quick," Enos ordered.
I grabbed the dustpan and handed it to Sarah. She took it, but the horse had gas.
"WOW! What a smell!" I said, holding my nose.
Eli was trying to coax the horse to go up the stairs. He had taken six steps and wouldn't go any farther.
"What's the holdup?" Sarah asked.
"He's stuck. I can't get him up or down," Eli complained.
The little one at the window yelled, "Mom's coming, Mom's coming!"
"Oh, na! Get that horse out of here quick!" Sarah screamed.
"I'm trying, but I can't get him up or down. Stand back. I'll try to scare him back down!" Eli shouted.
He lifted his arms up quickly and scared the horse back down and let the horse outside. As Eli led him out, Sarah followed with the bucket of water, mopping behind them. Sarah had just finished mopping the kitchen floor when Mother pulled up in front of the house.
"Come here, Jonas," Mother called.
Jonas picked a watermelon out of the buggy and carried it to the water pump to place it in cold water for our treat.
"Boy! Mom got us a watermelon," I said to Sarah with surprise.
"Did she?"
"*Ja.*"
"Did you get your work done?" Mother asked.
"*Ja,* but the kitchen floor is still wet," Sarah answered.
After all the evening chores were finished, we enjoyed the special treat Mother had brought home for us. This was unusual, since she had never done it before.

On the following Tuesday evening, a buggyful of Amish men came over to see Mother.

"Mother, what do the men want?" we asked.

"Stay out of the living room; it's about the watermelon that I bought last Saturday."

We stayed out to leave Mother alone, since we knew she was depressed and troubled.

When the men left, we asked, "How do they know about the watermelon?"

"Your cousin Jonas Williams saw me and offered to carry the watermelon to the buggy. On his way home, he stopped to see Uncle Judas and told him that he saw me. Jonas told me he didn't think anything about it. But Judas said the melon was something that wasn't necessary to buy. That's why they came over to see me."

Mother had left the living room to go to the kitchen to get away from the men. When she started back to the living room, she stopped and looked at the gun hanging over the doorway. She thought, *How I would like to use that gun on myself; then I wouldn't be a burden to anyone anymore. But what would my poor children do without me? Suicide isn't the answer.*

We children had really enjoyed that frivolous watermelon, and Mother's heart had rejoiced to see her children so happy.

I have to wonder what the Amish would have said back then if they knew what we children really did sometimes. We tried to overcome our boring life at home. No matter how much responsibility children are given, they still have to have some fun. Kids will be kids. We didn't have a box of toys to choose from. The girls in this settlement were not to have dolls that resembled real babies. They had to be rag dolls, dressed in Amish clothes. This was the Amish way of keeping their children from taking an interest in other dress styles as they grew up.

To have some fun, the boys made themselves stilts to walk on. Enos built a tunnel through the hay in the haymow. I can recall we were playing in the hay and every child had to crawl through the tunnel. When we were crawling through and were deep in the hay there was little air.

"I can't breathe," I said quickly.

"I can't either," Lizbet replied.

We all had to crawl backward to get back out. The opening was just big enough to crawl through. When everyone went in, it cut off the air supply. I advised the other children later not to try to go into a hay tunnel unless there were two openings for the air to circulate. Otherwise, your life could be in danger.

One day while Mother was gone, we children were home unsupervised. After dinner, Jonas, age seventeen, and Eli, age sixteen, were in a mischievous mood.

Eli said, "I wonder if a chicken would drink beer or even get drunk on the stuff?"

"Don't know," said Jonas, "but let's try it and see."

"*Ja.*"

They went back to the buggy and took a bottle out and opened it. Enos caught a banty rooster for them. Eli took the rooster and poured beer down its throat, a little at a time. Then he let it go. The banty wobbled back and forth. It was a comical sight to see a drunken rooster. We all had our fun for that day, and the experiment also satisfied our curiosity.

Mother told us a story of how she had given pigs some beer when she was a teenager. She said that the pigs were smarter than people.

We asked her, "Why?"

"The pigs wouldn't even drink the stuff," she replied.

"That's pretty bad stuff if a pig doesn't even drink it." This was Mother's way to tell the boys that beer was not good for them. She had seen the sixpack in their buggy.

Sometimes we would ask Mother how she knew what we were doing when she had her back turned toward us.

"I have eyes in the back of my head," she would say with a smile.

"No, you don't," we would say. But there were times when we thought she really did.

Hunting Season

One year when hunting season opened, the boys naturally wanted to go hunting. At the breakfast table, Jonas asked, "May I go hunting?"

Mother replied, "When you go hunting, you have to be very careful. I don't want anyone outside when you take that gun outdoors."

"Why?" both boys asked.

"Because that's how your grandpa died."

"Watcha mean?"

Sitting at the table, Mother told us another story.

"Grandpa always had a rule that the gun wasn't to be used on a Sunday. On Sundays he always slept in and the boys did the chores without him. One Sunday morning, a flock of blackbirds covered the trees and ground behind the barn. My brother Daniel went to the house to get the gun and checked to see if Grandpa was still in bed. 'Grandpa wasn't seen up yet,' I told him. Daniel took the gun and went out behind the barn. While my brother took the gun out, Grandpa had gotten dressed and walked out to the pigpen to survey the homestead. My brother shot at a bird and hit a tree branch. He heard a scream and ran to check to see what was wrong. He found Grandpa on the ground. He screamed for help: 'I shot Dad! I shot Dad!'

"Everybody came running. Mom sent one boy to the neighbors to go for help on horseback. While he went for help, the other brothers carried Grandpa to the yard. Grandma asked me to get him a chair. I ran and got it, and they sat him in the chair to wait for help to arrive.

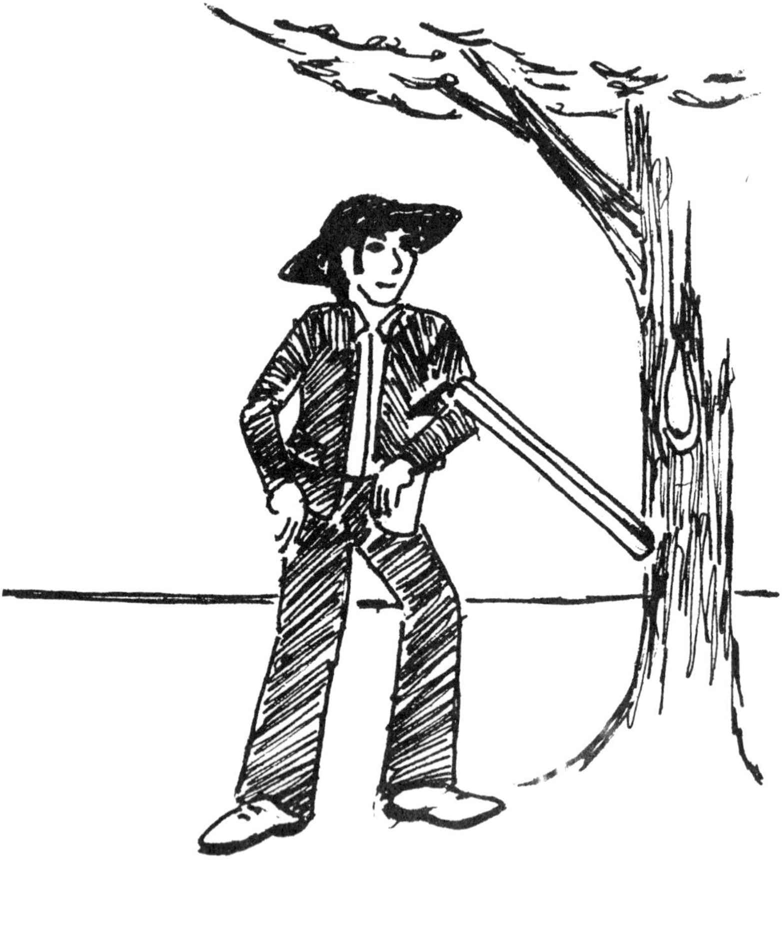

He was rushed to the hospital, and they operated on him. The bullet had just missed his heart. Three weeks later, he wanted to come home, so he was discharged from the hospital. However, his condition still wasn't very good.

"Several months later, my brother's glass of water was sitting on the table. Grandma wanted to get him a clean glass of water, but Grandpa said, 'No, I want a drink out of my son's glass.' After he had his drink of water, he died.

"We believe that was his way of saying he loved his son and wanted there to be peace between them. Daniel was forgiven."

"How long did Grandpa live after he was shot?" we asked.

"He lived for six months. My brother didn't kill him, but he shortened Grandpa's life. Daniel always blamed himself for killing Grandpa."

"How old were you?" I asked.

"I was nine years old."

"What happened to Grandma then?" one of us asked.

"Later my mother met a gentleman who wanted to marry her, and they were married. When my mother decided to marry him, we told her we didn't know if we could call him Dad. But as time went by, he was so good to Mom and us that before we knew it we were calling him Dad. Then they took a trip to the Colorado mountains and on their trip Mother took sick. When they came home, she went to the doctor's. We learned that she had cancer. She died a year later.

"What did your stepfather do then?" I asked.

"Well, his home had been in Plain City, Ohio, so he decided to go back to be with his children.

"What? Did he leave you in Kansas?"

"He asked us unmarried children to go with him. Actually, everyone was married except Brother Daniel and myself. My older sister said, 'You're not leaving with him,' but Daniel decided he was going regardless of what she said. I stayed with my sister, because my sister thought it didn't look right for me to go along."

Following this recital of family history and tradition, we all left the breakfast table and Jonas stated, "I won't be hunting around the buildings."

"All right; be careful," Mother replied.

We had the same rule at our house—the gun was never to be taken out on Sundays. Every time the gun was taken behind the barn for target practice, the boys would warn us not to leave the house.

One day after school, we saw several strangers hunting across the road in the field.

Enos said, "I'm going to check if they have permission." He rode up to them on the horse bareback.

When he arrived, he didn't know them, and so he asked, "Did you have any luck today?"

They answered, "Yes."

Enos asked, "Did you get permission to hunt here?"

"No, but we went over our limit with this rabbit we just shot. Why don't you take it?"

"No, that's all right; I don't want to take it from you."

"That's okay. You take it home for dinner." And one stranger handed Enos the rabbit.

"Thank you!"

Then the hunters departed and Enos rode back to the farm. On his way back, his horse spooked and started to run wild. When he came to a sharp curve in the road, Enos tried to hang onto the horse and the rabbit flew out of his hand into the air. The horse ran so fast that Enos barely made it into the driveway. When the horse arrived at the barn door, he made a sudden stop. He was huffing and puffing and acting wild. Patting him, Enos coaxed the horse to settle down. Then he jumped off and put him away for the night. We had seen him on the running horse and ran out to see if he was all right.

We asked, "What happened?"

"Those guys gave me a rabbit. The horse smelled the blood, and when a horse smells blood he goes wild."

"Where's your rabbit?"

"I lost it on the curve, trying to hang onto the horse. I'm going down and see if I can find it."

He returned shortly with the rabbit, and it was dressed and put in salt water to soak overnight.

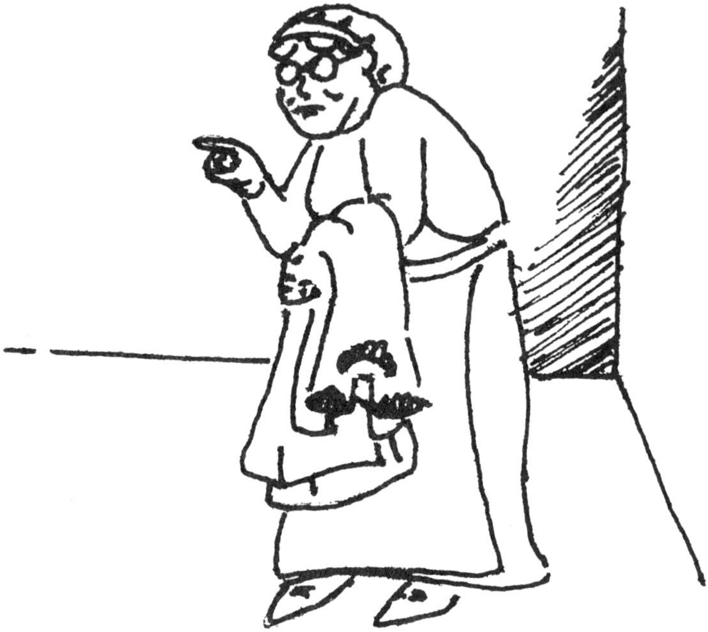

The Missing Dresses

Mom's oldest brother, Uncle Henry, was an average-built man with medium dark brown hair, a quiet gentleman married to a woman named Hattie. She wore the pants in their house. She even tried to boss everyone in the church numerous times concerning our family and the dress code of the Amish.

I believe Aunt Hattie would even have enjoyed taking her husband's place as preacher. However, the Amish tradition is that women are to be silent during church service. Following the service, however, the business meeting was opened to all members of the congregation. Hattie would always have her say and argue if everyone didn't agree with her. She was a pushy busybody.

Mother had just made new dresses for my sister and me. This was a treat, because we usually got new dresses only about twice a year. This was a big event for a young Amish girl.

We pulled the ankle-length dresses over our heads, pinning the front opening shut and feeling the little mandarin collar and the long loose sleeves. They were beautiful dresses. For church, we covered them with a white organza cape and an apron. A V-shaped cape was pulled over our heads and pinned at the waist in the back. In front the cape crisscrossed to the waistline and was pinned down with straight pins. The apron pinned on around the waist. A ribbon was tied around the neck so the cape was folded over and around the ribbon to hold the cape in place.

From pictures, I knew this was how early American

women dressed. Yet this was 1950. We were Amish and we were still dressing like pioneer women.

Sewing day was that one day a month when women from the church gathered to sew. This particular month, they had chosen our house, to help Mother. Mother told the children the women were coming to help with the sewing that day. When my sister Sarah heard they were coming, she ran upstairs to hide her dating dress in the old trunk. A dating dress was a dress to wear when going out with boys. Sarah knew her dress didn't conform to the dress code because she had made the hem to fall three inches below the knee instead of being ankle-length. Normally I wasn't in a hurry to get home from school, because I dreaded all those chores. But today I couldn't wait to get home because it was sewing day. When school was out, I didn't wait for my brothers and sisters. I took off skipping and running for home. A tomboy, I would rather walk the two and one-half miles than ride anyway. I was hoping I would have something new made for me when I got home. Thinking realistically, I knew I probably wouldn't, since I had a new dress already.

I arrived home about the same time as the others. We girls raced upstairs to change into working clothes, hoping there might be a surprise for us. My oldest sister thumbed through her dresses hanging on her peg. We younger girls did the same thing. We couldn't find anything new. Then Sarah checked the old trunk for her dating dress that she liked so much. Instead she found her dress gone. Lizbet and I noticed our new dresses were gone, too.

"Someone took my dress," Sarah cried.

"Ours are gone, too," Lizbet and I cried in unison.

Mother had quietly slipped upstairs and was standing in the doorway with an apologetic look on her face. "Your Aunt Hattie went through the clothes. I'm sorry."

"She took our dresses. Why?"

"She said the material was too worldly and against church rules, so she took them."

We couldn't believe it. It was hard for Mother to keep us in clothes. We had been hoping we would have something new when we came home. Instead, we not only didn't find anything new, but we found our new dresses that we had had been taken from us. It was hard enough for Mother to keep eight children in clothes without having anything taken away from us. Mother had ordered the material from a mail order catalog. The green material had a frosty look to it. We didn't see anything wrong with it. It was plain—not printed or patterned.

Mother sympathized with her three girls. "Don't worry. I'll see somehow that you get new dresses. Now go do your chores."

Mother tried not to show it, but she was sad and upset.

"Oh! Hattie makes me mad; she has no business going through our things," Sarah complained.

"I don't like her at all!" All three sisters agreed on this point.

The busybodies were working in the living room. Mother had gone back to finish what the women were working on.

Lizbet and I went downstairs and outside, away from the busy women. We were upset and didn't want to see them. The other children went about doing their chores, wishing the visiting women would leave.

While Lizbet and I were loading our arms full with firewood to carry to the house, Lizbet stated, "I wish they would all leave."

"*Ja*. I can't stand them," I replied, with an angry feeling inside.

When everybody had left, we went inside. Sarah asked, "Mom, what did the women sew today?"

"They made pants for the boys."

"Why did Aunt Hattie have to go through our clothes then?"

"I don't know."

"Oh! Those dummie people," I complained.

"They just had to stick their noses in our things, didn't they?" Sarah shouted in tears, continuing, "I wish they would mind their own business. Aunt Hattie is so afraid I'm going to look too good for the young fellows. Well, she doesn't have to worry, because with the styles here it's impossible to look good. No matter how hard you try. She's always sticking her nose where it doesn't belong. I'd like to cut it off for her."

"So would I," I agreed.

"Me, too," Lizbet added.

Our poor mother. She was caught in between. She wouldn't argue with us; she knew we were upset and had every right to be. There were times when she didn't know which way to turn. She would say, "Where there is a will there is a way." This was the family's saying as we tried to go forward instead of giving up.

The day after sewing day, Mother stated, "Alma, Aunt Hattie said she would pay you a dollar a week when you work for her in the summer." When I had enough weeks in to earn the material, Aunt Hattie went and bought the material and gave it to my mother. Mother said, "Aunt Hattie gave me the material for your new dresses."

I wanted to see it right away to see what color she had bought. When I saw it, I was so surprised. "Red?" I asked. "She got us that?"

"*Ja.*"

"I thought we weren't allowed to have red?"

"Well! So did I," Mother answered.

Aunt Hattie asked Mother how we liked our dresses. Mother told her what I had said. Aunt Hattie asked if the material was red. Mother said, "*Ja.*" Aunt Hattie had thought it was dark purple. When Mother told us this, we had to laugh. We were told that we weren't allowed to have red or white dresses. Red is evil and white is for purity. There is only one that is pure—Jesus. Mother made our dresses for school and we didn't say any more about the color. We knew Mother wouldn't get in trouble for buying the red material.

Later on, I asked Mother, "What did Hattie do with the green dresses?"

"She made me mail them to your cousins in Ohio."

"Oh! Okay."

And the subject was dropped.

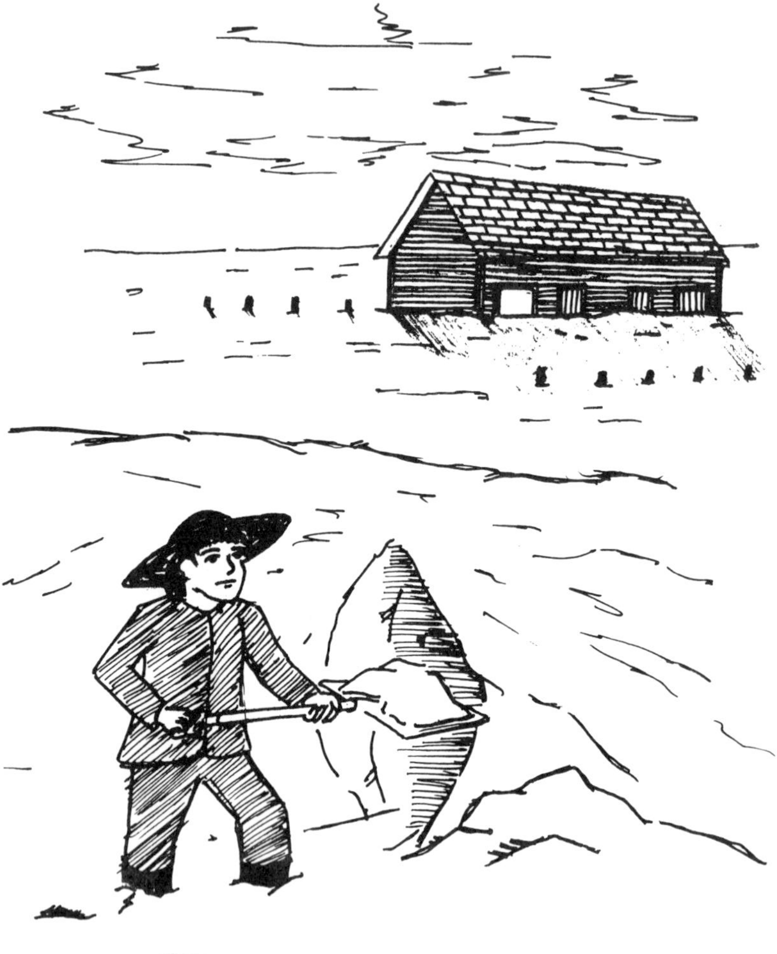

Old-fashioned Winter

Our winters in Iowa in those days of the 1940's seemed rough. It seemed to me then that when we got our first snowfall, it would always snow for at least two days. The second night, I remember standing at the window watching the snowflakes fall. Work on a farm doesn't stop because of inclement weather. It's just like the slogan of the postal service. "Neither rain nor snow nor gloom of night will keep us from our appointed rounds."

The older boys did the milking morning and night. After school, my sister Lizbet, just fourteen months younger than myself, helped me with the firewood. It was in big chunks and had to be chopped for use in our stoves. The finer the wood, the more quickly it catches fire.

A couple of wagonloads of logs were stored under our large walnut trees, and the ax was next to the woodpile. I would stand a log on end and cut it into two pieces. If it was a very large log, I would split it into four pieces. This was one of my favorite chores. I was a tomboy and liked the outdoors. As I cut the logs, my sister gathered up the pieces and carried an armload to the woodbox. There'd be one box beside the stove in the kitchen and one beside the heating stove in the living room.

We didn't think much about this then—it was an accepted thing that everyone did. But in later years, I realized that this was what the pioneers did as they carved out the new frontiers in our country. Yet at the time I was doing this old-fashioned chore, our country had forty-eight states and was civilized and modernized.

Carrying wood was done every day—summer and

winter. We carried more in winter to keep two stoves going. In summer, we'd carry wood for our cook stove.

It fell upon the girls to carry the water, too. From the house out back, down a small hill, between the pigpen and chicken house, we'd cross the cement wall at the steps, yet still had to go downhill to the pump.

In winter we could slide down on packed snow, but slippery snow made it that much harder to climb up with full buckets. On this day, Lizbet and I had filled our buckets with water and started back up the hill to the house. However, before we reached the top of the hill, Lizbet slipped and fell. The buckets went tumbling back down. I tried not to laugh, but it was too comical so I had to let out a laugh. I missed the buckets coming at me and slipped down the hill as well. Lizbet was angry and tried to pick herself up with her ankle-length dress tangled up around her legs.

"Oh! So *dumm*," I said. I tried to get up, saying, "Jack and Jill went down the hill to fetch a pail of water; Jack fell down and broke his crown, and Jill came tumbling after." Lizbet and I both broke out in laughter, trying to see humor in our exasperating situation.

"You look so funny, Lizbet."

"Oh! *Ja*, you do, too. I guess we better get some more water."

"*Ja*, let's try it again."

We both went down the hill, laughing on our way to fetch another pail of water while repeating the Jack and Jill rhyme. Sometimes it's easier to do something when you joke about it rather than get angry.

We carried water morning and night. We needed several buckets for drinking and cooking, for washing faces and hands, and for the garbage buckets, which later were sent to the hogs. If any buckets ran low, we'd have to go out again. When it came time for bathing, that was another problem. Our West Virginia tub (a round galvanized tub) held six buckets. We took baths one night a week. With eight to ten people bathing, we had a beaten path between the pump and the house.

Inside, on those cold nights it was so quiet that any noise seemed magnified. No wonder we were startled when we heard the sound of an engine. We lived pretty far out in the country and didn't get too many cars. Outside of the mailman's truck, we saw one or maybe two cars a week. That usually was the modern farmer who lived nearby.

The sound on this snowy night turned out to be that of a snowplow. It wasn't a very big one. The snow had a pretty big head start and was too much for the small plow to handle. It got stuck. A while later, a jumbo snowplow came along and pulled out the small plow.

"Never send a boy to do a man's job," mused Mother.

However, the next morning the older boys found the snow so deep, they couldn't get to the barn without using shovels first. They had to dig a tunnel to the barn so they could milk the cows. Although this was a practical and necessary task for the older boys, we younger children got a lot of fun out of the tunnel. Our first impression was, "Oh! How neat!"

"It's warm," we said.

"Just like the Eskimos," Jonas spoke up.

"Whatcha mean?"

"There are people that live in snow huts in Alaska."

"Oh, yeah? What do they eat?"

"You go get ready for school; you ask too many questions now."

When we walked to school that morning, we looked up on both sides of the road. All we could see was snowbanks, with a telephone line about three feet above the banks running to the modern farmer's house, and the blue sky.

We had cold weather along with that snow. Sometimes the temperature plunged below zero, once thirty-eight degrees below. Still, life went on. We just put on more clothing than usual. We had our long johns, heavy woolen capes for the girls, and bonnets, mittens, scarves, and shawls for the older girls and women. The boys had their heavy capes and earmuffs, too. Everything was in black material, as tradition dictated.

It was a dry cold, and we got used to it. When winter set in, it would stay cold until springtime. There would be snow on top of snow. After a snow had passed, the sun would come out and melt some, yet when night set in, the temperature would plunge back below freezing and leave a crispy crust on top of the tunnels of snow. We would walk with care on the high snowbanks on our way to and from school.

The Saturday following the first big snow, the boys took the old wagon's wheels off and put the sled runners on it. Wooden benches for us to sit on were placed in the wagon. The sled was a lot warmer than the buggy. Sunday morning, we all readied ourselves for church. We climbed into the box sled, which was covered with a canvas to keep us from getting frostbite in the bitter cold.

We weren't allowed to have a storm window on the buggy. This was one of the man-made traditions for our congregation. Their idea was if it's too cold for the people, it's too cold for the horses.

Since the Amish have church only on every other Sunday, the boys took advantage of their off-Sundays. When chores and breakfast were completed by 8:00 A.M., the boys dressed warmly and announced, "We are going ice-skating. The river is frozen solid, so we plan to skate down it. Two other farmer boys are going to meet us at the river at their homestead. We'll be back in time to do evening chores."

"Are you sure the river is solid?" Mother questioned.

"Oh, yeah. We took the ax down and checked to see how deep it's frozen," Jonas answered.

"How deep is it?"

"It's eight to twelve inches, Mom. Nothing to worry about. It's hard all across that river."

"All right, just make sure it's safe. Watch the spots for rapids where it may not be solid."

"We'll be careful and don't worry. Bye."

"Have fun."

During the day, the other children got out their homemade wooden sled and double-bladed ice-skates. They did some sledding and took turns with one pair of ice-skates. The skates were adjusted to each child's foot size and clamped to the shoes.

When it was time to do the evening chores, the boys were home. At the dinner table, the boys narrated the events of their exciting day. We all listened in silence as they recounted their adventures.

"We skated down the river, and our friends joined us when we got to their boundary line. When everybody had joined us as planned, we made a couple of safety rules. Jonas is the oldest, so he took the lead. A single file was maintained to keep a safe distance in case the ice might break. We decided to skate one way till noon, then make a turn and come back."

"That really was fun," Jonas interrupted.

"We could skate as fast as we wanted," Eli continued. "The whole river was all ours. We wanted to see just how far we could skate in a day. We didn't let no grass grow under us."

"Since I had the lead, I went as fast as I could. A

couple of times when the ice cracked I leaped across and yelled back, 'soft spot!' Everybody followed with a leap. At noon we arrived in Fairbank. Fairbank is eight miles from here if you take the road. There were a couple of spots where the river had rapids and it wasn't frozen hard. But it was totally exciting, trying to beat the soft ice in different places like that."

Monday evening, the boys did their chores and after dinner took their beloved skates in their hands and headed for the river. The boys knew what the river was like to Fairbank, but they wanted to investigate in the opposite direction, to Littleton, too.

When the boys came home, they were all excited.

"Mom, guess what's happening in Littleton?" Eli asked.

"I have no idea. What is happening?"

"Some people are ice fishing. They've got a tractor with a blade on it to scrape the snow off the river. Then they took an ax to open the river. They drag a net to lift the fish out."

The young ones were curious. "What are they doing that for?" one asked.

"Because the river is frozen so hard, no air can get to the fish. The fish will die this year because of lack of oxygen. So we gave them a hand. The men said if the fish die, it will cause bigger floods. We can have all the fish that we want," Eli stated.

"May we drive the horse and buggy to Littleton to get some?" both boys asked. "We told them that we couldn't take fish with us on our ice-skates."

"Sure! Go get them if they said you may have them."

The boys left in their horse and buggy with a feed bag. They returned with a bagful of fish.

We ate fish for breakfast, lunch, and dinner until they

were gone. Those fish were good eating while they lasted. Mother said, "Fish and rice are brain food." So we ate plenty of fish hoping it would make us smart.

At the breakfast table, Jonas revealed his wish. "I hope what we did will keep the river from flooding in the spring." Everybody had to agree.

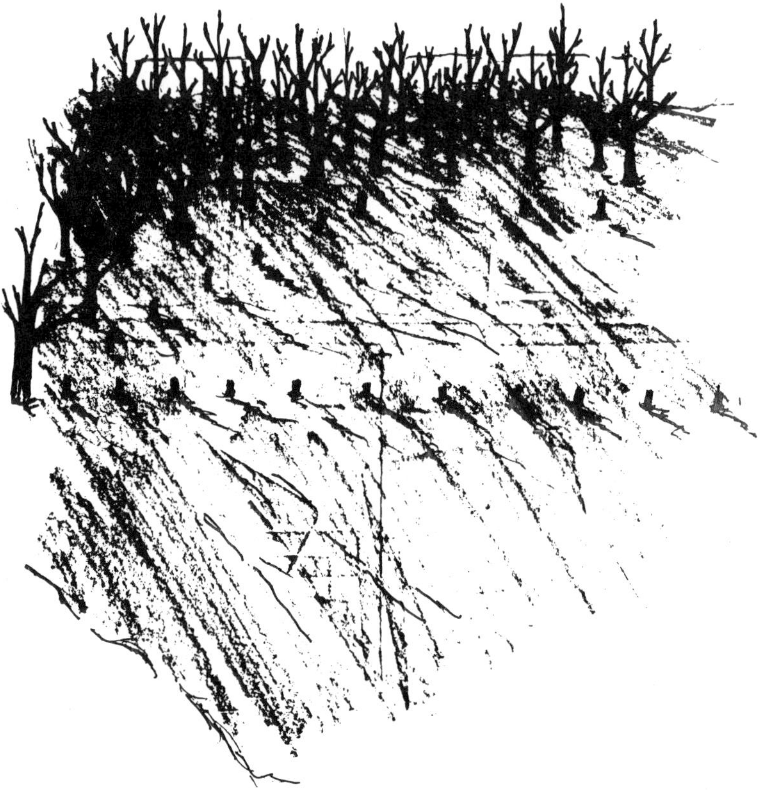

Eli's Disappearance

One Sunday in the spring of 1951, the sun was beaming down on the snow, causing it to disappear. As the snow melted, the creeks began to rise and rush into the river. The river rose over its banks, through the woods, and onto the tillable fields. The creek that ran behind the pigpen, chicken house, and outhouse passed along the garden and emptied into the wide river below. The creek rose to the garden. The river rose until it met the creek. The river was one-fourth mile from the house.

Every spring we had floods. The rising river would rush over our land, taking soil with it and covering the land with sand.

This Sunday morning, it was church Sunday. The Amish community had been wanting my brother Eli to join the church. To join the Amish church, a young boy or girl would have to go to a private room with the preacher for conferences on six church days. He or she would be taught the church rules and the church dress code. Then he or she would be baptised to become a member. Baptism was done by pouring water on the person's head.

Eli was getting ready for church. Mother and the younger children all readied themselves for church, too. We had to use two buggies to take our large family to church. Eli stated, "The bridges will be so flooded that we may never get across."

"Which way are you going?" Mother asked.

"I'm going to Littleton, across that bridge, because that one will be the last one to flood."

"We are going the other way," said Mother.

Mother, myself, and the younger children departed

in our large family buggy with a team of horses. Before we arrived at the bridge, we came to a line of six buggies and a car at a standstill. We pulled up beside another buggy and asked, "What is the holdup?"

"Two boys are caught in the high water," they answered. The people in the car were upset and angry. "Those boys treated their horse terrible. They should be turned in for mistreating an animal. The two boys tried to cross the bridge, since the water was only about four inches over the bridge. They had a young horse barely broken for their single buggy."

We couldn't see because of the bend in the road and the woods, so we pulled our rig up along the left side of the traffic, near the bridge, on the high part of the land. We stopped. The water was rising and rushing down the river, overflowing its banks and covering woods, driveways, and tillable lowland fields.

From this vantage point we could see the two boys. The boys had thought they could enter the driveway of the farm right beyond the bridge. They were halfway in the driveway when the water arrived so high and so fast that it reached the box of the buggy and went above the horse's stomach. The young horse was frightened and didn't want to move any farther, so it came to a complete stop. The boys stepped down into waist-high water. One boy tied the buggy to the fence post so it wouldn't be washed down the river. The other one unhitched the horse and coaxed it away from the buggy. The boys, one after the other, jumped on the horse's back and rode it to the homestead.

We watched until they arrived on high ground. Then all the people in line took turns turning around and returned to their homes in safety. When we arrived home, we didn't see Eli, so we thought he had made it across the bridge. When evening set in, we did our chores, but he still didn't come home.

A friend, David, stopped and asked, "Is Eli all right?"

Mother explained what happened that morning and told him Eli had taken the other road to church.

"Eli wasn't in church."

"He wasn't?"

Mother was worried now. She looked at Brother Jonas and told him, "Go to Littleton to see if that bridge is flooded."

Jonas was worried, too, and concerned for Eli. He promptly agreed to check the bridge. David left with these last words: "If you need help with anything, let me know."

"Thank you."

Jonas hitched up the horse and buggy and left to check the Littleton bridge. We had all lost our appetite for dinner, wondering where Eli was and what had happened to him. We waited and hoped Jonas would find some answers about Eli. Jonas returned home and had no idea where Eli was, saying, "This is a puzzle! The people in Littleton said that the river didn't overflow the bridge until noon. But that gave him plenty of time to get across before it overflowed."

It was dark, but we waited until eleven o'clock. Then we all went to bed and hoped that Eli would return before morning.

At daybreak, everybody went to check to see if Eli had returned home during the night. What a disappointment! No Eli! We did our morning chores, and then we gathered at the table to eat. One of my sisters, Sarah, stated, "Mom, you have one too many place settings."

"Sarah, go out and call Eli in for breakfast," my mother said in a soft, concerned voice.

We all looked at each other and at Mom. Due to her

worried appearance, we all obeyed with no arguments. We went to the table, except for Sarah, who went outside to call Eli in.

The Amish families have a silent prayer before and after their meals. After prayer, we would all start reaching and pass the food around the table. This day, the meal was silent. Everybody still had questions and was worried. Why didn't Eli come home? Why call him before meals? We all ate our breakfast and then said our silent prayer before we were excused from the table.

After breakfast, Mother told Jonas, "Go get the horse and buggy ready; we two are going to Littleton once more to double-check."

Jonas agreed. Mother readied herself and they went to town, leaving the younger ones at home.

As they were going down the country road, we who were left at home went to the kitchen window to watch them. They disappeared over the rolling hills, and then we looked down at the high water where the creek and the river united, no land in sight.

How was this possible? But it was possible. We were looking at it. We learned at our young age not by someone telling us a story, but by seeing it with our own eyes. It was hard to believe that a river that is so calm in the summertime could grow to be as dangerous as a roaring lion.

This Monday morning, the sun was shining. Spring was here to stay. At about 11:00 A.M., Mom and Jonas were returning home. We saw two buggies coming down the road. We all ran to meet them, yelling, "Eli's buggy's coming too!" We cheered, jumping and waiting for them to get to the house. However, as they pulled past the house into the driveway, the happy cheers ended. There was silence! Eyes were wide open with disbelief. Oh, no! Why?

We saw Jonas driving Eli's horse and buggy up to the homestead. We all went out to see them.

Jonas unhitched the horse with a younger brother's help. Enos, the younger brother, stated, "I see you found the horse and buggy. Where is Eli?"

"Don't know."

The girls asked, "Mom, where is Eli?"

"We don't know. The rig was in Littleton tied behind the gas station. Jonas missed it last night."

We all were disappointed. Mother asked, "Sarah, do you have dinner on?"

"Yes, it's on the stove."

We didn't feel like doing anything. Nobody did much, as on the first day of Eli's absence. We did our chores and that was about it.

For every meal, Eli was called, with a place setting on the table for him in his absence. Days had gone by and still there was no word from him or anybody of his disappearance.

Mother told us, "Life goes on and we have to continue."

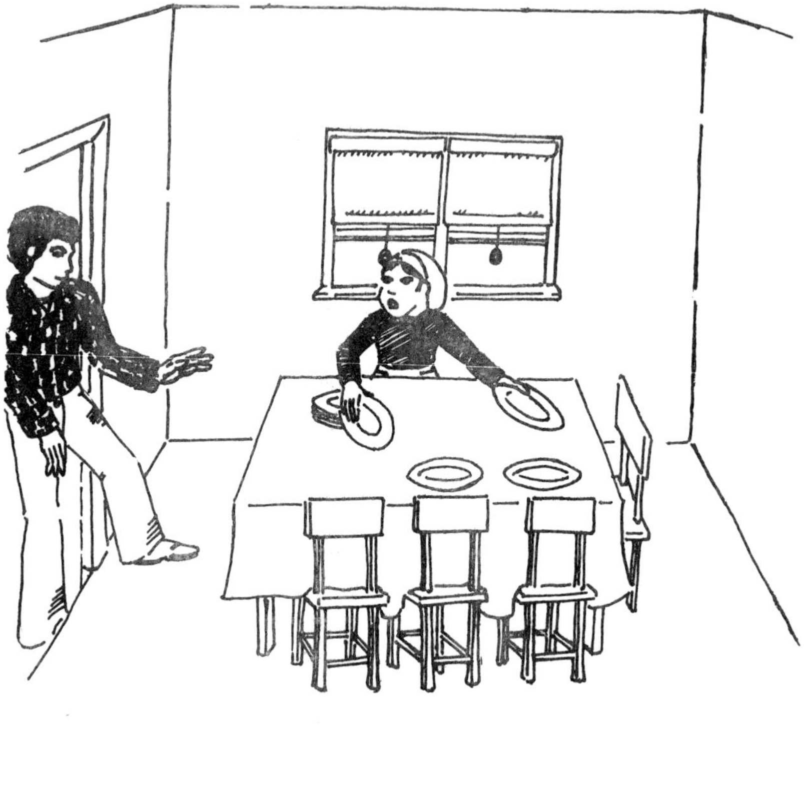

Shunning

After the high water had receded in the river and creek channels, their boundaries returned to normal. It was planting season and the garden and fields were being plowed and seeded. Everybody helped Mother and each other, because we were short one hand with Eli's absence.

Two weeks later, on a Sunday, the children did not go to church, thinking maybe Eli would come home. We weren't leaving home in case he did return. Eli didn't return. Four weeks passed; we wouldn't leave still, in hopes he might come home. That Sunday afternoon at around 4:00 P.M., the boys were getting ready to do the milking. We girls were getting dinner ready. We heard an engine down the road. We looked, but didn't recognize who it was. The car stopped in front of the house and took off again.

A voice yelled, "Eli's home! Eli's home!"

We were surprised and could hardly believe it. When I turned around from setting the table, he was standing there in person, dressed in a plaid shirt and blue jeans. He picked up the baby, and Annie ran to him. He swept her off her feet and hugged them both.

Junior ran and hugged Eli's leg, then decided that wasn't enough. Junior climbed up on the worktable and grabbed Eli around the neck to hug him. He just laughed; he had been homesick.

The other boys came running in from the barn to see their brother. Everybody wanted to talk to him at the same time. There was laughter in the home again. I stood back and enjoyed the rejoicing sight. I was relieved that Eli hadn't gotten caught in the high water. He was really alive.

Mother asked, "Are you hungry?"

"No. I'm not staying."

"Stay for dinner; we have a place set for you."

"No. My friend went to turn the car around, and then he'll be right back to pick me up."

Mother looked out of the window and commented, "Oh! He parked in the driveway. I hope Uncle Judas doesn't see it."

"Why?"

"Because the Amish tradition here is when one leaves home or the church, he isn't supposed to park his car on the home place."

"What?"

"That's what they call shunning," Jonas interrupted.

"Well, we have to go anyway."

Everybody pleaded, "Don't go; don't go."

"I'll be back again."

"When?" The young ones didn't want to let him go.

"I wanted you to know I'm all right and I'm working on a large farm about sixty miles from here, close to Waterloo."

"Come back and stay longer next time."

"All right, I will."

He left, but nobody was ready to see him go so soon. We were glad he was all right. His visit was a pleasant surprise.

I was relieved and said, "I'm glad he stopped to let us know he was okay." I realized then that Eli's leaving home was a reaction to the recent pressure on him to join the church.

Everyone went back to their duties again with relief. It was easier to do the chores now, but there was still sorrow because we missed him.

At the dinner table, I asked, "Why isn't Eli supposed to come home and park a car here?"

"Because he left home and he changed his dress code. He has his hair cut in a shingle," Mother answered.

"Well, I think he looks handsome."

Eli was five-nine, dark-haired, and well built for an eighteen-year-old boy.

"He really did look good," agreed Sarah. "I don't understand why it's so wrong to have different colors in our clothes."

"Joseph in the Bible had so many brothers; they wore plain clothes, too. But they mistreated him. Yet the Bible teaches that Joseph had a coat of many colors and he was the good guy," Enos commented. "Why don't the Amish believe in other colors then?"

Mother replied, "The Amish claim other colors are of the world. We are to look different from the world."

Although it would be hard to be the only ones making the change, the children weren't very happy with their traditions. These were man-made traditions.

On a Sunday two weeks later, Eli stopped in again. We all were just as happy to see him then as we were before. We went through the same exciting experience. This time his friend—whose name was Eli also—parked his car close to the bend down the road so we wouldn't get in trouble with the church.

"Eli, the people asked today if you were going to join the church," Mother stated.

"No, I'll never join the church here."

"Won't you come back home?"

"No. I've got a good job. I'm making eighty dollars a month, plus a place to stay. They are good to me, too."

"Stay for supper."

"No, I'd better get going before somebody comes through and sees the car."

No one wanted him to leave, but we were glad he had stopped by again.

"You will come back again, won't you?" Mother asked.

"Yeah! I'll be back." He kissed the young ones and left.

This time two weeks went by and he didn't stop back. A whole month passed before he stopped again.

Mother asked, "What could I do to get you to come back home?"

"I don't know. I'm not joining that church."

Eli stayed for a while, helping the boys with their chores, but he wouldn't stay for dinner. According to the local Amish tradition, Mother and Brother Jonas were supposed to shun him. To "shun" means that they were not supposed to eat with him or have anything to do with him.

Still, Eli's plate was always set at the dinner table and his name was called before we sat down to eat.

On Eli's next visit home, Mother asked, "Would you like for us to move away from here?"

"Where would you want to move to?"

"Let me check with the uncles in Ohio."

"All right."

In August, he visited us again. Mother stated, "I received a letter from your uncle."

"*Ja*? And?"

"They said they would have a house for us and there are jobs available there."

"Whatcha going to do with the farm?"

"We'll have an auction in the fall and rent the farm, then make our move."

"Sell everything?"

"We'll just take our personal belongings and a horse and buggy."

"Does everybody else want to go?"

"Oh, yeah!" we yelled.

"We're sick of these church people picking on everything we do," someone said.

The previous summer, the boys had met our neighbor across the river. He had an airplane and told the boys if they came over some Sunday he would take them for a ride. The boys told him they would hold him to that. On that following Sunday, we were invited to go to Uncle's house for dinner. The boys went over to see the farmer about the airplane ride.

The neighbor took them for a ride in the sky. When the plane flew over Uncle's farm, we spotted it and waved to them. The plane signaled back and started to do some fancy tricks. Later in the afternoon when we arrived home, the boys were already doing their chores.

Everybody went to church the following Sunday. Before church started, it was announced that there would be a meeting for the members after the service. After the service, the children were excused and only the adults remained.

Somehow the people knew Brother Jonas had taken an airplane ride. They wanted him to make a confession for taking that ride. He didn't think he did anything wrong. They told him they would expel him if he didn't make it right with the church. To keep peace in the community, he did what was demanded of him.

However, Jonas was upset with the church over this issue. He could see no wrong in what he had done. When we came home from church, everyone was upset over the matter.

The younger ones were fast learning that the Amish ways in Buchanan County, Iowa, were not in harmony with ours.

Not only that, Brother Eli wasn't coming back to stay as long as we lived there. Mother made arrangements to have an auction in November of 1951. When she made the announcment, oh, how the church members tried to talk her out of it! Having Eli back home with us again was more important to Mother than what the people felt about us making the change.

Eli had quit his job a month before the auction to help us get ready for the big day. He didn't worry about his dress code, and Mother didn't put pressure on him. It was great to have Eli fill the empty place at the table, and we didn't worry about the tradition of shunning.

Leaving Iowa

In November of 1951, the auction day was nearing. Everyone was excitedly running around to get ready for the big day. The girls helped package the household goods.

The boys, working in harmony, asked Mother, "Where do you want the machinery parked? What do we pack to take along to Ohio? Which horse do we take to Ohio? How are we going to handle the animals at the auction?"

Mother discussed it with the boys. "The farm equipment has to be parked close to the barn in a neat row. We'll take the hand tools to Ohio in a toolbox."

"Which horse do you want to take along?" she asked the boys.

"I want to take Esther," Eli said.

"No, I want to take my horse," Jonas stated.

Each boy had a good horse and didn't want to part with it. Mother decided that they both could go along. The horse Junior had taught all the tricks had to be sold, and so did the draft horses.

Eli stated, "The animals can't be parked in a row. How are we going to auction them off?"

"We'll have to leave everything in the barn, and when the auctioneer is ready for the animals, you boys will have to bring one animal out at a time so the people can see what is for sale."

Mother knew another Amish family that wanted to rent the farm. Uncle Judas wanted to get the rental agreement together for the renters, for Mother, and for Father's new guardian, a banker in Independence, who would be collecting the rent for us.

Uncle Judas wanted Mother to buy the fertilizer for

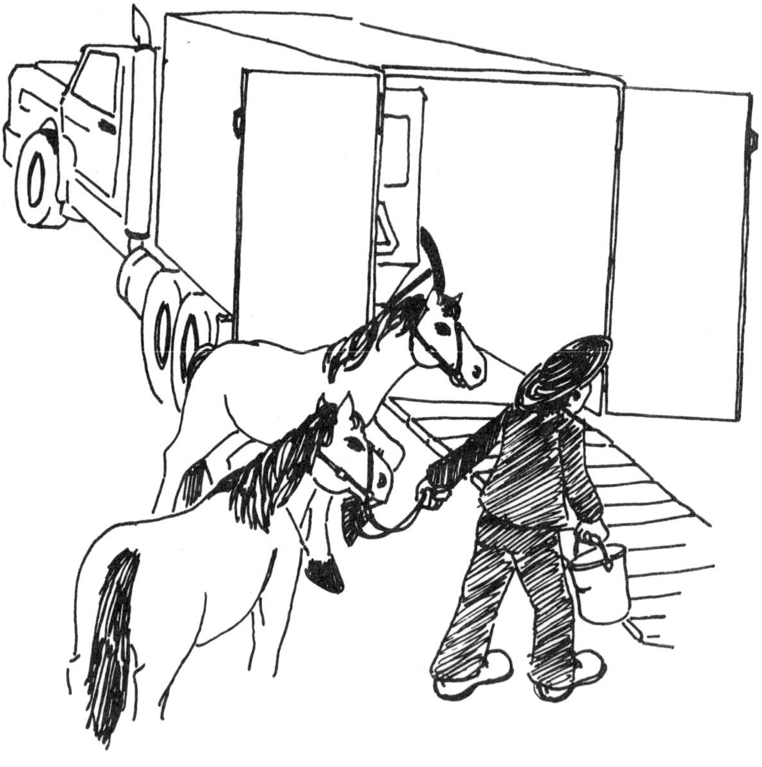

the renters. Mother said, "Do you think I'm going to buy fertilizer for the renters after you refused to let me fertilize those fields while I was farming? I won't even think of it."

"Those fields need to be fertilized," Uncle Judas said.

"That's what I've been trying to tell you for several years, but you always told me they didn't need it. Now that I'm moving out, they need it, but for all I care, you can buy the fertilizer yourself. I knew those fields needed fertilizer for years!"

Since we were leaving Iowa, arrangements had been made making a banker in Independence Father's new guardian. When that was done, Mother said to the banker, "Judas has taken all the money. Shouldn't I be entitled to get half since I'm the wife?"

"Didn't you get half?"

"No, I didn't get any of it."

"What did you live on then?"

Mother explained what and how we lived. The banker could hardly believe it and was shaking his head. "Your brother did that to his own sister and children?" he questioned.

"Yeah."

The banker made arrangements to get Mother's share for her.

Mother decided to move our personal belongings and household goods in a moving van. The family would travel to Ohio in a hired three-seater automobile, driven by a man none of us knew. The day after the auction, Mother was disappointed. The sale didn't bring in much money for everything that was sold. Of course, Uncle Judas was right there to take the money on auction day. Early that morning, everyone in our family was up, loading the semitruck and getting ready to leave for Ohio.

Before we left, we learned that Uncle Judas refused to give Mother her money. He was going with us to Ohio to personally deliver Mother's money to Uncle Eli Hershberger. Mother didn't argue with him. We children were packed in the automobile like sardines. The middle seat didn't have a back, which made the trip uncomfortable. Uncle Judas sat up front with the driver. We thought if our uncle hadn't come with us, it would've been a more comfortable trip. But we really didn't mind, because we were moving away from an unhappy period of our life, one that I really believed none of us would ever be able to forget. I was scared, not knowing what was ahead for us.

It was an eighteen-hour trip to Ohio. We arrived at Uncle Eli's homestead early in the morning on the day before Thanksgiving. Uncle Eli and Aunt Esther were just getting ready to do their morning chores when we arrived. Aunt Esther was happy to see us and welcomed us all to the house. She asked us if we wanted to go to bed.

We all nodded our heads, and Mother said, "I'm tired, but I don't think I could sleep right now."

We all were tired, but too excited to crawl in bed at that moment.

Then Esther asked, "Where's Jonas and Eli?"

"The boys are coming with the moving van. It's taking them longer because they have to stop to exercise their horses on the way."

"Would you like to have breakfast? I'll make breakfast now," Aunt Esther offered.

"No, we'll wait until the chores are done and eat breakfast with you," Mother replied.

Glancing around Aunt Esther's kitchen, I saw a green dress hanging up beside the stairway. I just stood there and looked at it.

Aunt Esther saw me and said, "Do you recognize that dress?"

"Is that the dress that Mom made me?"

Aunt Esther walked over and lifted the dress off the

hook, saying, "Ja, this is the dress your mother made for you."

"Are we allowed to have that kind of dress here?"

"You sure may," she said, hanging the dress back up.

Then I suddenly realized the move to Ohio was a good move and it would be different now. I was sure it was for the better, even though we hated to leave Dad behind.

"Aunt Esther, is there anything we can do to help with chores or breakfast?" we asked.

As we were helping her, we visited. While we were visiting, one of my sisters whispered, "Did you see Uncle Judas sitting at the doorway trying to listen to our conversation?"

Aunt Esther shook her head and stated, "Ja, he's eavesdropping."

"He's trying to hear what we have to say and probably doesn't approve," Mom replied.

"Well, we aren't saying anything that we have to hide," Aunt Esther commented, laughing.

While they were talking, I looked over and saw Uncle Judas sitting there listening. I could hardly believe it. As I was looking at him, a vision flashed through my head. I don't believe anyone saw the light except for myself. The light blocked the surroundings from me momentarily. It was as if a voice were saying, *Write a book about Iowa.*

I asked, *A book?*

Yes, write a book about your life in Iowa.

Oh, but I don't know how to even begin.

You will in time, and the voice left me.

I could never forget that moment, and I've asked myself over and over again, *Why am I supposed to write this book? Why me?* It came to be an obsession with me.

I had to write this book, even if it's against my family's wishes.

Epilogue

Today Brother Jonas is a married farmer. He and his wife have ten children. Brother Eli is married and has his own buggy shop. He and his wife have ten children. Sister Sarah is married to a factory employee. They have three children. They are foster parents for the county. Sister Polly died. Brother Enos is a married farmer, and he and his wife have five children. Sister Alma, the author, is divorced and has three children. Sister Lizbet is married to a man who is a carpenter and a farmer. They have four children. Junior is married. He has seven children and is a truck driver. Sister Anne is married. Her husband rebuilds automobiles. She makes Amish dolls. They have five children. Joseph Jay was the baby when we left Iowa. He is married and has three children. He is an assistant manager for the Gold Circle. We are living in Ohio except for Junior. Junior has his residence in Pennsylvania.

    Alma Hershberger has compiled: *Amish Taste Cookbook* (with over 500 recipes), *The Alphabet in Amish Life* (a child's book), and *The Art of Amish Cooking* (with 650 recipes). Annie's handmade Amish dolls are like the ones that pioneer children played with. They are seventeen inches long, washable, and come in boy or girl versions. For information on ordering dolls or cookbooks, please write: Art of Amish Taste, P.O. Box 375, Danville, OH 43014.

ART OF AMISH TASTE
BOX 375
DANVILLE, OHIO 43014

____Amish Life through a Child's Eyes @ $7.95 ...._____
____Art of Amish Cooking (650 Recipes) @ $9.95 ...._____
____Amish Taste Cookbook (Over 500 Recipes) @ $8.95 ...._____
____Alphabet in Amish Life (Children's Book) @ $2.00 ...._____
____Amish Doll (Girl 17") @ $18.50 each ...._____
____Amish Doll (Boy 17") @ $34.00 a pair ...._____
Plus Postage and Handling $1.00 each ...._____
Ohio Residents Sales Tax 5½% ...._____
Enclosed is a check or money order .... TOTAL _____

Name _____

Address _____

City, State _____ Zip Code _____
NO C.O.D'S

ART OF AMISH TASTE
BOX 375
DANVILLE, OHIO 43014

____Amish Life through a Child's Eyes @ $7.95 ...._____
____Art of Amish Cooking (650 Recipes) @ $9.95 ...._____
____Amish Taste Cookbook (Over 500 Recipes) @ $8.95 ...._____
____Alphabet in Amish Life (Children's Book) @ $2.00 ...._____
____Amish Doll (Girl 17") @ $18.50 each ...._____
____Amish Doll (Boy 17") @ $34.00 a pair ...._____
Plus Postage and Handling $1.00 each ...._____
Ohio Residents Sales Tax 5½% ...._____
Enclosed is a check or money order .... TOTAL _____

Name _____

Address _____

City, State _____ Zip Code _____
NO C.O.D'S

THE DRAGON RIDER
WHO SAVED THE WORLD

THE UNKNOWN PATH

TED DEKKER & RACHELLE DEKKER

Copyright © 2024 by Ted Dekker

All rights reserved. No part of this book may be reproduced in any manner whatsoever without written permission, except in the case of brief quotations embodied in critical articles and reviews.

ISBN (Paperback Edition): 979-8-9909639-0-0

Also Available in *The Dragon Rider who Saved the World* trilogy:

The Golden Egg (Book One)
ISBN: 979-8-9888509-9-1 (Paperback Edition)

Rise of the Fire Walker (Book Three)
ISBN: 979-8-9909639-1-7 (Paperback Edition)

Published by:
Scripturo
350 E. Royal Lane, Suite 150
Irving, TX 75039

Cover art and design by Manuel Preitano

Printed in China by Artful Dragon Press, a U.S. Corporation

CHAPTER 1

EMILIA COULDN'T GET HER LEGS TO WORK. Her body felt like stone. She was frozen in place. Voices filled the air, but the words were muffled as if she had cotton shoved in her ears. Motion near her feet drew her eyes, and she found the baby dragon staring at her.

The world sharpened and the events of the last half hour crashed through her mind.

She'd touched the egg.
It had hatched.
They wanted her to be its rider.

Emilia looked around at the others standing in the cave. Bastien and Amos, two of the desert elders she'd met only the day before. Saul and Marcs, hunters she knew by name alone. Torey and his son, Oliver, the two people in this cave she trusted. All were discussing how to get the dragon and Oliver, whose ankle was still swollen from the rattlesnake bite, back to the Guardian camp.

Oliver insisted he could hobble down if he had help.

Torey suggested they wait a few more hours before traveling.

Amos thought they needed to get the dragon to the Guardian camp immediately.

Bastien listened, his eyes filled with suspicion as they moved from the dragon to Emilia, as if they thought she might snatch the creature at her feet and run away with it. Did they believe she wanted anything to do with the dragon? Because she didn't.

"Amos is right," Bastien said. "We need to head for camp, even if we take it slower for Oliver's sake."

"The dragon could be carried," Amos said. "It's small enough. We could fashion a sling of sorts."

The others nodded, and Amos began drawing what he needed from the small pack on his back. Bastien stepped toward the baby dragon, and the creature tucked itself close to Emilia's legs.

Bastien squatted and reached a hand toward the small gray dragon. "It's alright."

The dragon hissed at Bastien's fingers and flicked its pointy tail at the man's hand.

"I don't think it likes you very much," Torey said.

Chapter 1

Oliver stifled a laugh and Bastien glared up at Emilia as if it were her fault the dragon wasn't cooperating. Bastien returned his attention to the dragon and tried to soften his features.

"Come now," Bastien said. "I won't hurt you."

The dragon maneuvered behind Emilia's legs to hide. It stuck out its tiny head and snapped at Bastien ferociously. Well, as ferocious as a little dragon could be. Emilia felt her mouth threaten a smile.

"Perhaps you could ask its rider to help you," Torey suggested.

Emilia saw anger flash in Bastien's eyes. He stood and crossed his arms over his chest. Clearing his throat, Bastien spoke to Emilia as though it pained him.

"The dragon does seem to respond to you."

"Of course it does," Oliver said, beaming. "The dragon chose her!"

Those words sent fear through Emilia's veins. She didn't want to be *chosen*. She looked down at the small creature, who turned its eyes up to her as if waiting for her to decide what to do next. For whatever reason, it trusted her.

Not 'for whatever reason,' her thoughts echoed inside her head. *It trusts you because you are its rider.* She swallowed her panic. She didn't want to be chosen. She didn't. She really didn't. The thought repeated on a soft loop in the back of her mind.

The chosen often don't want to be chosen, Torey had said.

Emilia pushed her thoughts aside and realized they needed to leave this cave. She lowered herself to one knee beside the dragon and it wiggled like an excited puppy. It sat back with a plop and gazed at her happily. She could see small gold flecks inside the creature's dark eyes. Its light gray scales shimmered in the torchlight. It was the size of a small dog, a couple of feet long and a couple of feet high. She imagined it weighed nearly twenty pounds, too heavy for her to carry back to Zion.

"We need to get you down to camp," Emilia said, feeling foolish for talking to a dragon. Then again, this mystical creature wasn't supposed to exist. Did it understand her?

"We've made you a carrier, so you don't have to walk," Emilia continued. "It's pretty far, so will you let us carry you?"

The dragon cocked its head to the side, considering her words, then turned toward Bastien and growled.

"It doesn't have to be him," Emilia said, and the dragon turned back to her. The dragon didn't trust Bastien. But then, neither did she. Maybe the dragon knew that. She motioned to Torey, standing a few yards

Chapter 1

to her right.

"This is Torey," Emilia said, "and I trust him. He's been kind to me. Could he carry you?"

The dragon peered at Torey for a long moment, then turned back to Emilia. It didn't growl or snap or hiss. Emilia took that as a yes.

She looked at Torey and nodded. He collected the makeshift sling from Amos and moved toward her and the dragon. The dragon hesitated and turned to Emilia again looking anxious, she thought. She wasn't an expert on baby dragon expressions.

"It's okay," Emilia said. "I promise."

The dragon's body eased, and it crawled into the sling, head hung low. It lay down, curled up, and wrapped its tail around its body. Torey rose and lifted the creature carefully. It was a snug fit, but the sling held the dragon. Torey gave Emilia a reassuring glance and she forced a smile.

Bastien threw a glance at Emilia that she couldn't read but it didn't feel kind.

"Let's move," he said.

"Don't worry," Torey offered beside her. "It'll work out as it should."

She wanted to believe him but didn't know if she did.

The Unknown Path

✦ ✦ ✦

The hours-long trek back to Mount Zion passed quickly. Emilia was lost in thought as they traveled. In what felt like no time at all, they reached the orchards in the Zion valley. The midday sun was warm overhead.

Emilia followed as Bastien led the group through the orchard toward the village. Before they'd left the cave, Bastien sent Marcs ahead to inform the desert elders of what had happened.

Now, as the buildings of Zion appeared through the trees, a pocket of dread opened in her gut. Marcs had informed the elders by now and news would have spread. She had no idea how Zion would respond. What would they expect of her now?

It was quiet as they walked. Wind coursed softly across her cheeks. No one was rushing to meet them. For a second, she felt relief. Maybe nobody knew yet.

Then she heard it: a soft melody of *ahhs* and *oohs* drifted on the breeze, cutting the silence. And then Emilia could see the Guardians gathered. They stood in two lines across from one another with a wide gap between them through the center of town. In their hands, they held flowers of all colors and types.

Their voices grew as Emilia and the others neared. She glanced back to see Torey, with the tiny dragon still snuggled up in the sling at his chest. The song drew

Chapter 1

the dragon's attention, and it poked its small head out from the cloth. It blinked against the bright sun and stretched its jaw wide in a yawn.

The dragon found Emilia's eyes and let out a soft screech. It seemed utterly unfazed by the scene. Did the dragon know they were singing for it? Had it been waiting for the people of Zion as they had been waiting for the dragon?

Nerves gathered in Emilia's chest. She swallowed hard as they approached the village. She saw their faces clearly now, eyes wide and hopeful. Some were filled with tears, others with excitement. But some held expressions of distrust and even anger, which could only be directed at her. In their minds, she wasn't qualified to be chosen, and she agreed with them. The whole scene made the hairs on the back of her neck stand up.

Bastien stopped before the gathering, and Clara stepped from one side to greet them. The song didn't stop but dropped to a low, melodic hum. Everyone seemed to know exactly what sound to make, as though they'd practiced for this moment.

But, of course they had, Emilia thought. The Guardians had waited for the dragon and its rider for over a century. Emilia could feel Clara's eyes and turned to meet them. They glinted with tears, and her face was bright with awe.

"I hoped to live to see this day, but . . ." Emotion cut

off her words. Clara's eyes moved from Emilia to the sling at Torey's chest. She stared for a long moment and then exhaled to control her voice. She turned to the rest of Zion.

"Today we witness and become part of a promise given to our people when the darkness seemed to consume all," Clara said. "A promise of hope and freedom. A dragon and its rider would come and create a way out from under the oppression of our enemies."

Clara turned to Torey and gave a nod. The man crouched and released the small creature from its pouch. The dragon lazily crawled into the open, and soft gasps filled the air. The dragon arched and stretched like a cat, then walked to Emilia's ankles and sat like a puppy, seemingly unconcerned now that it was with her. Before Emilia could react, Clara continued.

"The dragon has chosen its rider, and today we invite that rider to walk with the dragon all of her days. Together in union, you will be our salvation." Clara motioned down the pathway created by the people of Zion to a small table. Upon it sat a golden goblet.

"Come and partake of the blessed water. A symbol of the cleansing that you will bring to the world," Clara said.

The Desert Mother offered Emilia a hand as reality

Chapter 1

crashed into Emilia's mind. The notes from the gathering swelled once more into wordless song. They wanted her and the dragon to walk the path and drink to symbolize ... Emilia didn't know quite *what*, but everything in her wanted to run in the opposite direction.

This was their belief, not hers. Emilia didn't want to be a dragon rider. She didn't want to drink blessed water. She didn't want them to sing over her like she was some kind of savior. She just wanted to rescue her mother and go back to her life.

She felt Clara's warm fingers clasp her own and gently tug her forward.

The dragon gave a playful call and trotted beside Emilia. Flowers rained down over her as they walked the path now littered with a colorful rainbow of petals. A voice inside Emilia screamed for her to yank away from Clara and flee, but she couldn't seem to obey it.

They reached the table, the song still full, the path behind them covered in floral beauty. Clara released Emilia's hand, lifted the goblet, and held it out for Emilia. If she accepted, would she be bound to the dragon forever?

It was too much, and Emilia opened her mouth to say so, but nothing came out.

"Wait," a voice cried. The song wavered and Emilia glanced back to see Bastien striding forward. "Wait!"

The people quieted.

"This can't be right," he said. Some looked shocked by his interruption while others were nodding in agreement. His boots crushed fallen flowers. "Clara, she is an outsider."

"Bastien—"

"He's right," a male voice called from the crowd. "It should be someone from Zion!"

"But the dragon hatched for her," a small voice said. Emilia recognized the speaker as Izzy. A harsh correction from her mother silenced the child.

The Guardians erupted into discussion, some in defense of Emilia and others against her. Bastien called for quiet, and the crowd settled.

"The elders should discuss this," he said. "She's a child that doesn't even share our beliefs."

"The dragon chose her," Torey said.

"Something isn't right," Bastien said. "It can't be."

The dragon scooted between Bastien and Emilia and hissed. Children withdrew to their mothers as the tiny dragon barred its teeth.

"It appears the dragon disagrees with you," Torey said.

"Now you know the thoughts of dragons, Torey?" Bastien demanded. Before Torey could respond, Bastien continued. "My family has given everything

Chapter 1

to this cause, and no one believes in its truth more than me. Allow me this, Clara. Let the elders consider while the dragon and the girl rest. Then we can move forward, if it is agreed."

"I agree with this plan," Emilia said before realizing she was speaking aloud.

They all looked at her, surprised, and she lowered her voice before continuing. "I think there's been a mistake too. I can't be what you..." Tears filled her eyes and emotion clogged her throat. She was exhausted and afraid, and she had the sudden urge to lie down on the ground and weep. Emilia turned to Clara and pleaded. "Please."

Empathy settled over Clara's face and for a long moment no one spoke. Then the Desert Mother offered a comforting smile and nod.

"Very well," she said. Whispers from the crowd started to grow but Clara held up her hand to silence them. "The elders will meet and discuss all that's happened. Please don't be afraid. We'll have clarity to share soon."

She reached forward, laid her hand on Emilia's shoulder, and gave a squeeze. "Rest. We'll call for you soon." She nodded toward Maria, and the woman and her daughter Izzy escorted Emilia away.

The dragon started to follow, but Emilia held up a

finger to it. "No!"

Many watching gasped. Sudden regret yanked at Emilia's heart. The dragon paused and sat, looking up at her, confused.

Emilia softened her voice. "I just need a minute, okay?"

The dragon gave a soft squeal and Emilia hoped it understood.

Torey stepped forward and offered the sling for the dragon to crawl into. The dragon hesitated. Emilia motioned to reassure the creature, and the dragon crawled back into the sling.

Emilia turned away with fresh tears threatening her eyes and followed Maria toward her tent. She refused to look back.

"I'll come and get you when they're finished," Maria said, closing the flap behind her.

Finally, alone with her thoughts, Emilia curled up on the bed and cried herself to sleep.

CHAPTER 2

VICTORIA STOOD INSIDE the Keep's main sanctuary. Outside the large oak door, horses were being readied for the two-day journey back to Capital City. Victoria needed to return to the Grand Master. She'd already delayed the trip by a day, and she didn't want to draw unnecessary attention. Not with things in such a fragile state.

After a hundred and fifty years of searching for the golden egg, it was finally within reach.

Although in truth, it still hadn't been found, at least not by her. The dragon queen insisted it had been found by a chosen rider, which was the worst possible scenario.

Her service to the dragon queen was now more crucial than ever. She would be the Overseer who did what none before her could. She would slay the golden dragon and its rider. Even more, she would release the queen and her Reds now trapped in the belly of the Keep, returning the world to its true glory, bringing about the rise of dragons once more.

Lee, the Head Keeper, arrived at her side, a small tan satchel in his grasp.

"I've given you twenty vials of dragon's milk," Lee began. "Each will ensure your connection to the queen for about two days. Enough to last until the next New Moon Ceremony, as you requested."

"And the vials for the mother?" Victoria asked.

"Also there."

Victoria took the pouch from Lee and secured it on her belt. Lee handed her a heavy cloak, which she placed over her shoulders, and buttoned at her collarbone. The dark wool cloak fell to the tops of her feet and hid the satchel at her waist. Removing dragon's milk from the Keep had always been forbidden. The risk of discovery was too significant and protecting the secret existence of the dragon queen was an Overseer's top priority.

But everything had changed with the hatching. Victoria needed to be in constant communication with her queen. The dragon's milk not only allowed Victoria and the queen to speak with each other, but it also allowed the queen to track Victoria's movements.

Chapter 2

And the movements of anyone with dragon's milk in their system.

A ticking clock had started when the egg hatched, and the golden dragon and its rider needed to be eliminated before the infant dragon grew to find its power. If the golden dragon came into its fullness, it could not be destroyed, and the queen and her Reds would be trapped forever. Victoria knew from the journals of Malcolm, the first Overseer, who'd built the Keep, that most dragons grew to full maturity within a month of their hatching.

She had to move quickly.

The fact that the queen could sense the golden dragon meant it had to be close. Closer than Victoria would have thought possible. Unfortunately, the queen couldn't pinpoint the golden dragon's location. But Victoria was certain that if she could find the Guardians, she would also find the golden dragon. She was also quite certain that the girl, Emilia, had traveled south to find the Guardians.

But the warriors she'd sent to search for the girl had returned from every direction empty-handed. It was safe to assume that Emilia had found the Guardians. If not, her warriors would have at least found her body, destroyed by the desert.

Thus, the girl was Victoria's greatest opportunity.

She needed only to draw the girl out. Thankfully, she had Emilia's mother, the perfect bait.

A Keeper opened the large entry doors and gave Victoria a nod. The horses were ready.

Victoria kept her eyes forward and spoke. "In all things be vigilant."

"In all things be true," Lee responded.

The queen's presence whispered inside Victoria's mind as her steps echoed off the stone floor.

Take me to the hatchling. I will sense it as you draw nearer.

"Yes, my queen," Victoria whispered.

Destroy it and its rider. Do not fail me, daughter.

"I will not."

If you do, all will be lost.

Seven days ago, Victoria had questioned whether the prophesied egg would ever be found. Now she would be the Overseer to destroy it.

It was her true destiny.

CHAPTER 3

EMILIA WOKE WITH A START. She sat up on her sleeping mat, hot and gasping. Sweat collected across her forehead and made her shirt stick to her collarbone. She looked around and saw she was still in her tent. It was still day but not as bright as it had been. How long had she been asleep?

She took a deep breath and felt her heart slow. The last day's events ping-ponged through her brain, and she considered lying back down and yanking the covers over her head. Leaving her tent meant facing the people of Zion.

The desert elders.

The dragon.

The thoughts made her heart skip again. She stood, reached for the tent flap, and pushed through. The sun touched the surrounding rock walls as it set for the day. She could smell cooked meats and voices happily drifting across the evening air. Her stomach growled loudly.

"Sounds like you could use a meal."

Emilia spun and saw a young woman standing nearby with a small plate. Emilia could see steam rising from the bread perched there, and her stomach moaned. The young woman stepped forward and offered Emilia the food. Her suntanned face was paired with dark brown hair braided down her back, and chocolate eyes that looked at Emilia suspiciously.

"I'm Rachael, Bastien's eldest daughter," the woman said. Emilia remembered seeing her greet her father when he returned to camp days ago. "Here, eat."

Emilia took the warm bread. She could smell the honey butter soaked into the slice. "Thank you."

An uncomfortable silence fell between them. Rachael stared with an intensity that reminded Emilia of Bastien. Like father, like daughter. It looked like Rachael wanted to say something but thought it better not to.

"How long have I been sleeping?" Emilia asked, to cut the awkward tension. She took a bite of the bread.

"A few hours," Rachael replied.

"And you've been sitting here babysitting the whole time?" Emilia tried to tease.

Rachael didn't even crack a smile. Emilia swallowed her bread and her flight instincts flared. What she really

Chapter 3

wanted to do was run. Instead, she munched on the bread, trying to appear at ease.

"You're not what I expected," Rachael said.

"No?" Emilia wasn't sure what the woman was referring to.

"I've lived every day of my life waiting for the chosen rider," Rachael continued, "and I'm supposed to believe that you, a stranger and outsider, are the chosen one?"

Emilia didn't know how to respond. *No*, she wanted to say.

Rachael took a step forward. "How did you do it?" Rachael asked. "Hatch the egg?"

Emilia was taken aback. "I . . . What do you mean?"

Rachael cut her voice to a harsh whisper and her eyes darkened. "What trick did you use?"

"I didn't use anything."

"What do you gain from stealing our chance at freedom? What did the Grand Master offer you?" Rachael's whispers felt like daggers, accusing as if she'd already figured out Emilia's grand plan of deceit. How disappointing it would be when she learned that Emilia was just a sad girl with no plan at all. Chosen to be their rider? It would be a better story if it were all some grand plot. That would make more sense.

"Nothing," Emilia tried. "I don't even want to be the rider."

"Then surrender it!" Rachael snapped. "Tell the elders the truth and face your fate."

Emilia feared tears would spring to her eyes. Again, she couldn't find the right words. Could she just surrender the role to someone worthy, someone who wanted it?

"Hey," another voice came from Emilia's right. She and Rachael turned to see Oliver approaching with a concerned expression. "Everything okay?"

Rachael narrowed her eyes at the boy, then turned back to Emilia. "Do what's right, outsider." She turned on her heels and left, leaving Emilia's ears ringing and heart racing.

Oliver limped toward Emilia. If she had been a better friend, she would have checked his ankle. But her mind was consumed with self-preservation and the disgust she'd seen in Rachael's eyes.

Oliver reached Emilia's side and searched her face. "What was that about?" he asked.

Emilia wanted to tell him, but fear sliced through her chest before she could speak. She knew immediately the emotion didn't belong to her. It wasn't her fear. It must have shown on her face because Oliver took a step closer.

"What's wrong?" he asked.

Without knowing how, Emilia knew the fear

Chapter 3

belonged to the dragon. "Where's the dragon? Something is . . . I don't know."

"I think it's with the elders," Oliver answered.

The fear came again, innocent and simple, like a child crying for safety. It burrowed into her heart and caused her own pulse to rise. "Where are they?"

"In the Community Hall."

Emilia handed Oliver her plate and rushed toward the Community Hall. Her mind cautioned her to stop and think before running in, but her instincts screamed at her to protect the innocent dragon. She ran up the entry steps, into the main level, and headed up the winding staircase that led to the loft. It was where the desert elders had met with her before, and she hoped that's where they were now.

Their voices reached her as she took the last few steps, and then she heard the hissing dragon. Its terrified screech echoed as worried voices tried to soften and console. Emilia took in the scene.

The desert elders stood in the back corner, their faces concerned. Bastien was on one knee, his arms extended toward the opposite corner, where the dragon cowered. The dragon looked . . . bigger. A moment of surprise stopped her cold. In fact, it had almost doubled in size, which seemed impossible. It had only just hatched! Had it even been a full day? Its gray scales looked dark in the fading daylight, its teeth were bared, and its tail flicked back and forth.

"Get away from it!" Emilia demanded.

The elders turned to her, but Emilia kept her eyes on the creature. It snapped its head toward the sound of Emilia's voice, and the fear collecting in Emilia's chest eased.

She was feeling what the dragon was feeling, there was no other explanation. But she couldn't focus on that until she was sure the dragon was safe.

"Why have you cornered it?" Emilia snapped.

"We weren't trying to," Clara said. "It woke, and I think it was confused and started reacting. We were trying to calm it."

Emilia didn't wait for permission. She crossed the space without thinking and faced the council with her back to the dragon.

"He"—Emilia paused—"or she, is afraid of you." Emilia glanced down behind her and found the creature had moved into a more relaxed, seated position. It craned its neck at her and seemed to be trying to say something with its eyes.

A particular thought popped into Emilia's mind. An unknowable, specific thought that she suddenly knew. She swallowed and turned back. "He."

"He?" Clara asked, bewildered. "How do you know?"

Chapter 3

How did she know? There wasn't a logical answer. She just knew.

"He looks like a he," Emilia said and heard how ridiculous her answer was. How could a dragon *look* like a he?

The elders exchanged unreadable glances and backed away from Emilia and the dragon. All except Bastien.

"How do you know *he* is afraid?" Bastien asked, his eyes suspicious.

Emilia considered lying. Would it be good to be honest about something she didn't understand yet? She cleared her throat and tried to muster as much courage as possible. "I can feel it."

"Feel it? The dragon?" Clara asked. "Like you know it's male?"

"Yes," Emilia said.

"Fascinating," Torey spoke. Emilia saw the smile playing at his mouth.

"This is new information," Helen said. The older woman had returned to her seat at the long rectangular table. It held seven chairs along one side, one for each desert elder. Emilia had only met with them once, but knew their names and faces well. Clara, the Desert Mother, and Bastien, the protector, led the elders. Amos and his wife, Maria, Izzy's parents, occupied two seats.

Torey, Oliver's father, and Helen, who had the reputation of a fierce hunter, took up two more. Arthur, the oldest of the bunch, held the final seat. If Emilia had to guess, he was the one with the most attitude.

They all watched her.

"Of course, the information is new," Arthur said. "We had no way to know how the dragon and its rider would interact."

"I wonder if it will intensify with time?" Maria asked.

"I thought the dragon would be gold," Helen said.

"What other abilities will come from this?" Amos asked.

"Abilities?" Emilia whispered, but no one was listening to her. They were all talking at once, their eyes filled with wonder. It was as if Emilia and the dragon were something to be studied and understood. But Emilia was just a girl, and the creature behind her was just a baby.

But a dragon all the same. And one that had been nesting inside a golden egg for over a hundred and fifty years. Until Emilia touched it.

Emilia blocked out the voices and noticed Bastien, the only silent one, staring at her with concern.

I don't trust him, a voice said in her mind.

The voice felt strange. Which elder had spoken? Who was *him*? It didn't make sense.

Chapter 3

He doesn't like you.

"What?" Emilia asked.

Bastien's eyes turned curious.

He has mean eyes.

Emilia shook her head. She turned her head to the others still huddled in discussion, their eyes occasionally glancing up at her.

And a funny nose.

"Stop," Emilia said with more volume.

Your nose is also funny. So small in the middle of your face.

"It is not," Emilia said, her hand touching her nose. It wasn't that small.

"What isn't?" Bastien asked.

The room had fallen silent, and all eyes were on her.

"What?" Emilia said. Her mind was spinning.

Bastien crossed his arms over his chest. "You said '*It is not*'. *What* is not?"

"My nose isn't funny," she whispered.

Bastien looked taken aback, as though of all the things she could have said, he'd never imagined it would be that. Emilia felt like she couldn't breathe for a moment. Was she hearing voices now?

He wishes it wasn't you.

She was most definitely hearing voices. Or at least *a voice*. It was small and . . .

She whirled and dropped her eyes to the dragon. "Who wishes it wasn't me?" she whispered.

The dragon moved his eyes to Bastien and cut them to slits. *The one with the mean eyes.*

No way...

"Emilia?" Clara's voice.

Emilia's mind tried to process what was right in front of her. But it wasn't capable of understanding. Was she actually *hearing* the dragon's thoughts?

"Are you alright?" Clara asked.

Emilia met Bastien's eyes. "Did you hear him?"

"Hear who?"

"The dragon."

The room went still as stone and Emilia continued. "He thinks you have mean eyes."

Bastien's gaze widened with shock.

Unless she'd lost her mind, the dragon *was* talking. And from the expressions on the elders' faces, only she could hear him.

"How?" Clara asked, her voice low and soft.

"In my head," Emilia said. Fear gripped her heart.

"Unbelievable," Torey whispered. His eyes lit with awe.

You're afraid?

Emilia turned and locked eyes with the dragon.

Why?

"You're a dragon," Emilia whispered. "I've never

Chapter 3

seen a dragon."

I've never seen a girl, but I'm not afraid of you.

The dragon's eyes were bright and kind. His expression was soft. Her insides battled themselves, because, on the one hand, she still didn't want to be a dragon rider. But on the other hand, Emilia couldn't deny the pull she felt toward this amazing creature.

The elders remained quiet, though Emilia could sense their questions rising. She dropped to one knee, so she was eye-to-eye with the dragon. He'd grown at least a foot since before she had napped.

"You're really talking to me? In my head?"

Yes, it's the only way I know how.

"Can you talk to them?" Emilia motioned to the elders.

Why would I? They're not my riders.

His words buzzed in Emilia's heart.

"Why me?" she whispered. Tears threatened to escape her eyes.

I don't understand.

"Why did you pick me to be your rider?"

The dragon tilted his head to the side and seemed to smile. *I just followed my heart. And it found you.*

Tears slid down her face. Emilia was still afraid, but something in his words connected with her spirit. And for a moment it felt *right*.

CHAPTER 4

EMILIA SWALLOWED HER EMOTION and sniffed. The dragon had said his heart had led him to her, but what if his heart was wrong? Someone cleared his throat, and the sound yanked Emilia back to the loft, and the desert elders. She could see their fierce curiosity. This was the creature they believed would save them. They had questions. Emilia still couldn't wrap her mind around the fact that this dragon had hatched at her touch and could speak into her mind without using its mouth. What she did understand was she would protect him at all costs.

"They have questions for you," Emilia said.

The dragon flicked his golden eyes across the gathered elders and then back to Emilia.

Do we trust them? Are we safe?

We, he said, as if they were the same. Something

tugged at Emilia's heart. She felt a sense of belonging and realized she wanted to be part of his *we*.

"They've been kind to me," Emilia said, though a memory of Rachael's accusing eyes floated through her mind.

The dragon cut his eyes to Bastien, who stood in shock.

Even that one?

Emilia knew not even Bastien and Rachael would ever hurt the dragon. He was very special to them. "You're safe here."

"Tell him we're sorry if he felt unsafe," Clara said, stepping toward them. "That was never our intention."

"He can hear you," Emilia said as she stood.

"Oh," Clara said and moved her eyes to the dragon. She cleared her throat. "Welcome to Zion. We've been waiting for you." Emotion tinged her words.

The dragon moved to Emilia's side, his head reaching past her knees.

Why were they waiting for me?

Emilia was surprised by his question. Didn't he know? She turned to Clara.

"He wants to know why you were waiting," she relayed.

Surprise crossed Clara's face, and several of the desert elders exchanged curious looks.

Chapter 4

Clara kept her eyes on the gray dragon. "Don't you know what you are?"

I know that I'm a dragon and you're my rider. And I know I have a lot to learn.

Emilia told Clara what the dragon said and worry filled the elders' expressions. Their entire belief system rested on this small creature, and he didn't even know how significant he was to them. Emilia could see pricks of doubt. Maybe they'd been wrong about the prophecy.

They seem mad at me. Did I do something wrong?

Emilia gave him a small smile. "No," she said. "You're just a baby after all."

The dragon stomped his two front feet and fixed her with a stern look. *I'm not a baby.*

"You just hatched."

I hatched hours ago. I'm growing!

Emilia stifled a giggle at the sternness in the dragon's voice. "I see. How does that work? The growing?"

Don't you know things?

She couldn't help but laugh as he cocked his head. "Not about dragons," she said.

Why not?

Because he was the only one. Emilia was suddenly afraid to tell him. He would be completely alone in this world. The only one of his kind. But then, she would be too, in a way. The only rider.

She thought about her words carefully. "You're special. The world hasn't seen a dragon in a very long time."

Bastien interrupted. "So, it knows nothing about the prophecy?" he asked. "All this time, and he–"

"Will learn," Clara said, cutting off his fear. "Time is a great teacher, Bastien. Don't lose your faith."

The protector turned to Clara. "Don't question my faith. Although this dragon doesn't know its significance, its arrival means war is coming."

"Bastien—" Clara started.

"We know the birth of the golden dragon begins the time of change," Bastien continued. "He will grow quickly. He's already doubled his size."

See, the dragon said, *even he knows I'm not a baby.*

Emilia rolled her eyes.

"We should double the number of scouts to ensure our perimeter is secure," Bastien continued. "Make sure that everyone willing to wield a weapon is ready. The dragon and his rider need to be carefully guarded."

Emilia hated the sound of that.

"War is not our way, Bastien," Torey said.

"No, but it is the way of our enemy," Amos said.

"We shouldn't rush to chaos," Arthur offered. "The hatchling is still our secret."

"As far as we know," Bastien said. "But bigger forces

Chapter 4

have always been at work where the dragons are concerned. Better to be safe than sorry."

"I agree with Bastien," Maria said. "There's no harm in being on the defensive."

"When the enemy comes, turn the other cheek," Clara said. "How quickly in the face of uncertainty we disregard the great teachings."

The elders fell silent.

After a moment Bastien broke the silence. "The calling of our people has always been clear. Protect the egg and its rider. I'll not abandon that now."

Clara said, "We are also called to honor the way of the true prophet, Jack Solomon, who convinced our ancestors to lay down their weapons in the face of their enemies." Her voice wasn't angry. Instead, Emilia thought she heard sadness.

"I'm not suggesting we take war to the desert," Bastien said. "I'm suggesting we be prepared when war comes to *us*."

"An hour ago, you weren't even sure Emilia was the dragon rider," Torey said.

Bastien exhaled and faced Emilia. The room waited as he held her gaze. His expression wasn't kind, but it wasn't hateful either. A knowing seemed to pass between them. He didn't want her to be their rider, but she didn't want that either. For a moment she wondered if he, like his daughter, thought she had done something evil to gain access to the dragon. Did he share Rachael's suspicion that Emilia was part of a bigger deception created by the Grand Master to destroy their chance of freedom?

He dipped his head. "I'm the protector of this valley and all who are here. And I will protect her and the dragon with my life."

The weight of it all suddenly felt like a mountain falling on Emilia's shoulders. War? Protection? Enemies across the desert? Those enemies still had her mother. The thought drifted across her mind and shame opened a hole in her chest. She'd forgotten about her mother in the strangeness of talking to a dragon. Her heart ached.

The dragon pressed the top of his head lightly against Emilia's leg. Emilia looked down and saw the sadness in the dragon's eyes. Just as when she'd sensed his fear and come running, he clearly sensed her sadness now. They were deeply connected, she and this creature.

Because she *was* his rider. The truth was too great to run from now.

The dragon released a considerable yawn, and Emilia saw the weariness in his eyes. She, too, could curl up on the floor and sleep, even though she'd just

Chapter 4

napped for hours. Also, her stomach felt hollow, and the thought of eating crossed her mind. But that must be the dragon, because she'd rarely felt such a deep hunger.

Emilia turned to the elders. "The dragon is tired and hungry. He's growing quickly and needs rest and strength."

"Of course," Clara said. "We've never hosted a dragon before. What is best?"

The dragon smacked his jaw softly.

"Would you like milk or meat?" Clara asked.

The dragon gave her a sour look. *Meat? I'm not a monster. Fruits, flowers, plants, bushes. Bushes are yummy. And I will stay with you.*

Emilia nodded with a smile. "I think he's vegetarian. And he'd like to stay with me."

"I can't permit—" Bastien started, stepping toward her and the dragon, but the dragon jumped in front of Emilia and snarled.

Emilia curled her hands into fists at her sides. "I'm his rider. We'll not be separated." She was surprised by the force and confidence of her words. "We're not asking."

The dragon snapped his jaw loudly to assure them he felt the same.

Clara moved to Bastien's side and placed a hand on

his shoulder. "We're not trying to separate you. We're as new to this as you are. Please extend us this grace. We'll ensure you're fed, and Emilia's tent is big enough for both of you for now. Bastien, you can place guards on watch through the night. Tomorrow, we will make a more permanent plan together. How does that sound?"

Emilia exhaled and released the tension in her fists. She felt the dragon do the same and she nodded to Clara. Bastien also gave a tight nod and the room relaxed. Bastien left then, motioning for Amos to follow. They descended the stairs as they spoke in hushed tones about gathering their best people to guard the tent in shifts.

The other desert elders stood and left, leaving only Clara with Emilia and the dragon. She stared at Emilia for a long moment and then smiled, looking at the dragon. "I can only imagine what this day must have been like for you," she said. "For both of you. I'm sorry if we're clumsy figuring out what comes next."

She dropped her eyes to the floor and sniffed. When she drew them back to Emilia, they were lined with tears. "I've heard the stories of this moment since I was a little girl. I've hoped for it all my life, and now that it's here, I'm overwhelmed." She gently grabbed Emilia's hand. The dragon shifted but didn't snarl.

"I knew when I first met you that you were special,

Chapter 4

Emilia," Clara said. "I couldn't have predicted this"—she gestured to the dragon—"but I could feel something stirring inside you. And now I can see you're struggling to know who you are. Not who the world says you are, but who love says you are. I believe this journey will take you into the depths of love in ways you can't imagine. And, in the end, you'll discover a great truth. A truth that can save the world."

She placed her hand on Emilia's cheek. "Don't be afraid of this gift. If it calls, follow. If it whispers, listen. If it instructs, act. Bless the world, long-lost daughter of the true prophet." Clara leaned down and placed a kiss on the top of Emilia's head. A deep warmth spread through Emilia's shoulders and down her spine.

Emilia wasn't sure how to respond and was grateful when Clara quickly changed the subject.

"Let's go fill your bellies and ensure you sleep," Clara said, heading toward the stairs. Emilia followed, the dragon at her heels. Her mind buzzed with the Desert Mother's words and the hope reflected in her eyes.

So much hope.

There would come a moment when Clara would realize all her hope was misplaced, Emilia thought. She prayed she wasn't around to see the Desert Mother's disappointment.

CHAPTER 5

EMILIA FELT THE WARMTH of the sun across her cheek. She blinked open her eyes and pushed up from the sleeping mat. In the corner, near her feet, sat a heap of blankets. Unoccupied. A flash of panic sliced through her chest. The dragon should be nuzzled there, in a nest of sorts, which he'd created with his feet last night after they'd stuffed themselves full of dinner.

Only a few had spoken to them, but everyone in Zion had stared as they ate. Bastien and a group of hunters had followed them like flies. Emilia had been happy to tuck herself away inside her tent with the dragon as soon as they had finished eating. She'd intended to interrogate him, but he quickly made himself a nest of blankets and fell asleep.

Emilia launched herself off the floor and out through her tent flap. She quickly scanned the village in all directions but saw only the people of Zion doing their normal work under the early morning sun. She searched herself for an emotion that didn't feel like hers but felt nothing. Hopefully, that meant the dragon was safe.

Laughter, soft and full, floated toward her on the breeze. She rounded the tent and stopped at the sight in the field ten yards ahead. The dragon was there, bigger than he'd been the night before. His scales shone in the light as he happily bounced across the grass. Small knobs on his back were starting to sprout what she assumed must be wings. He nipped at the foliage and yanked sunflowers from the earth. Last night he'd gone to bed the size of a large dog, and this morning he was the size of a small pony.

The sight of him was rather unnerving. How could he grow so much so fast? Maybe he'd spent the whole night eating between naps.

People, children mostly, were gathered to the right of the dragon. Oliver and Brodie stood nearby. Izzy sat in front of the small group, her face worried, as the dragon snatched a sunflower and chewed it happily. The children watched, fascinated as the creature hopped into the air, tucked into a ball and clumsily rolled across the grass. Their laughter filled the air as the dragon turned to his adoring fans. A toddler

Chapter 5

clapped his chunky hands and cried out in excitement.

Emilia felt watchful stares and turned to see Bastien, Amos, and several others observing from the shadows of the Community Hall. Rachael stood among them. Even from this distance Emilia could read the coldness in her gaze, and again she couldn't help but wonder what Bastien and his daughter discussed behind closed doors. Surely this poisoning was his fault.

She turned from them and hurried toward the children. The dragon's head snapped up in her direction as she neared. His face broke into an expression that looked like a smile, and his sharp rows of tiny teeth shone brightly. It was both charming and frightening. She could hear them whispering something about her being the rider.

Rider, you're finally awake. The dragon's voice filled Emilia's mind as he bounded happily toward her. Oliver turned to her and offered a wave.

"Morning," he said.

"You shouldn't have left the tent without me," Emilia scolded. "I didn't know where you were." She sounded like a mother scolding an adventurous toddler. The children fell silent, and their excitement evaporated.

The dragon stopped, his smile falling. *You're upset with me?*

Emilia exhaled. "I was worried."

The Unknown Path

I thought you said we're safe here.

She had said that, and they were safe. She opened her mouth to say more but couldn't think of anything. She felt the children watching her. Felt the eyes of Oliver and Brodie. The eyes of the men in the shadows. They heard only her words, not the dragons.

When she first came to Zion, they watched her because she was a stranger to them. Now they watched her because she was the chosen rider. Emilia wished they weren't watching her at all.

I'm sorry I disappointed you.

Emilia looked back at the dragon and saw the sadness on his face. She regretted speaking in such a harsh tone.

"You didn't," she said. "I'm sorry."

The smile returned and the dragon spun in a circle. *Would you like me to hunt you some flowers? There are many here! The children said there are more outside the cliffs. We should go flower hunting!*

Oliver and Brodie walked closer. "The dragon is going to give Izzy a heart attack," Oliver said. Emilia looked at Izzy and could see her distress as she looked at the grass around their feet. It was littered with broken flowers.

The dragon turned to Oliver and stomped a foot. *Tell that boy I would never attack someone's heart!*

Chapter 5

Emilia felt a smile yanking at her lips. "That boy is named Oliver."

The dragon made a huffing sound through his nostrils.

Oliver. What a cute name.

Emilia chuckled and walked to the dragon's side. "He thinks your name's cute," she said, looking at Oliver. Several children giggled, and Oliver shot them a silly look, making them laugh harder.

"He isn't wrong," Brodie said, playfully punching Oliver's shoulder. "I've always thought that."

Oliver pushed Brodie back and the taller boy stumbled, chuckling. "And what strange name do they call you, dragon?"

The dragon shook his head. *I don't have a name. Do I need one?*

"It might be better than calling you dragon," Emilia said.

Where do I get a name? If there's a quest, I'm ready.

Emilia laughed. "There's no quest, you just pick."

The dragon looked confused for a moment and then light flashed through his bright eyes. *You're my rider. You will pick for me.*

"You want me to name you?" Emilia asked.

Yes. Anything you pick would be a great gift to me.

Emilia considered the dragon's words, and a

memory from her childhood leaked into her mind. Her father working in the Grand Master's stable. He was brushing a brown mare, a handsome steed with white tips in her mane. Emilia was with him that day. She couldn't remember why, but she was only seven or eight. She loved going to work with her father, seeing the animals and getting to ride.

Her father told her the horse was a gift to the Grand Master from an influential family in First Ring. Her father had been tasked with naming the creature.

"Darrian," he'd said.

"Why?" Emilia wanted to know.

"Because it means gift," her father had replied.

Darrian, she thought, what a perfect name. Her father's smile filled her mind and it nearly brought tears to her eyes.

Something gently nudged her shoulder yanking her back to the present. The dragon stood beside her; his face trained to hers. His snout softly brushed her shoulder.

You're sad.

Emili smiled and swallowed her emotion. "How about Darrian for a name?"

Darrian.

"That's a good name," Oliver said. "It sounds strong."

"Better than Oliver," Brodie teased.

Chapter 5

The dragon smiled. *Darrian, the great flower hunter! I accept.*

Emilia laughed and nodded. "Good, but maybe you could hunt grass?"

What a silly thing to say. Grass does not need to be hunted.

Emilia glanced at Lizzy, who was biting her lip with worry.

"See that little girl?" Emilia said, pointing to Izzy. "Her name is Izzy, and she loves flowers. I think it makes her sad that you're eating them all."

Darrian looked at Izzy and then walked toward the child. As he approached, the other children's eyes went wide, and many scooted away. He was a dragon after all. Darrian lowered his snout, so it was level with Izzy's face. The girl sat bravely without cowering.

Izzy, I don't wish to make you sad. Flowers are my favorite too.

Emilia joined them. "He's sorry if eating flowers make you upset. He loves them too, just in a different way."

Izzy never took her eyes off the creature. Slowly she reached out and tentatively placed her hand on the dragon's nose. Darrian closed his eyes under the small girl's touch, and a bright smile crossed Izzy's face. "The dandelions, the ones with the puffy white heads, are technically weeds. You could eat those ones," Izzy offered.

Darrian gave a nod. *Thank you, Izzy.* Then he jumped up and spun around. A surprised but excited gasp left Izzy's mouth, and the other children laughed at the dragon's playfulness.

Watch, I will show you the skills of my name, Rider.

Emilia watched Darrian crouch to his belly and slowly approach a collection of dandelions that waved in the soft breeze. The tall grass moved as he came upon his target. He stilled for a long moment, then pounced, yanked the dandelions from the ground, and drew them into his mouth with his tongue.

"Poor dandelions," Oliver said. "They never stood a chance."

Darrian swung around, beaming. The children fell into laughter and applause.

"Emilia," a voice called before she could congratulate Darrian. She turned to see Clara heading their way with Bastien and Amos in tow. Rachael, still standing in the shadow of the Community Hall, drew Emilia's gaze. She and Rachael locked eyes in a moment of stillness. Then Rachael turned and left. Emilia felt her gaze long after the young woman was gone.

Brodie broke the trance. "Here they come to ruin our fun."

Chapter 5

"I heard that," Amos said. "Don't you boys have morning chores to attend to?"

Oliver and Brodie gave Emilia a *good luck* nod and turned away. She wished they'd stay. Or better, she wished she could go with them.

"I hope you feel rested," Clara said.

Before she could answer Darrian was at her side, his shoulders tense.

Clara gave Darrian a nod. "I heard we should call you Darrian now. A very good name."

A gift given to me by my rider, he said.

Emilia smiled but didn't share his words. They were just for her anyway.

Clara addressed the children watching a few feet away. "We'd like to speak with them. Back to chores, all of you."

The children quickly scattered. Izzy stopped at Emilia's side and wrapped her in a tight hug. "Thank you," she whispered and then left. Her father, Amos, smiled sweetly after her and the sternness in his eyes melted. Memories of her own father made Emilia's heart ache.

Emilia turned her gaze back to Clara and raised a brow. "Yes?"

"We just want to better understand what the dra— what Darrian knows and doesn't," Clara said. "So we can . . ." She considered her words. "Prepare."

Prepare for what? Darrian asked.

For war, Emilia thought but didn't say. Instead, she looked at Darrian. "Do you want to speak with them?"

Darrian considered the three elders. *I have nothing to hide. Let them ask their questions, though my mind is still growing.*

Emilia turned back to Clara and gave a nod.

"Good," Clara said, then motioned to the grass. "Shall we sit?"

CHAPTER 6

EMILIA AND DARRIAN SPOKE with Clara for a while, answering as many questions as they could. Bastien and Amos stood by, ever watchful.

What did Darrian know about the prophecy? *That a rider would call to his heart, and he would awaken.*

What about the coming war? *War wasn't something he understood.*

And his purpose? *It wouldn't be revealed until he came into his fullness.*

What was that? *He didn't know.*

When would it be? *He didn't know.*

What did he know of his history? *Very little, but more would become clear with time.*

Did he know what Silvers were? *Yes, they had made him.*

What about the war against dragons? *Again, he didn't understand the idea of war.*

What about the true prophet, Jack Solomon? *Who?*

What did he know now? *That Emilia was his rider. That nothing could separate them and that he loved flowers but would not eat them because it made Izzy sad. Speaking of which, he was very hungry and would like to eat bushes and trees.*

Would he fly? *Of course, he was a dragon, and he had a rider.*

When? *Why did they have so many questions he couldn't answer?*

After about an hour of the same questions being asked in different ways, Darrian started yawning. Emilia had said nothing except to relay Darrian's replies. She had questions too but could see how tiring it was for Darrian. She would wait to speak with him until they were alone.

Clara ended the discussion, and Bastien escorted Emilia and Darrian back to her tent. The dragon curled up into a ball inside his nest of blankets and fell asleep.

The following two days passed in a similar cycle. Darrian slept most of the time, waking frequently to eat larger and larger portions of vegetation. He grew while he slept. He'd gone from small dog size to horse size in the four days since hatching. His wings had expanded to hang at his sides. They touched the ground unless he tucked them close. On the fourth day he could no

Chapter 6

longer fit inside Emilia's tent, so Bastien and others constructed a lean-to against the side of the Community Hall. They filled it with hay for nesting and hung burlap on the openings to protect it from the sunlight and wind.

When Darrian was awake, Emilia never left his side. They often spent their time in grassy fields, where wild foliage grew for Darrian to consume. He'd been scolded away from eating the trees in the orchards and the vegetables in the gardens. Sometimes, Emilia would walk with him among the cows and horses, where he joined in grazing hay and drinking from their troughs. But hay was sour, and he wasn't sure he liked it.

As he grew, he also gained knowledge, titbits of information that came to him each day. Emilia shared what she learned from the dragon with the elders, though no one could make sense of most of it.

"So, your purpose is to come into your fullness?" Emilia asked.

Yes.

"What does that mean?"

I don't know.

"Why aren't you gold?"

All dragons are born with gray scales, which change when they fully mature. I think my scales will be gold, like my egg.

"And when will you fly?"

Soon. I can feel it coming. And you will ride me.

"I won't."

You will. That's part of your purpose.

"Do you know what else my purpose is?"

You will grow into fullness as well. It's the way of the dragon and its rider. Though we will both make choices that could change the world.

"What kind of choices?" *I don't know.*

Emilia sat against a large oak as Darrian rolled in the grass under its shady canopy. She couldn't see Bastien or Amos now, but she knew they were close. They always were. She'd overheard them discussing the extra patrols being sent out daily. Today Oliver was with his father, ensuring the desert was safe and their enemies hadn't come knocking.

Oliver often walked with her and Darrian in the late afternoons. He had become Emilia's closest friend, and Darrian seemed to like him as well. Oliver told Darrian stories about the people of Zion and how they had come to watch over the golden egg. Darrian listened carefully, occasionally asking questions. Emilia also asked questions, but most of what Oliver said she knew already.

Jack Solomon was the true prophet who spoke of the ways of Yeshua. After the world was destroyed

Chapter 6

by wars, Red dragons had risen from the ashes and poisoned the minds of those few who remained. But Jack had befriended the Silvers and spoken about a way of love. His son, Noah, followed in his footsteps, and the ancestors of Zion had gathered to live in the world through love rather than fear. Two hundred years ago, the War of Dragons nearly destroyed all dragons and the ways of the true prophet.

Emilia always thought it odd to hear Oliver talk about the history of the world. His version was slightly different from what she'd been taught. The Guardians believed dragons could be good. Emilia had been taught all dragons were evil. Oliver believed the Order oppressed its people. Emilia believed it offered them protection. The people of Zion believed true power came from the source of love. Emilia had been taught that it came from humanity and following the laws that kept them safe.

Oliver's ideas made her question everything she believed. Hadn't her father warned her against the Order before he'd been taken from her? His words were crystal clear.

There is more to this world than you know.

Watching Darrian roll in the grass, she knew her father was right. It was hard for Emilia to believe she'd fled Capital City only two weeks ago. Two weeks since the death of her father and the separation from her mother. The wounds were still so fresh, and yet so much had changed. The people and place she'd called home were now the enemy. Could she ever go back to Capital City? Would she ever sleep in her bed again? Ever see Ruth?

Tears stung her eyes. Darrian stopped twisting his back against the ground and rolled over to face Emilia. Even lying on his belly, he towered over her now.

What's wrong, little rider?

Emilia blinked to clear the tears and sniffed. "Nothing."

You can't lie to me. I feel your distress.

She turned her eyes to Darrian. The gold flecks in his eyes were becoming more vibrant. His scales had darkened but still shimmered when they caught the sunlight. His leathery wings were tucked tight to his sides, and Emilia saw the first signs of ivory claws peeking out from his feet.

She no longer questioned if she was his rider. That truth was etched into her soul. She felt closer to Darrian than she'd thought possible. Not because they knew one another so well. Darrian hardly knew anything about himself. Rather, a mysterious yet undeniable binding united them.

For her part, Emilia wasn't sure she believed they

Chapter 6

needed to be free from the Order. She might be Darrian's rider, but she was still just a girl from Capital City. And more than anything, she just wanted to save her mother.

"I was thinking about my parents," Emilia said.

Darrian watched her thoughtfully. *They are important to you?*

"Parents are important to children, yes."

Dragons don't have parents, not like humans or animals do.

"Then where do you come from?"

Love or fear.

"What does that mean?"

Darrian considered her question. *I'm not sure. I just know that it's true.*

"Well, I come from Silvia and Korin Harker," Emilia said.

And thinking about them makes you sad?

Emilia dropped her eyes and struggled to control her sorrow. "My father is gone, and my mother is in trouble."

What kind of trouble?

"She helped me escape danger and was taken prisoner. At least, I think so. I guess she could be . . ." Emilia couldn't say it out loud. She wiped at the tears that slid down her cheeks.

Darrian scooted closer and laid his snout on Emilia's lap. *Don't cry, little rider.*

"It's my fault she's in trouble," Emilia said. "And I don't know how to save her."

Can I help you?

Emilia looked at the dragon and a surge of hope sprang to life in her chest. "She's far away."

But we will fly soon. Then could we find her?

Emilia looked around for Bastien or Amos, then dropped her voice to a whisper. "You would help me with that?"

Darrian lifted his head off her lap and gave a firm nod. *You're my rider! I will face anything with you.*

"It would be dangerous. And people would see you and know about you."

And that's bad because people and dragons have been at war in the past. He was repeating the stories Oliver had told.

"Yes," Emilia said.

But not the Silvers? They have no enemies. I come from the Silver dragons.

"Tell me about the Silvers," Emilia said. "Do you know anything else about them?"

I know they were helpers to mankind. They served love and peace. They didn't fight in the war between humans and dragons. They loved humans.

Chapter 6

New information, Emilia thought.

"And you don't remember the war?" she asked.

No. I wasn't an egg yet, but I know I was made because of it. Darrian closed his eyes, lost in thought. This was how his new information often came. Emilia imagined it was like suddenly remembering something forgotten.

A great darkness took over the minds of man and the Silvers knew their time was coming to an end. So, they created me to become light when the world was ready.

When Darrian opened his eyes, Emilia thought that they held tears. *The Silvers are gone. I am the only one left.*

"I'm so sorry," Emilia said, reaching out to touch Darrian's snout.

Darrian smiled, even as a tear fell from his eye. *Love can never really be destroyed, so I will see them again.*

"How is that possible?"

I don't really know.

He would soon, Emilia thought. It was clear he'd know more as he grew, and then he'd explain it all to her. Maybe even explain her role in all of this. She hoped they'd be able to save her mother.

✦✦✦

The Unknown Path

Emilia stirred and felt something rough scrape her cheek. Her mind was foggy, and she struggled to open her heavy eyelids. She opened her lips to speak and felt them tug against something pressed over her mouth. Panic erupted in her gut, but she couldn't move. Something was holding her down.

Emilia twisted with as much strength as she could muster and felt the sudden rush of falling. A beat later her back slammed onto a hard surface, and the air left her lungs. Pain rocketed across her body as her mind scrambled to process what was happening.

She tried to speak again, but her words were muffled by whatever was pressed across her mouth. Her hands were bound together at her wrists. Her ankles were tied as well.

"Struggle all you want," a harsh whisper said. "But you won't escape." The voice was familiar, but Emilia couldn't place it.

Emilia opened her eyes to darkness. Stars glimmered high above. She wasn't in her tent.

"I laced your food with a sedative," the voice whispered. "Stop struggling. It's useless."

Someone had drugged her and kidnapped her. Emilia could feel the effects in every inch of her body. Everything was too heavy, too dense, too sluggish. Why? Who?

Chapter 6

As if her attacker could read her mind, a small torch appeared, chasing away enough darkness for Emilia to make out recognizable features.

Rachael.

The young woman reached for Emilia's drugged body. Emilia yanked against her grasp, but she was too weak to pull away. Rachael shoved the end of the torch into the ground and Emilia realized it was sand. Dread fell into her stomach. They were in the desert.

Rachael yanked Emilia off the sand with a huff and threw her over her shoulder like a doll. The movement hurt and caused Emilia's mind to spin, but she didn't have the strength to resist.

She saw the horse a moment before Rachael swung her over the beast's saddle, belly down. She must have fallen from its back to the sand. Again, a question echoed through Emilia's brain. Why would Rachael do this?

Again, Rachael seemed to read Emilia's mind. "You have bewitched my people," Rachael said. "I don't know what darkness you used to hatch the dragon, but you're not the chosen rider. You're an outsider. The enemy. And I'll give my life to ensure you don't harm Zion."

Emilia tried to speak but her words were muffled by the cloth.

"Your lies won't work on me," Rachael said. "I see

who you really are." Rachael fastened Emilia's arms and legs to the horse, then grabbed her torch and the horse's reins, and started walking.

Emilia's heart started racing through the swirling fog in her mind. What would Rachael do with her? Kill her? Leave her in the desert to die? Was Rachael's father a part of this? He'd sworn to protect her, but maybe that was a lie for the elders' benefit.

"You may think this cruel," Rachael said, leading the horse, "but I have to save the dragon from you."

Darrian, Emilia thought. What would happen to him?

Her mind was still muddled, but she reached out to him with every cell. They were connected, but she didn't really understand how it all worked. Could he feel her now? Could he hear her?

Darrian! She cried with her mind. *Darrian, help me!*

The drug dug its claws back into her consciousness. It wanted to drag her back into sleep, and Emilia fought it with everything she had.

Darrian! Please hear me.

The sway of the horse's body and the drugs were too powerful to resist, and Emilia fell back into complete darkness.

CHAPTER 7

THE CAPITAL CITY DUNGEON GUARDS yanked a burlap sack over Silvia's head and dragged her from her cell. Shrouded in darkness, she stumbled into the fresh morning air, daring to hope that the sudden change to her predicament might be a good sign. Although the only good sign she cared about would be news that her daughter had found the Guardians and was safe.

They hoisted her into a cart that traveled quite far from the Central Tower, which housed the dungeons. No one said a word as the cart rumbled over rough ground. She could feel the sun's warmth and hear the morning calls of birds, so she assumed it was early in the day. Apart from that she was, quite literally, in the dark.

When they finally stopped, she was pulled from the

cart and led across uneven terrain. Something caught the hem of her skirt and snapped. A branch. Was she being led into the forest? Her heart skipped. Were they setting her free? She'd never heard of anyone being executed in the forest, but many were rumored to be exiled there. That was its own kind of death sentence, because few if any from Capital City knew how to survive on the outside.

Harsh hands grabbed her arms and jerked the burlap sack from her head. Air rushed across her face and sent a chill down her spine.

Rolling sand dunes with bunches of foliage and red rocks spread out before her. Her heart fell. The desert. Maybe they were going to execute her after all.

Compliance officers stood on either side of her, and others stood on guard close by, as if concerned she might make a run for it. She almost laughed at the thought. She'd eaten hardly anything in over a week, and proper sleep was nearly impossible in the dungeon. When she did manage to rest, nightmares of Korin's execution and Emilia's unknown fate haunted her dreams. She worried her legs might give out if the two compliance officers released their grip on her arms.

Victoria stepped out from behind the guards to Silvia's right. Fear and hatred spread over her as the Overseer approached with an easy stride.

Chapter 7

"Hello, Silvia." The Overseer wore a wicked smirk and held out a water flask. "I imagine you're thirsty."

Silvia eyed the flask, aware of her desperate need for water. She slowly raised her hand, grasped the flask, and yanked it away from Victoria, fearful that the woman might be playing a cruel trick. But Victoria only smiled as Silvia twisted off the top and filled her mouth with the sweet water. The liquid was cold enough to hurt her parched mouth, but she drank more, flooding her throat with enough water to make her cough.

She wiped her lips and offered the container back to Victoria, who held up her hand.

"That's for you to keep. A gift from the Order," Victoria said. She motioned behind her, and a compliance officer tossed a small pack at Silvia's feet. "Along with the contents of this bag. More than you deserve, considering your crimes."

Silvia glanced at the pack and then back up at Victoria. Something dark danced in the Overseer's expression. Silvia didn't trust the woman's intentions, but she clearly wasn't in any position to resist.

"It appears you've found favor with the Grand Master," Victoria said. "If it were up to me, you'd meet the same fate as your husband. But the Grand Master thought banishment would be a better end."

Better? People didn't survive the desert.

"For crimes against the Order and by command of the Grand Master," Victoria said, "you, Silvia Harker, are banished from Capital City and any city within the rule of the Order. The desert now holds your fate. Should you ever return to Capital City, or should you seek shelter in another city, you will be killed on sight. Do you understand the charges brought against you and the punishment rendered?"

Silvia opened her mouth to speak, and her voice came out like a whisper, "What of my daughter?"

Victoria's eyes flashed with something Silvia couldn't place, but it felt threatening. Then again, everything about Victoria felt threatening.

"Emilia?" Victoria said. "What of her?"

"I can't leave without her."

Victoria stepped closer to Silvia, her mouth pulled tight and her eyes vicious. "The desert will be your fate, as it was hers."

"Is she alive?" Silvia demanded.

To this, Victoria only shrugged. "Is she?"

So, Emilia must have at least eluded them. Silvia couldn't know for sure, but for now she would cling to that belief. Could Emilia have found the Guardians?

"Be grateful, Silvia Harkin," the Overseer said. "You are still alive."

And with that, the woman turned and walked for

Chapter 7

her horse. Within less than a minute she was gone with her guards, leaving Silvia alone to face her fate.

She gingerly reached down and lifted the sack from the sand, ignoring the pain in her muscles. She ran through the possibilities of her situation. Returning to the city was out of the question. There was nothing left for her there. Even if there was, she wanted nothing to do with the monsters who had killed her husband.

Trying to survive alone in the desert was also out of the question. She simply wasn't equipped to live by herself in the wastelands.

That left only one option. The Guardians. That's where she would find Emilia.

She'd studied her husband's map enough to know roughly where the Guardians lived, but she would be a fool to believe Victoria wouldn't have her followed. For all she knew, this release was an elaborate trick to get her to lead the Order to the Guardians.

First, she had to survive long enough to be confident they weren't following her. Only then would she find the Guardians.

Let the desert try and take her. If there was a chance Emilia was alive, Silvia would find her. Or she would die trying.

✦ ✦ ✦

From her perch on a nearby rise, Victoria watched Silvia Harker's form slowly enter the desert. The woman was a mere speck on the sand when Victoria finally dropped her eyes and dismissed the compliance officers standing by. Most headed back to the city as instructed. Two waited for her by their horses, twenty paces to the rear.

One figure remained at her side. Quinn, the Keeper who'd traveled with her from the Keep. A trained scout, hunter, tracker, and killer; Quinn was one of the Keep's finest warriors. He was now essential to her plan.

The man was massive, towering nearly a foot over Victoria, with broad shoulders. He wore the brown-and-tan sackcloth commonly worn by the Marauders to the west. The disguise would allow him to blend into the desert and convince any he met that he wasn't from Capital City. Not that Victoria was afraid he'd encounter many. His ability to remain hidden despite his size was one of the reasons he was here.

His head was shaved and his dark eyes were always focused. A thin scar ran from his temple to his chin along the left side of his face. It held a story of pain that Victoria would have to ask him about one day.

"You know what to do," Victoria said in a low voice. "Make sure she doesn't die."

"How close to death before I'm to intervene?" Quinn asked in his husky voice.

Chapter 7

"Only when absolutely necessary. Otherwise, stay out of sight."

Unbeknownst to Silvia, the water in her canteen was laced with dragon's milk. Just enough to allow the dragon queen to sense her. Victoria needed Silvia to find her daughter. She was certain the woman knew the way to the Guardians, but Silvia was also smart enough to assume that she was being watched. Silvia would die in the desert before she led trouble to her daughter.

Only when the woman was sure she was alone would she seek out her daughter and lead them to the Guardians and the dragon.

"Go," she said.

"As you wish, my lady." He gave a nod and turned to collect his horse.

Time is of the essence, daughter.

The queen's voice whispered in Victoria's brain like scurrying ants. She was drinking dragon's milk every day now, keeping her connection to her mistress unbroken.

"Can you feel the other woman?" Victoria asked.

Yes. She will lead you to the golden dragon?

"I believe so."

Do not fail me.

Victoria swallowed the lump of fear lodged in her throat.

"I won't."

CHAPTER 8

EMILIA WOKE AND CLAWED her way out of her mind's dark details. The reality of her predicament slowly returned to her. She lay on her belly across the back of the horse like a sack of potatoes. Her mind was less foggy, and she lifted her chin to look around. Her arms and feet were bound, and her mouth gagged. Though Emilia couldn't see from her position, it sounded like the steed was drinking.

The first colors of the day peeked over the eastern skyline. She twisted her neck slowly to see the mountain range that hid Zion. It was miles away. How long had they been traveling? And where was Rachael taking her?

Darrian! She'd called out to him in hopes he would hear her. Emilia didn't know how their bond worked. Maybe she was too far away. Maybe he was still too young to help her even if he could sense her.

Crunching sand drew Emilia's attention as Rachael rounded the horse. She noticed Emilia's open eyes and returned the water container to the saddlebag without saying a word.

Emilia tried to speak but only managed to gag with the cloth stuffed into her mouth. She coughed, trying to dislodge the gag, but the effort was hopeless. Rachael sighed and yanked the gag free.

She grabbed Emilia's chin, tilted her head slightly, and poured cool water into her mouth. Emilia felt instant relief as the water covered her tongue and slid down her throat. Rachael pulled the water away and dropped Emilia's chin.

"Scream all you like," Rachael said. "It will only draw the beasts of the desert to eat you."

"Why are you doing this?" Emilia asked. Her throat felt like sandpaper, and her voice sounded like she'd aged a hundred years.

"I thought I made that clear," Rachael said.

"I'm not what you think," Emilia said.

"Everything you say is a lie, so you should save your energy."

"Where are you taking me?"

"Back where you came from."

Dread opened like a bottomless well in Emilia's stomach. Rachael was taking her back to Capital City.

Chapter 8

"Please, they'll kill me if I return," Emilia said.

"Do they have a habit of killing their spies?" Rachael asked.

"I'm not a spy! I fled with my mother—"

"Enough! Save your words."

Tears flooded Emilia's eyes. She searched her mind for something, anything, that would convince Rachael of her innocence. Fear cut through her like a lightning strike, a storm of terror that she couldn't see her way through.

Darrian, she called in desperation. *If you can hear me, I'm in the desert. She's taking me back. I can't go back!*

Without warning Rachael untied her from the horse and freed her ankles. "Sit up!"

Emilia swung one leg over the saddle and sat, trying her best to ignore the pain caused by her movement. The rope around Emilia's wrists remained tight.

"Don't even think about returning to Zion," Rachael snapped. "I won't let you. I'm taking you halfway, where I'll leave you with enough food and water to return to your beloved city."

"If you truly believe me to be so evil, why don't you just kill me?" Emilia asked.

Rachael held Emilia's gaze for a long moment. She sheathed her knife without taking her eyes off Emilia.

"I want to protect those I love from you, but I'm no monster," the woman said. "I would never disrespect our prophet by murdering even a deceiver like you."

Prophet. Jack Solomon. Emilia knew almost nothing about him.

"If I go back to Capital City, they'll kill me," Emilia said. "Like they killed my father and probably my mother. Isn't that any different from killing me yourself?"

Rachael dropped her eyes, but not before Emilia saw a flash of guilt run across them. She moved around to the horse's mouth, grabbed the reins, and started walking again. "I'm doing what I must for the sake of my people," she muttered.

Rider.

She heard the word as a whisper and Emilia's heart lurched. She looked around and saw nothing.

Darrian! Can you hear me?

Nothing came. Had the wind toyed with her mind?

A prick of anger flared in her chest and then vanished. The emotion wasn't hers. Emilia knew the difference between hers and Darrian's. The anger had to be his.

Darrian! I'm in the desert.

As the first morning light spread, Rachael led the horse northward.

Chapter 8

Darrian, we're headed north.

I'm coming... His voice was impossibly distant, but it was his voice. He was coming.

He would be on foot. She had to give him time to catch them. It was her only hope.

Emilia considered jumping from the horse. If she could get both legs on the same side without Rachael noticing, maybe she could slide off and land on her feet. With her ankles free she could run back toward the mountain range, buy herself a few extra minutes for Darrian to find her. If she slid off and fell with her hands bound, she'd never make it to her feet before Rachael seized her.

Emilia carefully shifted so she was seated as left-facing as possible. She held her breath and carefully swung her right leg over to meet her left. She sat sidesaddle, waiting for Rachael to turn around and ask what she was doing. But the woman didn't turn.

Emilia moved her gaze to the ground, waited for a flat section, and then dropped to her feet. Pain shot through her bones, but her legs didn't buckle. Without risking a glance at Rachael, Emilia started running, pumping her legs with as much strength as she could muster.

Behind her, Rachael grunted in frustration. Her feet pounded in pursuit.

Darrian!

Hands grabbed at the sleeve of her shirt, but Emilia managed to pull free and keep going. A second later, Rachael caught her from behind, slamming her into the ground. The side of her face met the sand as she and Rachael tumbled down a small dune. They rolled, bodies entwined, and came to rest at the bottom of the slope.

The sand burned Emilia's eyes and mouth as she tried to catch a breath and push herself away from Rachael, but it was impossible with her hands tied. Rachael clasped hold of Emilia's left foot and yanked her back. Emilia let out a scream and kicked out at Rachael with her free foot. She connected hard with the woman's shoulder.

Rachael huffed in pain and momentarily released her hold of Emilia. Emilia scrambled backward.

"Stop!" Rachael demanded. "What are you thinking? Running is stupid. I have the horse, you fool! What are you hoping to do, run away into a desert without food or water?"

"Darrian!" Emilia screamed. She hadn't meant to speak aloud, but her words echoed across the desert.

A vicious roar cut the air and both girls jerked toward it. At first Emilia saw nothing, and then a shadow came into view. She looked up and saw.

Chapter 8

One hundred yards above, soaring silently, wings outstretched and dark against the dim light of early morning, flew the dragon.

Darrian.

He circled, tucked his wings in tight and dove, headfirst, towards the girls.

Rachael scampered backward and Emilia tucked and rolled into a ball as the shadow rushed them. Head to knees and eyes clamped shut. The beast landed heavily, pounding the ground. It shook under Emilia's body. Even with her eyes shut tight she could tell the world had darkened and she knew the dragon had landed over her.

Another roar ripped the quiet morning air, sending a shiver along Emilia's spine. She opened her eyes and saw Darrian's underbelly. Gray scales, four large, pillared legs in a protective box shape around her. A deep growl rolled through the dragon's chest, and relief flooded Emilia's body.

Darrian had grown since she'd last seen him less than a full day ago. And not just a tiny bit bigger, but enough to easily notice. Amazing.

Are you alright, Rider?

Emilia untucked her body and crawled out from underneath Darrian. His golden eyes met hers and she thought she might cry with relief.

"I'm fine," Emilia replied.

Darrian saw the bindings at her wrists and turned his head toward Emilia's captor. A rippling snarl escaped his bared teeth. Rachael shook in the sand before Darrian. She was on her backside, her face drained of color, and her wide eyes gawking at the dragon.

What happened here?

Emilia opened her mouth to answer when a new realization slammed into her mind. "You flew here. You can fly!"

I told you I would. I was only delayed because I couldn't get my wings to catch up with my desire.

Rachael let out a soft whimper that drew Darrian's and Emilia's attention. Her body trembled and her face was still pale as she pushed herself from her backside to her knees. "I don't know what dark magic she used to deceive you," Rachael said with a soft, shaky voice, "but I was trying to free you."

Darrian dropped his long snout, teeth still visible, and a threatening rumble rolled through his chest. Rachael closed her eyes and trembled.

What does she mean?

Emilia was angry and couldn't help but enjoy the terror playing across Rachael's face. This woman intended to lead her to her death. She should let

Chapter 8

Darrian release his full range of horrors down on Rachael.

But a small whisper of something Darrian had said yesterday tumbled like a weed across the plains of her mind.

They were helpers to mankind.
They served love.
They were made of peace.
They loved humans. All of them. And all of creation.

He'd been talking about the Silvers. He said they made him in response to a darkness that had come from humanity. And he was supposed to be the light, which was the only path to peace. Looking at Rachael's fear now, Emilia could feel that wanting the young woman to suffer was her own form of fear. But Darrian wasn't created to punish or harm. Would he if she asked him to? And if he did, what would that do to him?

Emilia exhaled and tried to release her anger. "She doesn't believe I should be your chosen rider because I'm an outsider," she told Darrian.

But my heart chose you. Why would it matter where you come from?

"You don't understand our world yet," Emilia said. "We've all been taught to fear one another." She turned her eyes to Rachael, who was staring at her. "When you've believed in something your whole life, it's hard to see anything else." Tears sparkled in Rachael's eyes, and for the first time she looked at Emilia as though maybe she wasn't something to fight.

Darrian didn't say anything. Instead, he moved toward Rachael. The woman froze, eyes opening wider and more fearful, then she dropped her forehead to the sand, bowing. Emilia also took a step forward.

"Darrian," Emilia warned. But the dragon ignored her.

He reached Rachael's quaking figure on the sand and lowered his head. The world seemed to pause as he laid his snout gently across the back of Rachael's neck, closed his eyes and exhaled warmth. Emilia watched the dragon for several long moments as the wind tickled her cheeks. And Darrian just sat with Rachael, offering her comfort. He finally lifted his head and looked down with what Emilia thought was compassion in his softened eyes.

Emilia could hear Rachael's soft cries as the woman released her tears into the sand. Then she slowly pushed back up to her knees and wrapped her arms around the dragon's neck.

The scene brought tears to Emilia's eyes though she wasn't sure why. Maybe it was the sight of someone releasing their fear and shifting from resistance to surrender. Maybe this was Darrian's purpose: to offer

Chapter 8

the people of Zion peace in the face of their fears. Even as Emilia thought it, though, she didn't understand how that would work. Or how that would allow them freedom from the Order.

Thunderous hooves approached, and Emilia turned to see riders heading toward them from the south. Panic seized her heart. "Darrian," she said.

Rachael released Darrian's neck, and the dragon looked at the approaching riders. Rachael stood but didn't look afraid. Instead, Emilia saw shame in her eyes.

"That's my father," she said.

A moment later the cavalry arrived. Bastien, Amos, Helen, and Torey trotted in, concern etched on their faces.

"Rachael?" Bastien asked, pulling his steed to a stop and sliding off in one smooth motion. "What happened?"

Looking more human and less fighter than Emilia could remember, Bastien hurried to his daughter. Rachael held up her hand, palm out, and he stopped. The others remained on their horses and watched.

"I made a terrible mistake," Rachael said. Fresh tears spilled from her eyes. "And I was wrong." She turned to Emilia. "You are the rider. I see now what I couldn't before."

The two girls stood in silence and Emilia wasn't sure what to say. It seemed they might stay that way forever, but Bastien moved.

"We need to get out of the open quickly."

Bastien motioned for Amos to collect Rachael's horse as he drew his daughter towards his steed.

"Emilia, come," Torey said. "You can ride with me."

She took a step and Darrian stomped his foot.

Nonsense.

Darrian looked at Emilia and a twinkle filled his eyes. She wasn't going to like this.

You'll fly with me, little rider.

CHAPTER 9

EMILIA SUDDENLY WISHED Darrian hadn't rescued her from Rachael. Terror dropped into the pit of her stomach, and she started shaking her head.

Come, Darrian said. *You have to learn if you're to be my rider.*

Torey seemed to sense what was happening between Darrian and Emilia and chuckled softly. Was her fear that obvious?

"I don't want—"

It's not a matter of want. You're my rider and you will ride. I promise not to drop you. And to catch you if you fall off.

Darrian said it so casually. Like people rode dragon's all the time. Emilia couldn't even think of a response. All her brain could do was conjure a horrible image of her plummeting to her death.

"You just started flying," Emilia reasoned out loud. "Surely you aren't ready to carry a person."

Do you doubt me?

"Yes." Honesty is the best policy, she thought.

Darrian huffed and shook his head. *Come, you'll see. I was made for this.*

The others had left, leaving Torey to bring her, but he now turned his horse away.

"Aren't you going to help me?" Emilia asked.

Torey looked over his shoulder and spoke in a playful tone. "A dragon rider should learn to ride a dragon." He continued on his way, and left alone, Emilia swallowed her panic. This was really about to happen.

Darrian lowered his belly to the sand so that Emilia could climb aboard. She moved to the dragon's side and saw a flat place along his back. It sat in the center a foot from the base of his neck. The scales weren't as sharp and harsh. As if he'd been created with a spot for her to sit. A place where his scales wouldn't hurt her.

Grab onto the tops of my shoulders and hoist yourself up.

"I don't want to hurt you," Emilia whispered.

You won't.

She did as she was told. With a leg on either side, like straddling a horse, Emilia sat atop her dragon, her

Chapter 9

feet hanging just in front of his wings. Her heart nearly stopped as he moved to stand. She leaned forward and wrapped her arms around as much of his neck as she could.

Tuck your heels against the flesh at the base of my wings. That will stop you from falling backward.

Emilia followed his instructions and a small yelp of panic sliced through her lips. She couldn't do this. This was crazy. People weren't supposed to ride dragons!

Emilia felt a chuckle vibrate through Darrian's throat. How could he think this was funny?

"Wait, I'm not ready," Emilia said. Her voice was high and shrill.

Darrian neither responded nor waited. He pushed off the sand and into the air. His wings flapped and a scream left Emilia's mouth. She yanked tighter to his neck and shut her eyes as the morning wind whipped across her face.

Gravity pulled against her as Darrian climbed into the sky. Her feet slipped, dragging her legs back across Darrian's wings. She clung desperately to Darrian's neck, feeling like she might slip at any moment.

Use your heels, rider! If you choke me, we will both fall.

Emilia sat frozen in place. She couldn't get her body to respond. She felt Darrian dip and her heart leaped into her throat. *Don't fall, don't fall, don't fall!* It was the only thought that pierced her panic.

Rider, you must help me.

Again, Emilia didn't move.

EMILIA!

Her name screaming through her mind, and she opened her eyes. Which was immediately a mistake. The ground was far below them. From this distance if Emilia fell, she would die.

Darrian flapped his wings hard, drawing them higher into the sky.

Tuck your heels! Ease your grip! I will not let you fall.

Emilia turned to see her feet dangling along Darrian's sides. She yanked them up, one at a time, and forced her heels back against the stiff tendon at the base of Darrian's wings. There was a small notch there that she hadn't noticed before. Again, as if the place had been made for her, her heels pressed into the small, notch, giving her more stability.

Good. Now ease your hold or I won't be able to breathe.

Emilia turned her eyes back to his neck and slowly unwound her tight grip. Her skin had gone white along her hands and forearms from the pressure of her grasp. The wind pulled her hair away from her face and stung her cheeks as the early morning cold sliced into her body.

Chapter 9

Cling to my sides with your knees, keep your heels in their places. Hands grip the scales at my neck.

Emilia did everything as Darrian instructed. The dragon leveled out from their climb a moment later and the world stilled. Wings outstretched; Darrian sailed across the breeze like a bird. The sky was warming with the rising sun hung overhead. Emilia's breath caught in her throat as the beauty of the landscape below her spread out like a beautiful canvas of the desert with the mountain range to the south.

Up here, the world was quiet. Peaceful. Perfect. Tears chilled on Emilia's cheeks and she smiled. A rumble of laughter vibrated through Darrian under her legs and a giggle escaped her own lips. She eased her grip as they flew straight and level, daring to sit up slightly.

She was flying!

On the back of a dragon!

"Is this real?" Emilia whispered. Her words were nearly silent on the wind.

Yes, little rider.

"It's beautiful."

Darrian tipped slightly to the left and then to the right, wings still wide as he used the wind to guide him. Amazing that he'd learned to fly so quickly. Emilia squealed and tucked close to his neck. She was still a bit terrified.

The sound of Darrian's laughter rippling through the sky.

"It's not funny, Darrian!" Emilia snapped.

No? Then how about this.

She instinctively gripped his sides tighter. "Darrian? Don't—"

But then he was folding his wings and diving toward the sand. A yelp ripped from Emilia's throat as her backside lifted off Darrian's back. She clamped her thighs with all her strength and pulled her chest closer to Darrian's neck too panicked to cry out.

The rush of wind against her face was both terrifying and thrilling. After a long moment of freefall, Darrian expanded his wings, caught the air, and leveled out gracefully. She gasped, which shifted to a giggle that she couldn't stop.

That was fun, she thought. A strange and yet true realization.

Hold on.

Darrian flapped once, then twice. Next, he tucked his wings and barrel rolled straight through the sky. Emilia's head and heart filled with joy and terror in equal amounts as the world spun around her. She closed her eyes.

Don't close your eyes, little rider.

Emilia forced them open as the world leveled out again and the wind pulled them toward the mountains.

Chapter 9

"How did you know?" Emilia asked.

I know you.

Emilia smiled. Never in her wildest dreams could she have imagined this moment.

Shall we go higher?

Emilia's heart leaped at the thought. But she exhaled to steady herself and looked up to the clouds overhead. She held her knees tight, ensuring that her heels were steady in their notches, and readjusted her hands.

"Yes," she said.

She couldn't see Darrian smile but felt his joy spread through her like fire. He pointed his snout up and beat his wings steadily as they climbed toward the clouds.

And then through them. Emilia felt the wisps of clouds play over the skin of her arms as they climbed further toward the sun. Once above the cloud, the world opened up. A vast blue sky that held the hanging sun.

She would need to remember a cloak the next time she flew, she thought. It was cold up here. The idea struck her as odd, and she laughed. Only minutes earlier she'd loathed the idea of riding a dragon, but here, above the clouds, a new sensation erupted inside her.

Belonging. She belonged up here on the back of a dragon. She'd been so afraid to fly and now she never wanted not to fly. She wouldn't be the same person when they touched back down to earth. Darrian was changing, but so was she.

Are you alright rider?

Emilia smiled. "Better than alright."

I knew you would take to it like a bird. We were both born for this.

Emilia chuckled. "Because you know me so well." It was meant to be teasing, but Darrian glanced at her over his shoulder and his eyes were sincere.

Because my heart led me to you and called you forth for a reason. This is part of you now. It always has been.

The words weren't new. Darrian had said a variation of this many times. But it played across Emilia's heart differently up here above the clouds. An image of Rachael filled her mind. She'd gone from doubting to believing so quickly that Emilia hadn't processed it. Something bigger was happening here. Something true and certain. Maybe it was time for Emilia to accept it as well.

She smiled with the thrill that filled her chest.

Let's see what other tricks we can do.

Emilia hunkered down, thighs gripped and hands steady. Apparently, a ready position for flying on the back of a dragon.

"Okay," she said, excitement lacing her voice. "Show me what you got."

Chapter 9

Darrian chuckled and it shivered under her legs. *Hold on, little rider.*

CHAPTER 10

TIME FLEW AS ANOTHER FULL DAY with Darrian came to an end. It had been two days since Emilia rode Darrian from the desert back to Zion. When Darrian and Emilia returned to the village, she on his back, the mood of the people had shifted.

Rachael was taken before the desert elders privately to face what she'd done. Emilia wasn't sure what happened in that meeting, but every time she saw Rachael, the woman smiled at her with bright eyes.

Oliver told Emilia that Darrian had awakened the entire town when he discovered her missing. He was desperate to find her, roaring against the dark sky while trying his best to leave the confines of Zion's boundaries. Bastien and several others tried in vain to calm the dragon. In frantic desperation, he leaped into the air, attempting to fly. He crashed to the ground on his first few attempts, Bastien screaming at him to stay put. But once the dragon spread his wings and flapped them, he took to the sky without a second thought.

Bastien, Amos, Torey, and Helen had followed on horseback. Oliver said the entire town went silent after they left. No one knew what to do. And no one went back to sleep until they returned.

"I was really worried about you," Oliver admitted.

Emilia had smiled and playfully knocked her shoulder against his. She would have worried about him too, she thought. "Don't worry, I was just learning to fly."

Bastien was concerned with Darrian and Emilia flying outside of his protection. Still, they couldn't very well keep to the sky above Zion. So, they ignored Bastien's stern gaze and flew beyond his boundaries every time they practiced. Which was as often as possible.

Darrian and Emilia were born for the skies.

Some of the children wanted to ride Darrian, and the desert elders quickly created a rule that no one but the rider was allowed to put themselves at such a risk. This didn't make the children very happy, but their parents were the first to agree with the elders and enforce the rule. Darrian said only the rider was meant to ride him anyway, though he told Emilia he might make an exception for Izzy if he could. The little girl

Chapter 10

had endeared herself to him. In fact, Emilia was sure there wasn't a soul that met Izzy who didn't love her.

The air swept across Emilia's shoulders as she now comfortably held her place on Darrian's back. The insides of her knees were blue with minor bruises, and the muscles in her thighs ached from flying, but she didn't care. Something about being above the world made her feel safe. The clouds erased her troubles and cleared her mind.

Hold tight, Rider, Darrian said.

Emilia leaned into Darrian and squeezed her knees. Her heels were firmly in place and her hands locked onto Darrian's scales. The dragon turned right and pulled his wings in close. The motion propelled them forward and down through the clouds.

When they emerged, the massive caldera where Zion had been built came into view. It looked like a wide, shallow well; surrounded by the towering cliffs that became mountains reaching in opposite directions. Fields, orchards, and grazing pastures gathered at the south end; the humble buildings and homes clumped in the middle. People dotted the ground like ants scurrying about their chores.

Darrian aimed for one of the south fields and opened his wings to slow their descent. They caught the wind and glided low across the buildings. Squealing children rushed to the fields, and ran along with Darrian and Emilia, as they flew toward their landing.

Emilia noticed that Darrian was coming in too quickly for a graceful landing.

"Pull back, Darrian," Emilia said.

I can't, Rider.

She braced for impact. He bounced hard once and couldn't get his feet under him properly. Emilia lost her grip and threw her body sideways to avoid being flung over his head.

She hit the ground with a thud and rolled across the golden wheat, flattening stalks as she went. The ground rumbled with Darrian's impact. Shouts of concern from the children rose into the air, but Emilia couldn't see them from where she lay in the vast golden field.

Darrian bounded over and nudged Emilia with his snout.

Are you alright?

"Yep," Emilia said, pushing herself up to her backside. "The landing could use some work."

Yes, well I'm not full grown and you are heavy.

Emilia chuckled and shook her head. She checked and ensured nothing was broken or scraped beyond a sore shoulder, which would probably bruise. Another battle wound, she thought. Her body had never taken so much physical strain. It was painful but rewarding.

Chapter 10

She could feel herself getting stronger. Not just from the dragon riding, but from crossing the desert, hiking with Oliver, and working with the people here in Zion.

"It's all my muscle," Emilia teased. She stood and saw the tops of the children's heads as they came rushing toward them through the wheat stalks, Izzy in the lead.

"Are you guys okay?" the little girl asked through labored breaths.

I am a mighty dragon! A little fall won't hurt me, flower girl. Darrian sat tall and raised his snout proudly.

Emilia rolled her eyes and answered. "Yes. We're fine."

Izzy smiled as the other children appeared, all talking at once.

"That was so cool!"

"You fell out of the sky like a bird."

"A really cool bird with scales!"

"Oh, I want to fly so bad."

"I wish I was a dragon rider."

"I wish I was a *dragon!*"

Darrian laughed and crouched low, so his head lay across the ground. A few children giggled and scampered up his back. He wouldn't fly with them, but he'd gotten used to trotting them around as if he were a massive horse. A few bigger children secured smaller ones tightly in their laps as Darrian pranced through the field toward town.

Emilia smiled and took Izzy's hand as they followed.

"Are you ready for tonight?" Izzy asked.

"I guess," Emilia said. "Though I'm not sure what I'm supposed to be ready for."

"The bonding ceremony," Izzy said. "They say it's to symbolize your connection with Darrian."

Emilia thought back to when she and Darrian had returned to Zion together. Many people wanted them to participate in this ceremony that day, but it hadn't felt right. Emilia had been filled with fear and uncertainty. She felt different now. Ready.

"Do you think it'll change me?" Emilia asked.

Izzy smiled up at her. "I think it already has."

Emilia stopped and looked down at the small girl—a child of Zion, someone she'd been told all her life was her enemy. She loved this little girl.

"You're pretty smart," Emilia said. "You know that?"

"Yes, of course," Izzy replied.

She sounded like Darrian. It made Emilia smile.

✦✦✦

The sun was setting and evening shadows were spreading across the valley as the people of Zion gathered for the bonding ceremony. It was a ritual the Guardians

Chapter 10

had waited a hundred and fifty years to carry out. They stood on either side of a wide path, flowers of all kinds gathered in their hands. Their voices joined in a beautiful melody, without words, that evoked deep emotion.

Darrian and Emilia waited at the head of the path as the Guardians looked on. Many men had placed flowers in their shirt pockets and arm bands while the women wore them in their hair or around their necks. All their eyes were lit with fire and wonder.

All these flowers are making my stomach growl.

Emilia put her hand on Darrian's side. "Try not to eat any."

It will be hard.

She chuckled softly and gave him a pat. He stood beside her at least three feet taller than a horse, towering high above her head. She didn't know how large he would get, but his growth came in bursts, and she knew he wasn't done. It was hard to believe that Torey had carried Darrian into Zion in a cloth sling only a week earlier.

Emilia turned her eyes forward. Clara waited for them at the end of the path, standing proudly, a dozen flowers braided into her hair, and a high-top table at her side. The golden chalice stood upon it. The Desert Mother nodded for them to come forth.

Emilia walked down the aisle, Darrian at her side.

The beautiful song of Zion's people surrounded them until they reached Clara, and the voices trailed off in harmony. Clara addressed the quiet crowd.

"We are here again," she said, and a few chuckles peppered the crowd. "I'll just skip to the good part."

Emilia smiled.

"As we have all now witnessed, the dragon has most certainly chosen his rider," Clara continued. "Tonight, we invite that rider to walk with the dragon all her days." She faced Emilia and Darrian. "Together in union you will be our salvation." Clara reached out to the chalice and brought it before Emilia and Darrian.

"Come and partake of the blessed water, a symbol of the cleansing you will bring to the world." Emilia took the cup first, nervous energy coursing under her skin. She still had doubts and fears. She still wasn't sure she could be their salvation or even what that meant. But she was ready to walk with Darrian as his rider, wherever that took her.

She lifted the chalice to her lips and sipped the chilled water. It tickled her throat and made her arms tingle. She knew it was just regular water, but the circumstances made it taste different. Then the dragon dropped his head and opened his jaw, so Emilia could pour the water into his mouth.

Darrian swallowed and the people of Zion burst

Chapter 10

into celebration. Emilia laughed and gave the cup back to Clara.

"Tonight, we celebrate with feasting!" she said. "May you be blessed, as you bless the world."

More cheers rose into the twilight sky, and Darrian opened his mouth to roar with the people. No one shuddered, no one cowered. The roar only invigorated them. He was their promise of freedom, as was Emilia.

A small voice in the back of Emilia's mind warned that she could never deliver what Zion expected from her, but it was hard not to get swept away in their excitement and joy. So, she did, and she loved every moment.

✦ ✦ ✦

The feasting lasted until the moon stood high in the sky and children started to doze off in their parents' laps. Emilia was spinning in wild circles with Izzy when she felt Darrian drift away. She stopped twirling, let her head clear, and then went in search of the dragon.

She found him behind the Community Hall, staring at the night sky.

"Quite a celebration, huh?" Emilia asked as she approached.

Yes, little rider. Unlike anything I have seen.

"You've only been hatched for a week, so that's not

saying much," Emilia teased.

Darrian didn't respond with his usual playful scowl, and Emilia knew something was different.

"What's wrong?"

It's time to go.

Dread dropped heavy in her belly. "Go?"

Yes. I'm being called.

"By whom? You can't leave me."

You misunderstand, little rider. You will come with me.

The dread turned sour in Emilia's gut. "You want us to leave? And go where?"

Darrian looked down at Emilia. *We were always meant to leave, Rider. Don't be afraid.*

"I am afraid."

The place calling me is safe. I must follow the call so I can continue to grow into my fullness. As must you.

Emilia swallowed and held Darrian's eyes. She didn't understand, but she knew they had to go. "Will we come back?"

I believe so.

"When?"

When we are ready.

That gave her pause.

"Where is this place?" she asked.

It is where I was made.

Chapter 10

Darrian turned his eyes back to the stars.
The Silver Towers, he said.

CHAPTER 11

SILVIA TOOK REFUGE under the shade of a lone juniper tree. It was one of few that grew across the desert canyon lands, and she was thankful for its protection from the sun. Three days ago, she was banished from Capital City. She'd traveled slowly at first and not directly south toward the Guardians as shown on Korin's map, fearing she was being followed.

She did her best to watch for trackers but hadn't spotted any. Then again, she wasn't a tracker and hadn't spent time in the desert lands. If she was being followed, would she even know? She walked for nearly fifteen hours that first day, eventually collapsing from exhaustion among a small collection of boulders. After slowly draining the water the Overseer had given her, she altered her course.

Using the stars, she'd headed south. She had a good

memory for details, but she'd spent the last week inside a dark dungeon with little sleep and less food. So, she hoped she was remembering the map correctly.

The warm midmorning sun woke her the second day, and with a small curse she rushed to collect her things. She'd slept more than she intended. That was when she found that the contents of the bag were gone. A small animal must have taken most of her food, leaving only a few dried crackers and a gnawed-on bread stump. Her leather water flask was also in terrible shape. Tiny bite holes had allowed the water to seep out.

Silvia had tried to mend the flask by tearing off a small piece of fabric from her skirt and wrapping it around the nibbled section. The patch was practically useless. She would run out of water by the end of the day. Food as well. Hot tears had filled her eyes and she considered turning around and heading back for Capital City. But that meant death. Being caught in the desert without food and water would also mean death.

Her only option was to find the Guardians before death found her.

Silvia's legs, stiff and sore, groaned through another day of walking. The second day came with a bright sky void of cloud cover. The sun smothered her with heat as she'd slogged across the sands toward the southern

Chapter 11

mountain range. That night, she dropped in a heavy heap, exhausted.

The morning of the third day, Silvia struggled to push herself up from the sand. She had run out of water and food over ten hours ago, and her body felt half dead. Despite her exhaustion and aching muscles, she managed to continue south. As the sun made its way to the middle of the sky, Silvia slumped sat against the juniper tree and sank to her seat, praying the shade would renew her strength.

The sun seemed hotter today and the wind more vicious. Her lips were chapped and cracking. Her hands were dried and sunburned. Thankfully, the rest of her skin was covered by the long-sleeved dress that hung to her ankles. After her food had run out, she'd used her sack as a makeshift hat to protect her head from the sun.

The worst part of the desert wasn't the sun, the wind, or the rolling sand that seemed to get into every crack of clothing. For Silvia, it was the endless silence. It was her cruel mind that warred against her, replaying every painful moment of the last two weeks.

Tears threatened to drain her body of even more moisture every time a picture of Korin flashed through her mind. She couldn't stop the spiral. She'd never see him again. Never hold his hand, or kiss his lips, or see his smile. His voice would never warm her soul as his presence warmed her heart. She'd spent hours mourning him during her imprisonment, but she feared it would never be enough.

As Silvia gained control of her grief, her mind waged another war with thoughts of Emilia. Her failure as a parent stole her breath and made her steps labored. Even now as she laid her head against the juniper, her heart ached. She took deep breaths to steady her heart and remind herself that Emilia was not lost.

She was with the Guardians. She had to be.

A mother would know if her only child was dead. She would sense it in her bones. But even this belief didn't lessen the intensity of her pain.

Silvia closed her eyes and felt the weariness of her body dragging her into sleep. She couldn't stop yet. The longer she was in the desert, the more danger she faced. She pushed herself to stand on shaky legs and kept going.

Her stomach had given up growling and just ached for food. Her throat was as dry as the sand, and even swallowing hurt. The minutes turned into hours as the sun offered no grace from its relentless torture. Tears again boiled up inside her as Silvia shook her head and stilled. Glancing around, she saw rolling dunes, scattered rock formations, and brush. Endless desert in every direction.

Chapter 11

She would never find her daughter. She would die in this desert and Emilia would be an orphan. The pain brought her to her knees as her mind spiraled into darkness.

"I'm sorry," she whispered at the sand. "I'm so sorry."

The harsh, hot wind whipped against her frame and yanked at her clothes. She screamed at the invisible force called the Order and pounded her fist on the sand. "Haven't you taken enough?"

Her voice echoed into the sky as anger tore through her chest.

"I gave you my loyalty my whole life and you killed my husband!" Silvia shouted. "He was a good man who just got lost. Where's your grace? Where's your understanding?"

Alone in the desert and on the brink of insanity, she couldn't control her outburst. It was as if the dam around her heart had broken.

Something moved in the corner of Silvia's eye, and she snapped her head to her right. Several yards off, a shadow moved across the sand. A shadow shaped like a human.

Emilia?

Silvia pushed herself to her feet and staggered toward the form. She couldn't make out details, only that it was too small to be a grown man or woman. It disappeared over the dune just slightly west. Ignoring reason, Silvia followed.

"Emilia!" she cried. "Emilia, it's me, baby."

A small voice in her mind yelled for her to stop. She was wasting her energy and strength. It couldn't possibly be Emilia. What would she still be doing in the desert? She couldn't have survived out here alone for so long.

But Silvia ignored the small voice of logic and hurried after the illusion. Trekking up the dune, she slipped at the top, and fell forward. Her chest slammed against the wind-blown sand and the air rushed from her lungs. She coughed and rolled to her side in agony. Silvia paused only a second as she struggled to get a proper breath before pushing up to her knees and searching for the figure.

It was nowhere to be seen.

"Emilia! It's your mother! I'm here. I've come for you."

The desert was nothing but a valley of sand. There wasn't even a place to hide. Her logical brain tried to tell her that the only way a figure could have disappeared was because it had never existed.

"Emilia," Silvia whispered through her dread.

She'd been chasing a ghost. Her mind was playing tricks on her. She was seeing things that weren't real. Emilia wasn't here. How could she be? Silvia glanced

Chapter 11

over her shoulder back to the lone juniper tree. She'd have to retrace her steps. It wasn't that far, but in her weakened state, it looked like a distant land.

Silvia knew better than to weep, but she was powerless in the face of her sorrow.

She should stand.

She should make her way back to the juniper.

She should control herself.

She should fight.

But she was so tired and hungry and thirsty and weak. Silvia lay back against the sand and told herself she needed a minute to regain her strength. Only a minute, then she'd continue. Even as she thought it, somewhere in her psyche, she knew it wasn't true. Her mind warned that if she closed her eyes, she might not get back up.

But Silvia ignored the warning and quickly fell asleep on the hot sand.

✦ ✦ ✦

Quinn watched as Silvia stopped to rest against a juniper tree. It was tall and lonely in the sandy terrain. He was more than a hundred yards behind her, keeping to a rocky nook. He'd been following Silvia for nearly three days now, watching as she wasted energy, lost her food and water, and slept longer than she should. It was clear the woman had no idea how to survive the desert. But that was precisely why the Overseer had sent him. To ensure she didn't die.

Good thing, because without him she absolutely would.

Following her tracks on horseback a half mile behind during the day, and only drawing closer at night, Quinn matched her impossibly slow pace. He'd almost collected Silvia when she ran out of water, but the Overseer had given strict orders.

Only in the face of certain death was he to intervene. So, he didn't. Not yet.

He'd followed Silvia as the afternoon sun moved across the sky, watching the desert for other signs of life and keeping a close eye on her tracks. He held back when she'd stopped to rest against the tree. Not a surprise. Without food as fuel, she was resting more often than she walked now.

Quinn sighed and took the opportunity to water his horse. He then found a high rise from which to survey the sprawling desert.

That's when he'd spotted the scout through his scope. A single man, hardly distinguishable from the sparse desert foliage, but most definitely a man, astride a horse. Different scenarios quickly played through Quinn's mind.

Chapter 11

It wasn't unusual to encounter Marauders now and then, but the man wasn't dressed like a Marauder, and it was unlikely a Marauder would wander alone this far north. It could also be one of the fabled Guardians, but they were rarely seen, and never for more than a moment. They were the ghosts of this desert.

His pulse quickened. Perhaps he had indeed stumbled into a lone Guardian. Quinn could track the rider back to the Guardians, which was the whole point of releasing Silvia to begin with.

But following the lone rider would mean abandoning his orders. That wasn't something Quinn did. Ever. So, he would only move closer and identify the rider.

Quinn could hardly remember a time before being a Keeper. He was an orphan, taken in by the Keepers when he was a small boy. They'd earned his undying loyalty by offering him protection against a world that would rather see him outcast or dead. He'd earned the Keepers' trust by hunting, following commands, protecting his brothers and the Keep, and always placing the Keepers of the dragon queen above all.

He hadn't learned about the queen until he was a young man, and he'd still never seen her. Though a master hunter and tracker, Quinn still had his station, which didn't include seeing the queen. But he felt her there, breathing in the depths of the Keep.

Some men sought to rise above their station. They

longed for the adoration and praise of others. They felt dissatisfied with what was given and always wanted more. Quinn had never been that kind of man. When the Keepers had taken him in, he was one breath away from death, broken by unkind hands and lacking the protection of parents. He was starving and sick, sleeping in his own filth. No one had ever given him kindness until the Keepers. They fed, taught, and loved him in their own way, and he wouldn't dream of asking for more.

Silvia, who had begun crying into the sand and yelling against the sky, suddenly went quiet. Then she was moving, chasing after nothing. Hallucinations, Quinn thought. But watching her removed his sight from the rider, and when he glanced back the man was gone.

Quinn cursed under his breath, quickly dismounted, and walked in the direction of the scout. He moved gracefully, hunched low over the terrain in case the rider was as skilled a tracker as himself. He worked his way to another high point, looked back to see Silvia staggering up a dune, and quickly used his scope to check for signs of the scout.

Nothing. Only someone who had spent a lifetime living in the desert could vanish so quickly. The Guardians were skilled hiders, and Quinn knew he wasn't

Chapter 11

likely to find them or their tracks now unless they too were tracking the woman. Likely just a lost Marauder anyway. They were a nuisance but posed little danger alone.

Quinn quickly made his way back to his horse. The woman had stopped on top of the dune and dropped to her knees. Still at a safe distance, he watched Silvia lie flat on the sand. Quinn lifted his scope to get a better look and watched as her chest rose and fell with life.

Her eyes were closed, but she was still alive, so Quinn sat down to wait and watch. If she didn't move for another hour, he would bring her fresh water. But he would not intervene unless he was sure she was finished. Those were his orders.

And so, the Keeper waited.

And watched.

CHAPTER 12

EMILIA STOOD BESIDE DARRIAN as the people of Zion gathered around. It was midmorning, and soon she and Darrian would be in the sky headed toward a place that he was drawn to but had never seen.

After Darrian announced last night that it was time to leave, Emilia and he had gone to the desert elders. The discussion had been fraught with uncertainty, but Darrian hadn't budged. He was being called to fulfill his purpose, which meant he had to return to the Silver Towers.

Emilia had never heard of such a place, but Clara knew of it, at least from their stories. Their ancestors knew it as the place where the Silvers had lived. The true prophet and his son, Noah, had traveled to the high towers that were said to be cut straight into the sides of towering cliffs, accessible only by dragon flight.

The Unknown Path

According to all Emilia knew about the world, the Silver Towers would be empty. All the Silvers had been killed. Even the Guardians believed that. But it didn't stop Emilia from wondering what it might be like to fly up to the massive cliff sanctuary and find dragons.

We should leave, Rider. We want to cover as much distance as possible before dark.

Emilia nodded. When he'd first mentioned going to the Towers, Emilia asked if he knew how to get there. No, he said, but his soul did. She would have to trust him.

"I still don't think this is a good idea," Bastien said. The same thing he'd been saying for the last twelve hours.

Rachael stood by her father's side, a sack of food in hand. "Father," she said, "if they need to go, we must let them."

She stepped forward and handed Emilia the bag. It contained apples, bread, cheese, dried fruit, nuts, and water. Enough to keep Emilia fed for a little while. Darrian didn't know how long they would be gone, but they planned to return to Zion when finished.

Emilia smiled at Rachael. It was hard to imagine this same woman had kidnapped her only three days earlier.

"Be safe until we meet again," Rachael said.

Chapter 12

"Thank you," Emilia replied.

Bastien said nothing else, but his face was stern. Emilia imagined it would remain that way until she and Darrian returned. Clara gave Emilia a tender embrace.

"Oh, daughter of the true prophet, we will miss your face around here," Clara said.

Emilia dipped her head. "Thank you for all your kindness."

"Until we meet again," Clara said.

"Until we meet again," Emilia answered.

Torey stood close and gave a handsome wave. He looked at Emilia like a proud father, and Emilia's heart burst with gratitude for the man who'd defended her from the start.

"So," Oliver said, drawing Emilia's attention to where he stood by Darrian. "You're really leaving."

Clara and the others took a couple steps back as if to give her and Oliver a moment alone. She felt her cheeks and neck flush with heat. She wished Oliver was coming. This would be easier to do with him beside her.

"Yeah," Emilia said.

"I gotta say when my father and I found you in the desert, this was not how I saw things playing out," Oliver said.

"How did you see it?"

"I thought you'd be more trouble than you were

worth," Oliver teased. "And really annoying."

Emilia chuckled. "I can be pretty annoying."

Oliver laughed and offered his hand for Emilia to shake. She looked at it, then wrapped her arms around his neck. His body went tense for a second, but then he relaxed, and hugged her back. Until Zion, the only real friend Emilia had had was Ruth. Now she also had Oliver.

She pulled back and noticed his cheeks flush like hers, but his eyes were bright.

"Until we meet again," she said softly.

"Until we meet again."

Oliver walked away to join the others waiting as Darrian lowered his neck so Emilia could climb to his back. When Emilia had settled in, Darrian stood and turned from those watching.

"Wait!" a small voice called.

Darrian turned around and Emilia watched Izzy run toward them. She was holding a bag full of colorful flowers.

"For you, Darrian," Izzy said. "In case you need a snack on the flight and get sick of bushes."

Darrian bowed his head in thanks, allowing Emilia to reach down and take the sack. She rolled the top tightly and did her best to place it inside her pack without smashing its contents.

Chapter 12

Tell her I will be forever grateful for this gesture, and I'll smile when I think of her for all my days.

Emilia repeated what Darrian said, and Izzy smiled so brightly she looked like she might burst. With that, Darrian turned. Emilia gave a final wave over her shoulder as the people of Zion began shouting their good-byes.

Darrian leaped off the ground and into the sky. As they climbed toward the clouds and headed for the cliffs surrounding Zion, the children raced after them. They jumped, shouted, and waved frantically as Darrian and Emilia left them behind and crested cliffs.

Emilia focused forward, holding tight, ensuring her heels were firm. Her heart ached a bit and she felt a sudden rush of tears.

We'll be back, little rider.

Emilia trusted Darrian completely, but it still pained her to leave the Guardians. She leaned forward as the dragon's wings drove them higher into the sky with impressive speed. Together they sailed on the wind toward the distant Silver Towers.

✦✦✦

Oliver had watched as Darrian and Emilia crossed the clouds and disappeared from view. And just like that, the rider and her dragon were gone. Zion seemed momentarily frozen as they watched their hope for salvation vanish.

The children had run across Zion, chasing as far as they could, waving and yelling their good-byes. But that was several hours ago, and now the children seemed unusually quiet. All of Zion felt quiet. A strange feeling lingered. For a hundred and fifty years they had protected the egg and waited for the chosen rider to appear. And then the rider had come in the most unlikely of girls. The excitement, fear, and anticipation of what would happen next had filled the small community of Zion with a renewed sense of purpose.

Now they were gone. Emilia said they'd be back, but when? And until then, what were they supposed to do? Go back to everyday life? That felt impossible. A hand fell gently on Oliver's shoulder as he pulled fresh water from the well. He turned to see his father's kind face.

"You okay?" Torey asked. "You've been very quiet since she left."

Oliver nodded. "It's just weird that they're really gone."

Torey offered an understanding smile and gave his son's shoulder a squeeze. "Change is challenging but necessary for growth. I feel this is the beginning of something new."

Chapter 12

Oliver turned his eyes back to the sky, wishing Emilia and Darrian would reappear. He already felt her absence. He was about to open his mouth to say so when shouts cut off his words.

"Bastien! Clara!" Oliver whipped his head toward the sound and saw Marcs atop his horse, cantering across the field toward them. He'd been scouting the last two days and wasn't due to return until this evening. Which could only mean trouble.

Bastien appeared from the Community Hall with Clara on his heels.

"Marcs," Bastien said, his tone worried. He also knew Marcs's early arrival couldn't be good. "What is it?"

Marcs reined his horse to a stop and jumped down. "There's a woman in the desert."

"A woman?" Clara asked.

"Yes, I watched her only briefly, but I believe she's being trailed by a Marauder."

Clara gasped. "This far south?"

Bastien scowled. "What makes you think she's being trailed by a Marauder?"

"Because I saw him briefly," Marcs said. "He wasn't wearing Capital City clothes. He was well hidden and keeping his distance from her. I almost missed him entirely."

"And what of the woman?" Clara asked. "Was she also a Marauder?"

"She looked like she was from Capital City, though perhaps exiled. By the look of her tattered clothing, she is distressed and exhausted. But it was her cries that stuck me. She was calling out a name over and over, chasing shadows as if lost to this world."

"What name?" Torey demanded. Oliver had noticed that the expression on Marcs's face was peculiar. Like he wasn't sure he should say more.

"Emilia," Marcs said. "She was crying for her daughter, Emilia."

That brought a hush to them all.

"Emilia's mother is wandering the desert?" Torey asked.

"We can't know that for certain," Bastien said.

Torey glared at the man. "Why else would she be calling out her daughter's name?"

Bastien ignored him. "Did the Marauder see or follow you?"

"I would never return to Zion unless I was certain I wasn't being followed." Marcs sounded offended. "I lost sight of the Marauder, but the woman . . ."

"What?" Torey asked.

"She looked near death when I left."

"We have to go after her," Torey said.

Chapter 12

Bastien waved a hand of dismissal. "Are you mad? Not if she's being watched by Marauders."

"We can't leave her in the desert!"

"We can't risk our security!"

Torey opened his mouth to protest, then shut it. Of course, Bastien was right. Oliver's mind tumbled over the news. If it really was Emilia's mother, what was she doing in the desert this close to Zion? Was she looking for Emilia? Had Capital City sent her? Why was a Marauder following her?

But above all those thoughts, one came through clearer than the others. *What if she died?*

Oliver had lost his mother. He knew that pain. Emilia had already lost one parent. Losing both would crush her.

"She'd never forgive us if we let her mother die," Oliver said. "If Emilia was here, she would already be in the air, searching for her mother."

The others, who'd been talking amongst themselves, fell silent at these words.

Oliver looked up at Bastien and held his eyes. "If she returns and finds out we did nothing, she'll never trust us again."

Oliver's words hung in the air for a long moment.

"She might not be Emilia's mother," Bastien finally said. "It's too much of a risk."

Anger swelled in Oliver's chest. "So, we do nothing?"

"We protect this town and all of the lives here," Bastien said in a tone that made it clear his decision was final. He turned to walk off but not before sending Torey a look that said *get control of your son*. Marcs and Clara followed Bastien as they discussed extra security around the perimeter.

"This isn't right," Oliver said.

His father shook his head. "It doesn't feel right. But what if Bastien's right?"

"What if he's wrong?" Oliver snapped. "What will you tell Emilia when she returns?"

Torey exhaled and ran his fingers through his hair. "I'll go to the elders. We'll do what is best for all. Please try to understand."

Oliver hesitated but then gave his father a nod and reluctantly returned to his chores, though this mind never left Emilia. He knew how she would respond if the woman crying her name in the desert died. Or worse, was taken by a Marauder. It made staying focused difficult, and a few hours later he nicked the end of his thumb with a knife while whittling.

He'd done all he could manage and was still waiting to hear from his father, but no news came, which Oliver knew wasn't a good sign.

They weren't going to do anything.

Chapter 12

They were going to let Emilia's mother die in the desert for the safety of the tribe.

Oliver shut his eyes and tried to be rational. She wasn't one of them. She was from Capital City. A Marauder was following her. They weren't just protecting Zion; they were protecting the dragon and Emilia. It was the sensible, smart choice guided by a code that had served them for generations.

Still, it felt wrong to him. Terribly wrong. He couldn't let Emilia down like this.

Oliver tossed the stick he'd been aimlessly whittling and stood, scanning the village. The day was ending. Soon the sky would be dark and the stars bright. Darkness would be his ally.

Oliver spotted Brodie leaning against a fence, tossing the last of the feed into a long wooden trough. Satisfied that he wouldn't draw any unnecessary attention, he crossed the center of town toward the pastures.

"Hey," Brodie said, seeing him approach.

Oliver waited until he was close enough to keep his voice low. "I need your help."

Brodie emptied his bucket and turned to face Oliver with a knowing look. "I was wondering how long it would take you."

"Take me to what?"

"To go after Emilia's mother, assuming it's really her."

The response surprised Oliver. "You heard?"

"Word travels fast. And the answer is a most definite yes."

That was easy. So, Oliver wasn't the only one who disagreed with the council's decision. That fact alone boosted his confidence and sealed his own decision.

He leaned against the fence next to the taller boy. "If we get caught, we'll probably be in trouble forever."

A smirk pulled at Brodie's lips. "Trust me, Emilia will change that. It's them, not us, who will be in trouble."

CHAPTER 13

EMILIA AND DARRIAN had been flying for hours and her thighs were killing her, but the wonder of flying distracted her from the discomfort. The sun was sinking below the western skyline, and fiery pinks decorated the clouds. The horizon was stunning from this vantage point, but soon it would be dark and freezing, even wearing the hide coat she'd brought.

Darrian was scouting for a place to camp for the night when a small forest appeared to the south, a few miles off. *We can take cover there*, he said.

Emilia leaned into the sharp turn as Darrian winged toward the trees. After a few more flaps of his wings, he tucked them along his sides and dove. Emilia had done this a dozen times, but the feeling was always the same—a thrill of adventure and fear of falling wrapped up into a bursting ball of energy that rattled her bones. It always brought a smile to her face even as her heart thundered in her chest. At the last moment, Darrian opened his wings, caught the breeze, and drifted to the sand near the edge of the trees.

He landed with a heavy thud and shook out his wings, then lowered his head so Emilia could slide to the ground. Her feet hit the dirt and she slowly straightened her aching legs. She stood still for several long moments, not sure she could walk, so stiff were her muscles.

"Let's find a clearing in the trees to build a fire. We don't want to stay out here in the open," Emilia said, heading into the trees. "Follow me."

The foliage was so tight in spots that Darrian couldn't squeeze through, and they had to backtrack. They had wandered for a good ten minutes, and Darrian had started to complain that they could be flying, when they finally reached a clearing protected from the wind and wandering eyes.

"Here," she announced. "It's perfect."

Finally. I don't know how humans manage all this walking.

"Well, we aren't carrying around a thousand-pound body," she jested. "Now be useful and break off some dead branches with those big teeth of yours."

Ten minutes later, next to a heaping pile of wood, enough to build a house, Emilia started building a small fire the way Oliver had shown her. After a few

Chapter 13

failed attempts, a humble flame ignited. Thrilled, Emilia carefully stoked the flame until it grew large enough to offer warmth. The sun was gone, and the stars were out. It had been a perfect day.

"How much farther do we have?" she asked as Darrian munched on the flowers Izzy had provided. She ate crackers and dried fruit from her sack. Not much, but she was incredibly grateful for the food.

It's hard to know, but we're getting close. Maybe another day.

"And you just feel it drawing you?"

Yes, little rider. It lives in my heart, and I know the call.

Emilia still didn't understand how such a thing was possible, but he was a dragon, and she was just a girl.

Darrian's head snapped up from his snack and his body went rigid.

"What is it?" Emilia whispered, startled. She could hear nothing out of the ordinary.

Darrian remained still, then slowly stood. Emilia could feel his concern.

"Darrian! Say something!"

Someone else is here.

Emilia drew her eyes carefully around the small clearing encircled by large trees. The light from her fire was small and did nothing to illuminate anything past the trees.

A blurred motion to the right caught Emilia's eye. The shadows there seemed to move, and a moment later a figure stepped out from behind a tree. Emilia backed close to Darrian, who had turned his head toward the stranger.

The figure emerged from the cover of darkness, hands raised, and slowly removed the hood that shrouded its face. It looked to be a rather small, old man with dark gray hair and a matching thick beard that hung to his chest. His cloak was humble brown, draped across his shoulders, and skimming the tops of heavy black boots.

His eyes were still in shadow, but even from ten feet away Emilia knew the man was staring at Darrian.

"Blessed Scales!" the old man whispered.

"Who are you?" Emilia challenged, not knowing what else she might say.

"I mean no harm," the man replied. "And I'm alone."

"Saying something doesn't make it true," Emilia shot back. Darrian growled—she could feel the vibration at her back.

The man huffed, amused, and lowered his hands. "You're a smart girl. And you have a dragon."

Jump on my back and we will flee, Darrian said.

Not yet, Emilia thought. Besides, her supplies— which she desperately needed—were scattered about.

Chapter 13

They couldn't just flee.

"I swear by the Scales that I haven't come to hurt you," the man said, sensing her fear.

"My dragon will eat you if you come any closer," Emilia said.

I would never do such a thing!

The man laughed and shook his head. "That would be a sight, as I know most dragons are vegetarians."

He knew about dragons? "How do you know that?"

"My people know many things about dragons," the stranger said. "Though I have never seen one." The man took a couple more steps forward.

"And who are your people?" Emilia asked.

The old man hesitated, as if searching for the right answer. "They're deadly and stuck in old ways of being. Which is why I'm no longer with them."

"You didn't answer my question," Emilia said.

The man smiled. "You're right. My people are called Marauders. They live far to the west, and I live here in the forest. They call me the Hermit."

That's an odd name, Darrian said.

Marauders. Ruth had told her scary stories about the people living far to the southwest. They'd steal your belongings and leave you for dead. Oliver had mentioned they had hunted Guardians before the Guardians found safety in Mount Zion.

Her face must have reflected her fear.

"I can see you've heard of my people," the man said.

"A little," Emilia answered honestly. "Enough to be wary of trusting you."

"Again, you prove to be intelligent. Good. You'll need smarts out here."

"You live alone in this desert? By choice?"

"That's a long story," the old man said. "But in short, yes. My brother and I disagreed on how our people should live, so I left."

The man took another step and Emilia could now see the deep blue of his eyes staring at Darrian with wonder.

"A rather small dragon," the man said softly. "Black."

Darrian growled.

"I've offended it?" the man asked.

"Him, you offended him," Emilia corrected. "And he's a golden dragon, just too young to show his true colors."

The man's eyes went wide. "So, the Guardians' prophecy is true? The golden dragon will hatch at the touch of a chosen rider. Are you that dragon rider?"

Emilia swallowed and fidgeted. It was strange to hear others call her dragon rider. It was something she was still getting used to.

"It is said that before the War of Dragons, some could speak with the dragons," the Hermit said. "That

Chapter 13

the dragon's voices echoed in their minds, and their minds alone. Does the dragon talk with you, girl?"

"Yes," Emilia answered.

The man smiled. "Fascinating."

"How do you know so much about dragons?"

"The Marauders come from the original line of dragon followers. They called themselves the Scalers. They have always believed the dragons to be gods of this earth."

Emilia remembered Oliver's mention of Scalers. She also remembered he'd said they hated Silvers and the true prophet. That didn't bode well for her.

"But you don't believe that?" she asked, testing the waters.

The Hermit considered her question. "I believe the archaic ways of blood and violence are outdated. I also believe more war will not grant Marauders the power they believe they're due. But my beliefs are of no consequence to you. I promise not to harm you or tell anyone of what I've seen here."

Emilia wasn't sure she should believe him. "Why would you protect us?"

"Because I want nothing to do with any of it. I spent years trying to help my people see a different path, which got me nowhere. I'm better out here on my own."

You should give him a new name. You're very skilled with names.

Emilia smiled despite herself, and the Hermit flashed a look from her to Darrian.

"Did he just speak to you?" the man asked excitedly.

Emilia nodded. "He thinks Hermit is a terrible name."

The man looked shocked for a second and then let out a chuckle. It surprised Emilia, but then she too found it funny.

"He's right," the man said. "An actual dragon. I thought I was going mad when I spotted you flying through the clouds at sundown."

Worry snuffed out Emilia's joy. "Do you think others saw too?"

"There are no others out here," the Hermit said. "You're safe." Then the man turned as if to leave.

"Where are you going?" Emilia asked.

"I just came to see if madness had actually come for me," the Hermit answered. "Now I'll leave you."

"How do I know you won't just wait in the woods until I fall asleep and then kill me?"

The man turned, humor playing in his eyes. "You still don't trust me?"

"What have you done to gain my trust?"

The Hermit nodded and tapped the side of his skull. "Smart. You'll do fine, dragon rider. But I wish for you to be free of worry. So, may I present you each with a

Chapter 13

gift? Amongst my people, giving a gift ensures loyalty."

Without waiting for an answer, he lifted his heavy brown cloak and produced a small sack. It was tied to his belt, and he quickly unclipped it. He opened the top and rummaged through until he found what he was looking for. "Ah," he said yanking the item free. "This is for the dragon." He paused and then continued. "Does he have a name?"

"Darrian," Emilia said.

"Meaning gift! What a perfect name for such a creature." He held out his hand. "May I give you this gift, Darrian?"

The dragon hesitated, then gave a nod, and the Hermit approached. Emilia couldn't slow her racing heart as the man neared and opened his hand. On his palm rested a round, thick medallion on a thin, black, leather strap. The medallion was gold, about two inches across and half-an-inch thick, inscribed with symbols that were foreign to Emilia. It had dots and dashes, with curved lines, like backward letters. A language she'd never seen.

"It's beautiful. What does it say?" Emilia asked.

"It says *Baw Sulu Tee*, which means 'king among mortals.' Fitting for a dragon, yes?"

Emilia looked up at the Hermit and found herself more curious. How did he have something like this? Or maybe all Marauders held beautiful golden medallions.

It is very shiny. I accept. Darrian bowed his head and Emilia took the necklace from the Hermit. "I'll keep it for you," she said to Darrian. "We'll have to find a way to get it around your huge neck."

Or you could wear it for me, he said.

"And for you, dragon rider," the man said as he pulled something else from his belt. It was a small dagger, which he held by the blade. The hilt was made of the same gold as the medallion, with letters etched on the blade.

"A fierce weapon for such an intelligent young girl," the Hermit said. "*Kato Sue*, Aim true."

Emilia took the dagger from the Hermit's hand and held it in hers. It was light and smooth. The blade was only four inches in length.

"Now," the Hermit said. "If I come back, you can stab me." He gave a chuckle at his own joke and Emilia found herself smiling. Then he turned to leave again, stopping at the tree line and glancing back toward them. Taking a final look at Darrian, he moved his eyes to Emilia, and his smile fell.

"I don't know where your journey will take you, but whatever you do, don't go to the Marauders. Only pain and death wait for you there."

Then he turned and vanished into the dark forest.

CHAPTER 14

OLIVER AND BRODIE SNUCK out of Zion while it slept, riding on two of their strongest stallions. They used the stars and moon to guide them through the desert, moving fast. Over dinner, Oliver had pressed his father for enough details to calculate where Marcs had found the woman.

Guilt pricked his skin. Oliver and his father had always been honest with each other. And although technically he hadn't lied, he had indeed deceived his father, which left him feeling terrible. But Oliver reminded himself that he was saving Emilia's mother.

It took them three hours at a nearly impossible pace to reach the high dune where he suspected Marcs had witnessed the woman, and another half hour to find Marcs's tracks. Securing the horses to a small bush, they shimmied up the dune and stared down at the broad desert.

The Unknown Path

The moon was full, giving them plenty of light without a cloud in sight, and Oliver had brought their most powerful scope. He scanned the sands carefully. Endless dark dunes dotted with sparse foliage and occasional rock outcroppings covered the desert. But no bodies.

"Anything?" Brodie asked.

Oliver didn't respond, which was response enough. Maybe they were too late. Maybe the Marauder had taken the woman away. Or maybe she hadn't survived the desert afternoon?

Then he saw her. Or at least he saw a clump of tan fabric lying on top of a much smaller dune below to their right. His pulse spiked. It had to be her! The clump was motionless, curled in on itself. It almost seemed part of the desert.

"Found something," Oliver whispered. A terrifying thought crossed Oliver's mind. *What if she was already dead?*

He shoved the thought away and slowly swept his binoculars in every direction of the body. The Marauder could still be here.

They needed a plan.

✦ ✦ ✦

Chapter 14

Quinn had watched Silvia lay motionless for hours. He waited for the night to bring darkness and a cool breeze that would hopefully revive her. If she didn't wake then, he would deliver a distinctly Marauder-looking flask of water to her side, retreat, and then wake her from a distance. A thrown stone or branch should suffice. If all went well, she would wake, drink the water, and then, revived, lead him to the Guardians.

She would know she was being followed, naturally, as leather water pouches didn't just fall out of the sky to save dying women in the desert. But she would assume a Marauder had delivered the water. She had little choice other than to continue on her way, hoping a kind soul had saved her, and then left.

A dozen times while watching Silvia, Quinn had considered trying to track down the scout. But the Guardians were said to the most skilled trackers, who knew every grain of sand in this desert. The scout would be long gone by now. Regardless, his mission was clear. Keep Silvia alive.

Now waiting in the darkness, Quinn chewed a handful of sunflower seeds, biting their salty shells and removing the seed with his teeth. It gave him something to do and kept his mind awake. It was cold now, nearly midnight.

It was time to move.

He spit broken shells from his mouth and stood. He scooped up the flask of water and a small bag of food, scanned the desert a final time and then started toward the fallen woman.

✦ ✦ ✦

Oliver ran through different scenarios as the midnight breeze cut through his coat. If the Marauder was still out here, he hadn't made a move. What would be the purpose of watching a slumped figure? And being this far north, a Marauder would surely be just passing through. As far as the Guardians knew, they didn't concern themselves with outcasts, and avoided outsiders of any kind unless they were a threat.

Brodie shifted beside him, growing impatient. "We're running out of time," he mumbled. "We still have a long ride back. We should go to her now. She's obviously—"

"Look!" Oliver interrupted, seeing a shadow moving across the sand from the north. "It's him!"

"The Marauder?" Brodie rasped.

"He's walking toward the woman!"

Brodie grabbed the scope from Oliver's hands and peered down the dune. Could it be the same Marauder Marcs had seen? But why would he wait so long to rob

Chapter 14

or kill a lost woman who was clearly destitute?

"You're right," Brodie whispered. "It's him."

Fear spiked Oliver's gut as he exchanged a glance with his friend.

They could wait and see what the Marauder did. Or they could rush in and try to save the woman lying on the sand. The woman who was probably Emilia's mother.

The man approaching was large, but he was just one man. Brodie was also large for his age, and Oliver was skilled with a knife and the bow now slung across his back. If they waited, they could be too late. There was no telling what the Marauder would do with the woman.

"We go," Brodie said, seemingly thinking the same thing as Oliver.

Oliver considered their options again. "He isn't looking for us," he whispered. "We can move close enough for me to bring him down with an arrow to his leg. That juniper to the east."

Brodie studied the juniper tree, then the man below, and finally nodded. "Let's go."

How many times had they stalked game in this same way? Too many to count.

They kept low, keeping to the far side of the dune as they raced toward the small lone tree jutting out from several boulders.

In less than a minute they reached the boulders.

"Hurry, he's almost on top of her," Brodie panted. "Any closer and you risk hitting the woman."

Oliver whipped his bow around and withdrew an arrow. "You doubt my aim?"

"I'm just saying. That's probably Emilia's mother."

True. Enough said.

Brodie dropped to a squat behind the boulders as Oliver nocked an arrow and drew the bow, taking aim at the Marauder now only ten feet from the woman. It was dark, too dark, and his fingers trembled. He shifted his aim for the man's legs. If he missed, the arrow should plow harmlessly into the sand.

Deep breath, he thought. It steadied him.

He stilled his breathing, let a beat pass, and released the bow string.

✦ ✦ ✦

Quinn approached Silvia with quick, easy strides. The sand was soundless beneath his feet and, as he neared Silvia, he checked for signs of awareness. He could see her face now. Her eyes were still closed, and her nostrils flared slightly with deep, even breaths. Good.

He stopped and studied her for a moment and

Chapter 14

was about to close the distance between them when something sharp brushed the side of his thigh.

Pain rushed down his leg, and he jerked back. An arrow was lodged in the sand to his right.

Quinn spun in the direction the arrow must have come from. Sixty yards away, a tall body flew across the sands, racing toward him. Marauders!

Quinn launched himself to meet the invader, yanking two blades from either side of his belt. Another arrow flew and struck the meaty part of Quinn's upper arm. He grunted as the arrow spun him around.

Surprised, he drew his eyes up and saw another figure standing beside the juniper, nocking another arrow in the bow. So, there were two attackers.

Quinn dropped from the archer's line of sight as the closer enemy closed the distance between them in long strides. He yanked the embedded arrow from his arm and tossed it aside.

The running attacker carried a heavy club raised high overhead. Quinn ducked and swiveled away as the assailant's club fell in a mighty swing. It barely missed Quinn's injured arm, and he used the moment of the assailant's recovery to ram his elbow into the man's back.

The attacker stumbled with a painful cry but kept his footing and pivoted toward Quinn, poised for another assault. Quinn caught the invader's face in the moonlight and noticed he wasn't a man but a boy. The revelation stalled Quinn for a moment as the boy gritted his teeth and surged toward him again.

Quinn jumped back and blocked the club with his blades. He thrust up and pushed the boy's club back. Then he attacked, stepping forward and slicing at the tall figure with his knife. The boy jerked back, but Quinn's blade tore open the boy's tunic.

The boy glanced down, distracted for a second, and Quinn moved before he could recover. He bent at the waist and used his head like a battering ram, knocking the boy from his feet and slamming him against the sand. With a grunt, air rushed from the boy's chest. The boy tried to roll away, but Quinn didn't allow him to rise.

In three long strides, he was over the boy, dagger raised.

In the next breath, he slammed his blade deep into the boy's exposed chest.

✦ ✦ ✦

Oliver rushed out from behind the brush as the Marauder slammed into Brodie's body. He flew across the sand, desperately trying to restring another arrow.

Chapter 14

But he was unsteady. Terror gnawed at Oliver's gut. The next seconds slowed like dripping water from a faucet.

Brodie hit the sand hard.

The Marauder rushed.

Brodie tried to roll away.

The Marauder seized Brodie and poised one of his blades overhead.

And then plunged his knife into Brodie's chest.

Oliver staggered and then raced on as a terrible gasp escaped Brodie's lips.

"No!" Oliver cried and the Marauder yanked his blade free.

Oliver dropped his bow and pulled his dagger free as he approached. His mind darkened.

He would kill this man.

Still twenty paces out, he threw his dagger. The Marauder was on his feet and blocked the blade. The clang of metal on metal punctuated the night air.

Oliver pulled up, realizing his mistake. He had dropped his bow. His knife lay uselessly on the sand beside the Brodie's prone body. He was without a weapon, mind numb.

The Marauder rushed him, and at the last possible moment, Oliver managed to get his feet moving. But that movement took him backward and he had little control. He stumbled.

The Marauder reached him before he could regain his footing, slammed his foot against Oliver's chest, and sent him flying back through the air. His seat hit the sand first, followed by his head, which crashed into something hard.

Pain exploded up his spine.

The world spun and before Oliver could form another thought...

It went dark.

CHAPTER 15

AS PROMISED, THE HERMIT didn't come back in the night to murder Emily. In fact, he didn't return at all. When the sun rose, Emilia and Darrian returned to the skies. Following the call to the Silver Towers, they traveled another twelve hours before Darrian announced they were nearly there.

They'd had to fly lower due to the graying clouds that promised rain. Emilia was grateful they were close, because flying on a dragon during a rainstorm seemed like a bad idea.

Darrian flew around a steep mountain and into a deep canyon in a rugged landscape, surely impassible by horse or foot. There, at the end of the gorge, towered massive, stone-faced cliffs; and near the top, carved into the stone, the Silver Towers came into view. The sight of it took Emilia's breath away. Even from this distance it looked massive.

Made entirely of stone, it resembled a temple or castle of sorts. A large, pointed steeple rose from the center. A dozen openings, long and oval, large enough for dragons to enter, lined the face of the structure. The stone was covered with long vines of ivy, though the stone shimmered through the ivy as if it was made of diamonds. A large oval platform and what looked like a main arched entrance stood at the tower's base, which was at least a thousand feet from the canyon floor. It was twice the size of the others and sealed with long timber planks.

"Wow," she said.

Darrian remained silent, but she could feel mixed emotions sweeping through him: a thrill of new discovery, deep sorrow, a small edge of fear, gratefulness. All jumbled into one ball of conflicting feeling.

This was where he had been made, and where the Silvers who had made him were killed.

Darrian flew down and landed on the bottom platform. She sat on his back, staring in wonder. Behind them, the deep canyon remained as quiet as stone. The towers rose, old but majestic, before them. Everything was perfectly still. Abandoned.

Emilia had known that would be the case, because the Silvers had all been destroyed in the War of Dragons. Still, her heart had secretly hoped to be

Chapter 15

greeted by them.

The air was chilling as the sun faded, drawing the high tower into the coming night. Darrian lowered his neck, and Emilia slid down to the stone platform. They stared at the massive boarded-up entrance.

"I wonder who made this?" Emilia asked.

He remained silent.

She looked up at him. "Are you okay?"

I don't know how to feel, he said. Which was true because she could still feel his bundle of emotions and couldn't characterize the whole of them any better than he could.

Emilia left Darrian and placed her hand on the timber planks. They were stacked flush, one on top of the other, with no gaps she could see. She dragged her fingers across them, looking for a way in. A sharp splinter sliced her finger and blood sprang to the surface. She hissed in pain and yanked her hand away. "Ouch!"

Are you alright?

"Yes," she said, sucking on the end of her finger. The cut was far more than a prick. She would have to be careful with her finger. "We're not getting in this way."

A voice calls me forward. Darrian took a step toward the timber-covered archway. *Do you hear it?*

Emilia heard nothing but the soft thud of his paws as he approached.

"No."

Darrian didn't respond. Emilia stepped back as he neared, and when he was within six feet of the archway, the timber planks began to tremble. She froze at the sight, blinking hard to ensure the long flight hadn't affected her ability to see clearly. No, she thought. The timber was vibrating. Then turning to sawdust.

Starting on the edges and working its way to the middle, as if a thousand invisible termites were eating away at the wood, the planks dissolved. Slowly, but then with increased speed, a massive arched hall leading into the towering temple appeared.

"Whoa," Emilia whispered. "How did you do that?"

I didn't.

"But it opened for you."

Darrian stared at the mound of sawdust along the floor. The wind picked it up and swirled it around their feet. He lifted his head. *We should go inside.*

Fear crept up Emilia's back. She peered through the entrance and saw dark shadows covering most of the floor and walls. Her breath came slow and shallow while her heart raced.

Don't be afraid, little rider.

Darrian walked through the arched entrance and, taking a deep breath, Emilia followed. Inside, the walls and floor were covered in a thick layer of stale-smelling

Chapter 15

dust. They were in a sizeable round room with a domed ceiling. An atrium, perhaps, with a huge arched hallway to their right, which Darrian immediately entered as if drawn by an unseen force. Everything was massive—but of course it was, because it had been made for huge dragons.

She followed him down the passage, and they soon entered a second room nearly as large as the atrium. It too had a large domed ceiling with large cutouts in the stone revealing the sunset sky. The walls held more archways leading deeper into the towers. The floor was made of a smooth white marble, and in the center sat a large white fountain that was dry.

As Emilia approached the fountain with Darrian, she noticed layers of dust and wondered how long it had been since water flowed through it. Assuming it had been water. For all she knew, liquid light might have flowed through this fountain. It was, after all, the most impossible place, constructed of dreams.

But this was no dream. It was as real as her own body.

They stood silently for a little while as Darrian circled to the far side of the fountain, his attention acutely fixed on the towering spout where something—probably water—had once gushed.

"What is it?" Emilia asked.

I know why I was brought here.

He closed his eyes without another word, inhaled deeply, and then blew a forceful breath out through wide-open jaws. The air swirled around the fountain, drawing up the dust. A gurgling sound erupted at the fountain's base, and within seconds, water started to trickle out of the top. Slowly at first, and then gushing out. The water flooded the fountain's stone basin, which quickly began to fill.

One at a time, lanterns around the room lit up. The flickering flame ignited in each glass lantern, chasing the shadows from the room and casting an orange hue across the floor. Emilia watched in stunned silence. Just like the timber planks across the entryway, this room was reacting to Darrian.

He dipped his snout into the fountain and drank deep. She wondered if she should drink as well, but the idea felt strange. This was a place for dragons, and she was just a girl.

He raised his head, satisfied.

"So why *were* you brought here?" she finally asked.

His eyes darted to her finger. She glanced down and saw a couple drops of blood from her cut had dripped onto the fountain's edge.

"Sorry," she said.

Come.

Chapter 15

Emilia walked around to where he stood. "What is it?"

Show me your finger, he said, lowering his head so his eyes were just above her.

She lifted her hand toward him. He shut his eyes, and a large tear slipped down his cheek and landed on her wounded finger, seeping into her cut with a tingle.

She watched in stunned silence as, before her eyes, the cut sealed shut and vanished as though it had never been. Perfect pink flesh met her gaze where a bloody puncture should have been. She blinked and looked up at Darrian, who smiled.

I've come to receive my gifts, he said.

"Your gifts?" She glanced back at her finger.

Gifts that will help me come into my fullness and do what I've come to do.

"Your tears just healed me!"

Healing waters of peace. He said it like he'd always known this.

"Will there be more gifts?"

Yes, but not tonight. I must rest, as should you, little rider.

Emilia nodded as Darrian moved to the wall, turned in a circle, and laid his scaled body along the base. Suddenly feeling exhausted, Emily moved to snuggle down alongside Darrian, glad for his warmth.

"What else do you think we'll find here?" She whispered as she placed her folded hands underneath her head.

Sleep, little rider. All will be known soon enough.

Emilia wasn't sure she'd get her mind to stop spinning with the marvel of what had just happened. It was the last thing she remembered before falling into a deep slumber.

✦✦✦

Emilia.

She jerked her eyes open as the soft voice echoed in her mind like a whisper. Must have been in her dreams.

She pushed up from the hard ground and looked around. Darrian still slept behind her. The fountain flowed peacefully, filling the air with a comforting sound. The sky through the domed ceiling cutouts was turning from black to blue with the coming of a new dawn.

Emilia.

This time she was sure she heard the voice chasing away the last of her sleep.

She scrambled to her feet and glanced back at Darrian, who was gently snoring in sound sleep. It wasn't his voice in her head.

Chapter 15

Emilia, come.

She spun to an arched hall on the far side of the fountain, sure the voice had come from that direction. On the other hand, that seemed impossible, because if she wasn't mistaken the voice came from her own mind, as Darrian's did when he spoke to her.

Come to me, daughter.

Now the voice seemed to be outside of her and definitely from the passageway ahead. It was warm and inviting, and the word *daughter* briefly made her think about her father. But she knew this wasn't him.

Who did the voice belong to?

She hurried across the room and entered the arched passage, then continued down it, not bothered by the fact that the hallway was almost completely dark. Within thirty paces, she could faintly see stairs leading up, lit by small lanterns. She took the stairs carefully, as the warmth called to her like beckoning fingers.

Reaching the top of the stairs, she felt a chilly breeze sweep across her shoulders. Tingles spread down her spine as the wind played with her hair. This must be a balcony or something outside. She stepped out onto a semicircular platform much like the one she and Darrian first landed on, except much smaller.

The view from this small landing was stunning. Tall mountains stretched high and wide, but she wasn't looking at the same canyon they'd flown through earlier. Here, a bright green forest filled with lush trees met a crystal river that flowed through vast golden fields. It looked like a painting. She'd never seen anything like it.

The platform had no railing and was covered by a stone canopy, as though the space had been scooped out of the mountain. In the middle sat a simple, backless wooden bench. Far too small for any dragon.

Emilia. Come. Sit.

Maybe she *was* still dreaming. No, it was all too real. But dreams also felt real.

Either way, the voice felt . . . safe. Strong and certain. Inviting without a hint of uncertainty. She didn't know a voice could feel safe, but this one seemed to reach into her bones with reassurance. She walked across the platform to the bench and slowly sat.

"I'm here," Emilia whispered. A warm, gentle breeze flowed over her as if responding with approval, which she knew couldn't be true. It was only wind. But that wasn't true either. This was no dream, and the wind was more than wind.

The time is coming, Emilia.

"What time?" Emilia asked.

The time for transformation. The time to understand your purpose.

"Because I'm the dragon rider?"

Chapter 15

No. Because you are mine.

Emilia felt her heart skip.

"Who are you?"

I am the alpha and the omega, the beginning and the end. I am true love, and I call you my daughter. Some have called me Yeshua, but no human word can hold me, because my true name is in the wind. If you listen for my voice, you will know.

She immediately believed the source of those words calling to her heart. She was hearing the voice of something greater than the entire world. God, she thought. The voice that had called itself Yeshua had to be the voice of God.

"And who am I?" she said.

You are my daughter.

His use of the word *daughter* flooded Emilia with warmth again. But then an image of her father being executed filled her mind, and she felt the familiar sorrow that had hidden in her mind all these weeks. Father was gone. And her mother...

She couldn't imagine losing her. It would be too much!

"I lost my father," she said.

And my heart aches with you for the loss you feel. Life brings challenges to all. But you will soon learn that your father can never be lost. Neither the father who brought you into this world; nor I, your father throughout all of time. Set your heart on me, dear daughter. I will make your burdens light and your work easy. The path is found in the way of love that the Guardians have spoken of.

His words brought her a deep comfort that chased away her sorrow. Sitting here now at the Silver Towers, she was suddenly sure that nothing could *ever* go wrong. But knowing that didn't qualify her to save the Guardians from the Order. She was still just a girl.

"I don't really know the Guardians' ways," she said. "They're strange to me."

The voice chuckled, not in a dismissive way, but in the way that might say, "I know what you mean." *The way of love is lost even on the Guardians,* he said. *That way is much simpler than any human knows. Soon all will see that love can never coexist with fear. Love can only be forgotten, which is what leads to fear.*

"I'm not even sure what that means. And I really don't think I'm qualified to be the dragon rider just because the golden egg hatched for me."

Ah . . . But in time all will become clear. I have called you and I ask you to follow. Fly with me, little rider. I am, and always have been, with you, closer than your own breath.

Emilia sniffed. She hadn't even realized she started crying as tears ran down her cheeks. The voice stirred

Chapter 15

something profound in her chest, something that had remained hidden until now, here, hearing the voice of the wind called Yeshua.

"What if I'm not ready? What if I'm afraid?"

Fear is a lie encountered only when you forget who you are. But even then, I am always with you, from the beginning to the end.

The wind whipped over her cheeks, drying her tears and filling her chest with reassurance. Emilia closed her eyes and rested in the safety.

You will be tempted to defy love. You will want to pick up the sword in fear. Remember always that those who live by the sword, die by the sword. Instead, you will show them the way of love, dear daughter. I am that way. Only the way of love can save you and the world.

She was about to ask for clarification, but before she could, something touched her right knee and she opened her eyes, startled. A pure white dove sat on her knee and looked up at her, head cocked, eyes focused.

Emilia smiled as another dove sailed in on the wind and landed on the bench beside her. A dozen more came over the next few seconds. Each one settled down and curiously eyed Emilia. She giggled, surprised by the sight of so many.

"Where did you come from?" she asked. She remembered her mother once telling her that doves were often a sign of peace. As she looked at them, she decided her mother must be right. They were peaceful little birds.

I left you a gift, daughter.

"A gift?"

Under the bench. Take it.

Emilia leaned over, and the dove on her knee fluttered off to join the others perched nearby. She found a small box only a couple of inches long and high, made of wood like the bench, and pulled it into her lap. She lifted the lid. Inside, resting on purple silk, was a vial of liquid. It shimmered through the glass as Emilia lifted it to take a closer look. The fluid had a golden hue and was thick like oil, moving slowly as she tilted the vial side to side.

When the time comes, this gift will help you see.

"See what?"

All in time, daughter. For now, remember that I will always be with you. I have always been with you. Nothing can separate you from me. When you fear, remember that you have only forgotten who you are.

More warmth flooded Emilia's chest as she held the vial to her heart and exhaled.

Emilia!

This voice was familiar and worried. The second it echoed in her mind; the doves scattered to the sky and flew away. The breeze lingered a moment more, then

Chapter 15

seemed to follow the birds.

Darrian was awake.

✦ ✦ ✦

Emilia found Darrian where she'd left him in the fountain room.

I woke and you were gone, he said.

"Sorry," Emilia said. She wanted to tell Darrian what had happened, but held it close to her heart for now. *In time,* she thought. Instead, she said, "I was exploring."

Come. We must go beneath.

"Beneath?"

Darrian didn't answer. Instead, he walked to another arched passageway, and Emilia followed close behind. She couldn't explain it, but something about this place filled her with ease. It was as if the walls themselves held the spirit of the Silvers who'd once lived here, dragons that had been a friend to humanity. Helpers. They were the personification of love, Oliver had told her. They might no longer be physically present, walking the halls of the Silver Towers, but their love and souls seemed to lace the very air she breathed.

Darrian led her down a hallway to another set of stairs that dropped into darkness. But she wasn't afraid. As Darrian descended, lanterns came to life just like they had in the fountain room. He was following another call, and excitement tinged Emilia's pulse.

The stairs descended deep into the mountain, and in time they came to a massive, towering cave larger than any Emilia had ever seen. It seemed to have no ceiling—and maybe it didn't. Maybe she was looking into a starless sky.

The ground was rocky and littered with ash. In the center was a black lake, small as far as lakes go, inky and still. The walls were covered in soot, charred and black. Darrian approached the lake and peered into its depths.

Emilia realized that the lake wasn't actually black. It was pure and clean and reflected the darkness from above, so it looked black. Deep beneath the surface, at the lake's very center, something glowed. She leaned forward to ensure she was seeing correctly. At the bottom of the lake sat a glowing ember about the size of a pumpkin. And judging by the boiling water that surrounded it, the object was hot. Was that even possible?

She turned to Darrian and saw him staring at the ember with fixed fascination. His blue eyes reflected the hot ember, so that they seemed to glow.

Without a word, Darrian leaped into the air and dove into the water.

Chapter 15

She jumped back from the splash and watched his huge body vanish into the depths until she could no longer see him at all. Then the ember went out. The lake once again became perfectly still. Had he eaten it?

Her heart was pounding. Had he actually eaten the glowing ember? But that seemed rather far-fetched. Then again, she supposed that everything about dragons was rather far-fetched—as far-fetched as Yeshua speaking to her on the balcony. And that had happened for real, so maybe Darrian really had . . .

The water suddenly boiled to life, and Darrian burst through its surface and flew high into the air like an arrow shot straight up. He opened his mouth to roar. From his gaping jaws, flame erupted.

Emilia stared in shock as the fire licked the darkness.

Darrian could breathe fire.

CHAPTER 16

OLIVER STIRRED AND OPENED his eyes. In the fog of coming to, he felt himself swaying but had no idea where he was until he managed to sit up. It was day, and he was on his horse, hands tied to the saddle, and feet secured in the stirrups. Ahead of him a few horse lengths to his right, two more rode on a second horse, crossing the desert. The wind was strong and gusty, whipping sand across his body. It took a moment for his memories to return.

Brodie had been stabbed.

Oliver twisted his head, looking for his friend, but he didn't see him. Panic gripped him as he turned back toward the lead horse and now saw that it carried the Marauder and Emilia's mother, Silvia. He and Brodie had failed spectacularly.

"Where is he?" Oliver croaked. His throat felt as dry

as the sand. "Where's my friend?"

The Marauder gave Oliver a glance. "Buried in the desert where he belongs."

A terrible desperation swallowed Oliver whole. Buried meant dead. *No! He can't be dead!* But even as the thoughts fought for support in his mind, Oliver remembered the way his friend had been stabbed. Center of the chest—a wound no one could survive.

"You murdered him!" Oliver managed to utter.

The man said nothing. He didn't even glance back. Oliver stole a glance at Silvia, who was bound and gagged in front the man and looking at Oliver with terrified eyes. Emilia's eyes—that much was plain to see.

He swallowed. *Dear God, what have I done?*

She turned away, powerless.

Their predicament was so overwhelming that he almost missed the obvious: they were headed north, not southwest toward the Marauders' home. Perhaps their captor wasn't a Marauder.

"Where are we going?" Oliver demanded.

"Capital City," the man answered, looking back at him.

"So . . . So, you're not a Marauder."

The man turned ahead. "I am in the service of the Overseer, who will want to meet you, Guardian."

Chapter 16

✦✦✦

They traveled ceaselessly for two long days, during which time their captor said almost nothing, not even his name, and he allowed them to say even less.

Oliver kept his eyes on the horizon, hoping for sight of any rescue. His father and the others would be scouring the desert for signs of them. They surely had found the site where Brodie was killed, but the strong winds had probably covered most of their tracks. As the second day plodded past, he gave up hope of rescue. Maybe he didn't deserve it anyway.

Capital City came into view near the end of the second day, and by the time their captor led a fully secured and gagged Oliver and Silvia into the city, the stars were out. Soldiers met them and threw a bag over the mother's head. She struggled against her restraints as they threw her into a caged cart and galloped away.

His captor led Oliver toward a palace at the city's center.

He watched as the city neighborhoods went from poor to rich. He'd never been inside Capital City, but Emilia had told him about it during some of their many talks. They had rings that signified the citizens' status, and the sight of these, even in the dim light, was unsettling. Starving children begged for food on dirty streets in the outer rings, while the privileged dined and laughed in decorated cafés closer to the palace. The whole scene felt surreal, and he wondered why Emilia hadn't run away sooner. It was all quite disturbing to him.

His captor yanked Oliver from the seat of his horse and hastily led him up a grand staircase and through wide double doors. Once inside, he didn't have much time to study the palace, but even at a glance, he couldn't miss the opulence. Thick velvet curtains, shiny marble floors, gold-plated window frames, and towering stone pillars. He'd never seen so much wealth.

He was quickly led into a small, dark room and forced into a wooden chair. Across from him, a woman with piercing eyes studied him, and he immediately guessed that she was the Overseer his captor had mentioned. Intensity was carved in every line of her sharp face. Dark eyes and dark hair, long dark dress. Darkness seemed to seep from her skin.

The man who'd murdered Brodie spoke quietly into her ear. She listened, then nodded, dismissing the man from the room. Two guards stood along the wall behind the woman. Oliver imagined more were stationed outside the closed door.

"Do you know who I am?" the woman asked.

Oliver hesitated. "The Overseer."

Chapter 16

She smiled. "Good. I hear a friend of yours met an unfortunate end at the hands of my man."

The way the Overseer spoke so casually about Brodie's death made his blood boil. She would pay for this with her life one day. Even though it wasn't the Guardian way, he would make it his way.

"What do you want?" Oliver spat out.

The Overseer exhaled and motioned behind her. "You're angry. We've started on the wrong foot." A guard stepped forward and produced a water flask.

Oliver's throat ached.

"You must be dying of thirst," the Overseer said.

The guard lifted the flask to Oliver's mouth. Despite his anger, his body was in desperate need of hydration. He took several long swallows, water dripping from the corners of his mouth, before the guard withdrew the flask and returned to his post.

"Better," the Overseer said. "Now, you must know that I alone can ensure that you and Emilia's mother are fed and made comfortable."

The Overseer knew Emilia and her mother. The truth dropped like a stone into Oliver's gut. What had he walked into?

"That is, until you're executed for your crimes against the Order," the Overseer said, leaning back with a glint of pleasure in her eyes. "Surely you didn't think you would live through this without making some clear choices, did you?"

"If you're going to kill me either way, then why are we talking?" Oliver snapped.

"Because I want the dragon, and you know where it is. That information will buy your life. Choices."

The words cut Oliver like a blade. She knew about the dragon? How?

"I know more than you could imagine. You and your Guardians are in way over your heads." She folded her hands on her knees and continued. "The question is, how do you want to spend your final days? Starving in a dark cell, or comfortable with a full belly? And if you are plainly forthright, I might even let you live."

Oliver felt as deeply unnerved as he could recall ever feeling, but he sat perfectly still, trying not to show his fear. "You'll never find them," he said.

She gave a small laugh and leaned forward, nothing but hate in her eyes. All signs of humor vanished. "I already have."

The ticking of the clock on the wall was the only sound for a few long seconds. Oliver tried to think of anything he could say to help him or his people, but his mind was blank. He was exhausted. There was nothing.

The Overseer tapped her fingers together impatiently. "Nothing to say?" she asked.

Chapter 16

Oliver would sleep with rats in the sewer before helping her, and his expression must have communicated precisely that.

"Very well, damp and dark it is," she said. She stood and started for the door. Stopping at Oliver's side, she placed a hand on his shoulder.

"I'll give you a little time to reconsider. All I need is the name of your dragon rider and her location. We don't need you for this, but it would make life a little easier. The offer stands."

With that, the Overseer left the room.

Oliver swallowed. So, she didn't know the rider was Emilia. That was something, he thought.

The guards hauled him out of his seat and dragged him below the palace to the dungeons. Only when the gate of his dark cell closed and the sounds of the guards' retreating boots fell silent did Oliver crumple to the cold, damp floor and weep.

✦ ✦ ✦

It was impossible to tell time in the depths of the dungeon. Hours or days might have passed. Oliver cried himself sore, then found the boundaries of his black coffin with his fingers, then went back to weeping until he fell asleep. He dreamed of his father and how disappointed he'd be with Oliver's deception. He thought of Emilia and how sad she'd be about her mother. He thought of all the children in Zion and prayed they didn't end up in a cell like this one.

Something clinked in the distance, and he shot up from where he lay. He waited for more noise, and when nothing came, he lay back down. Then something did scuff the ground closer to his cell door, and he pushed all the way to his feet.

"Hello?" he called out.

"Shh," someone responded. Then in a whisper, "Come to the gate."

Oliver stepped forward cautiously. The stranger on the other side of the bars lit a match. The flame illuminated the space enough for Oliver to see that the stranger was a boy, no older than himself, with dark eyes and a near-shaved head. The matchstick he held was about three inches long, but would burn quickly.

"I can get you out of here," the boy whispered.

"Who are you?" Oliver asked.

"A friend." The boy held up a thick iron key.

"But who?"

The boy frowned. "Do you want my life story, or do you want me to try to save you?"

Fair enough.

Oliver gave a swift nod as the matchstick burned

Chapter 16

to its midway point. The boy cursed under his breath until he finally popped the lock open.

"Where did you get—"

"Not now," the boy interrupted. "Hurry!"

He yanked the gate open and motioned Oliver to follow. Oliver didn't hesitate.

The kid struck another match, and they hurried down the long stone walkway that led away from the cell before turning down a passage on the right. The boy let out a hiss as the matchstick burned to his fingertips and then went out. Oliver paused, and a second later another matchstick flared to light. The boy threw Oliver a devious smile, and then continued around another corner and to a small staircase.

The boy paused at the bottom and listened. Hearing nothing, he took the stairs two at a time. Oliver followed the boy into a stone corridor. It was impossible to tell where they were, but the air up here was less stuffy, surely closer to the surface.

The corridor was wide and short, with a heavy wooden door at the end. They reached the door, and the boy held up a finger for Oliver to wait for his signal. He stretched up onto his toes and looked through the small square cut-out high in the wood. A minute later he gave Oliver a nod and pushed the door open.

Oliver followed him into the open air, letting the

fresh breeze fill his lungs as he looked around: mud and grass underfoot, wooden fences, feeding troughs, a simple stable.

"We run for it," the boy said, pointing to the stable twenty yards away.

Oliver nodded and the two raced across the open air. Fear thundered with Oliver's footsteps as he pushed himself forward. He was tired and weak, but he'd rather be killed right now than go back inside that cell to wait for a more formal execution.

The boy slid around the corner of the stable and stopped, Oliver right on his heels. He looked out to make sure they hadn't been spotted, then turned to give Oliver a grin.

"Halfway."

"Halfway to what?" Oliver asked, panting.

"We don't have time for all your questions," the boy said. "But I'm Zac."

Oliver gave him a nod. "Oliver. At least tell me why you're helping me?"

"Is it true that you're a Guardian?" the boy asked, eyes wide. He seemed impressed by the thought, so Oliver leaned into it.

"I am, and more skilled than many other Guardians."

"Not everyone in this city believes in the Order," Zac said. "Many of us are waiting for a change. Just like your

Chapter 16

people wait."

Oliver's father had always claimed that there were some, though few, who lived in Capital City, but believed in the ways of Seers. This boy was clearly among them.

"How did you know I was in the dungeons?" he asked the boy.

"We have eyes and ears in the places that count. And that stupid spy led you straight through town," Zac said. The boy strode to a pair of horses already saddled. "You don't have a lot of time. I used the guard change to sneak you out, so any minute now the new shift lead is going to see you're missing."

Oliver joined him beside one of the horses. It was already prepared, including saddle bags that looked to be stocked.

"Who are you with? Why send a boy?"

"Are you saying a small boy who can sneak around is less valuable than a big hulk who is easily seen?" Zac shot back defensively. The boy definitely had an edge.

"No, I meant no offense. Just trying to understand."

"No need. Just get out and go back to your people. Tell them what we did for you."

Oliver nodded. "I will."

"I'll lead you to the edge of the southern border here," Zac said. "You have another hour of darkness before sunrise, so you should go unseen. Then the rest is up to you."

Zac handed Oliver the reins, then climbed atop the second horse. He motioned with his head, and Oliver mounted his steed quickly. Zac clicked his tongue and led his horse out the back of the stable.

They rode quietly and kept to the long shadows of buildings as they made their way to the border, just as Zac had explained. They had to backtrack twice to avoid being seen, but finally the desert came into view.

Zac pulled his horse to a stop. "You're on your own from here," he said.

"Thank you," Oliver replied. He felt like he should offer more, but the sun was already starting to rise.

"Don't let the desert kill you after I did all this work."

Oliver gave the boy a small grin. "I know the desert. I'll be fine. You should come with me."

"No. My place is here. Good luck, Guardian." Then Zac turned his horse and casually trotted away.

Oliver looked out at the desert. For a moment he considered that not two hours ago he had faced certain death. Now the desert called him home. Could it really be this easy? He shook the thought free. The Overseer had told him she already knew where the Guardians were. Was she bluffing? In case she wasn't, he needed

Chapter 16

to get to Zion fast. And he'd have to stop and collect the body of his friend along the way.

Grief pressed against his throat as he kicked the side of this horse and headed into the desert.

CHAPTER 17

"IS IT DONE?" Victoria asked the boy, who pulled his mount next to hers.

"As promised," the boy said. "Though I'd be suspicious if I were him. Pulling all the guards made it pretty easy."

"I don't care about his suspicions," Victoria said. "He has nowhere else to go but back."

The boy shrugged and Victoria reached into her pocket and pulled out a hefty fistful of coins. "You've done the Order a great service." She placed the money in his hand, and his eyes lit up with delight. As an orphan, that amount would keep him fed and give him a roof over his head for a long time.

"If you need anything else—"

"That will be enough. And if you ever speak of this to a soul, I will throw you in the dungeons until you starve."

The boy's smile softened. He offered a curt nod before hurrying off, satisfied. Quinn rode up to fill the boy's empty place.

"Everything is in place," Quinn said.

I can feel him. Stronger than the first, the dragon queen said in Victoria's mind. She closed her eyes to savor the presence.

She'd spiked the water in the boy's saddle bag with dragon's milk. The queen's milk. They couldn't give him too much milk or his eyes would start to cloud over and the Guardians would know he'd been poisoned. Heavy use of dragon's milk did that to all humans. Which was why Victoria was cautious about how much she herself took.

The queen had demanded to know why they hadn't sent the army after Silvia. Because they weren't sure the woman would lead them to the Guardians, Victoria had answered. But now they had dragon's milk in an actual Guardian. The boy would undoubtedly go home. And home was to the Guardians and their dragon.

This time there could be no mistakes.

This time they would all follow the boy.

"We'll let him get a day ahead, then follow," Quinn said. "If our warriors travel only at night, we'll stay out of sight."

Victoria nodded. She and Quinn would lead an

Chapter 17

army of one hundred after the boy, who would lead them directly to the Guardians.

Time is running out.

"I know, my queen," Victoria said. "We will have them in three days' time."

Prepare your blood. Do not fail me again.

The queen was referring to the fact that a dragon could only be killed with a weapon dipped in the blood of a human whose heart belonged to another dragon as the record made clear. Long ago all had known that. Today, it was lost to time but as true as always.

If she were to encounter the golden dragon, she knew what she had to do.

"I will not fail," she said.

CHAPTER 18

THREE DAYS HAD PASSED since Darrian breathed fire. Three days since Emilia had sat in the presence of Yeshua's voice on the high balcony. In a mysterious way, they had both been filled with a spirit of wonder and power that neither of them could put into words. It was their source of life, their only true need, their purpose.

They'd lingered for a day, exploring the Silver Towers, neither of them ready to leave. Emilia had such a deep sense of peace within these walls. She spent plenty of time sitting on the bench and feeding the doves, or staring out over the gorge as Darrian flew high circles before joining her on a different large balcony.

She told Darrian about the gift of oil she'd received, though she still had no idea what it was for. She'd also told him she would be tempted to defy love, and that those who lived by the sword also died by the sword. That was the way of the world when lost in fear.

I was born with that awareness, he replied. *And I will allow you to take your journey however you see fit. I'm here to serve, not correct.*

Strangely, she felt no anxiousness about any of it, nor by what her role might be as a dragon rider. She felt only a deep calm, knowing that whatever happened, even if she died, she would be just fine.

Darrian breathed small bursts of fire to ignite the fireplace they'd found on another level, then sat beside its warmth, talking about what his gifts could mean.

"You're still gray, so you haven't molted yet," Emilia observed.

I have more growing to do.

"So, receiving your gifts doesn't bring you into your fullness?"

No, little rider, not yet.

She was tiny compared to him now. Since leaving Mount Zion, Darrian had grown bigger and faster. He was nearly a full-size dragon, albeit a smaller dragon, he thought. Perhaps five horses long and two high, not including his neck and head, which were the size of yet another horse. They'd found a rope, which Emilia had tied to one of the large scales where his neck met his back, so she could climb up his leg when he stooped

Chapter 18

low. Even with his neck flat against the ground he was too tall to mount without the rope. He thought he probably wouldn't get much bigger, but he didn't know.

He was still small walking through the oval openings in the Tower's face, which made Emilia wonder how big the silver dragons must have been.

Eventually, they decided they needed to head back to Zion.

Leaving the Silver Towers was a bit of a sad affair. Something within those walls had changed her. A new cavern in her heart had opened, and what flowed from it was calming and blissful. The problems outside the stone arches didn't affect her. Or exist.

But the farther she and Darrian got from the Towers, the less peace she felt.

It took them two full days to fly back, and as the sun sank low in the desert, Mount Zion rose high before them. Her heart surged. She was struck by a feeling of homecoming that warmed her bones and made her pulse quicken. Imagine that! Home! The only thing missing was her mother.

But as the humble buildings and sweeping fields surrounding Zion came into view, she began to feel anxious. What if something had happened in the week while they were gone? A lot could happen in that much time.

She started to feel guilty for forgetting about her mother while she fed birds on the wooden bench at the Silver Towers. Then, the feelings had felt transformational, but now they felt selfish.

A small figure pointed up at Darrian as they crossed over the towering cliffs and dove for the field just beyond the village. Most of the Guardians were already gathered, and even before touching down, Emilia knew something dreadful had happened.

Just ahead, crumpled on the ground, a woman wailed into the sky. Others sank to their knees around the woman, holding her as she wept bitterly. Clara, Bastien, and Torey moved away from the grieving circle and hurried toward Darrian. Clara offered Emilia a tight smile. Her eyes were also teary.

"What happened?" Emilia asked as she slid down Darrian's leg.

Emilia's eyes were drawn back to the weeping woman and, standing just behind her, Oliver. His face was blotchy, and his eyes were red from crying. He lifted his distraught face and caught Emilia's gaze. It took everything in her not to rush to him and hug him tightly.

"Emilia," Clara said softly. "We're glad you've returned."

"Are you safe? How was the journey?" Bastien asked.

Chapter 18

Even his stern tone had softened. Something terrible had happened.

"I'm fine. What happened?" she demanded.

Torey placed a steadying hand on Emilia's shoulder. "Brodie..." He stalled and pain lurched in Emilia's chest. She held her breath as Torey searched for words.

"He died. Oliver brought his body back just before you arrived."

"No," Emilia's voice was a whisper. "I...How?"

"It's a long story but he was killed in the desert."

Alarm spread through her. Her eyes returned to the wailing woman. Brodie's mother. Emilia hadn't recognized her until now. Oliver was gone. She searched and saw him stalking off toward the orchard, his hands balled at his sides.

"There's more," Torey said.

Emilia fixed him with a demanding glare. "Tell me everything."

It took a few minutes for Torey to run through the events of the last few days. He told her everything they'd learned from Oliver, about how they'd gone to rescue her mother. About how Brodie had been killed and Oliver taken captive. Tears blurred Emilia's vision by the time he finished.

She didn't know what to say. Darrian approached and Torey stepped away to give her a moment to process.

Her mother was alive, but Brodie was not. Silvia had gone out looking for Emilia, but she was taken captive once again. The Overseer knew about the dragon and its rider, although she evidently didn't know Emilia was that rider.

The peace and comfort of the Silver Towers drained away in a few minutes. Darrian unfolded a wing and wrapped it around Emilia as she turned and hugged one of his front legs. It was solid like a tree, and his wing large enough to block the fading sun.

She cried into his scales. She cried for Brodie and for her mother, and when she couldn't cry anymore, she went looking for Oliver.

✦ ✦ ✦

As she crossed the field into the orchard, Emilia thought twilight was a beautiful time. Even on a day like today when the world felt impossibly sad. The sky was dark blue as the sunset faded, and the stars began to make their appearance. Darrian had flown ahead and found Oliver.

He was sitting against a tree, covered in shadows that hid his face, though she could hear him sniffing back his tears. She could imagine what it must be like to lose one's best friend because, in a way, her mother had

Chapter 18

always been her best friend and, for now at least, her mother was lost to her. So was Ruth, who was another best friend.

She didn't say anything as she approached, and Oliver kept quiet as well. Emilia walked to his side and sat. She just wanted him to know she was there. He lifted his head after a moment and looked at her with bloodshot eyes.

"I'm so sorry, Emilia," Oliver whispered.

"No," she said. "You don't have to apologize to me. You tried to save my mother." She blinked back tears. "This isn't your fault. It's the Overseer's."

"The Overseer," Oliver echoed bitterly. Their common enemy.

Several more beats of silence passed between them.

"I'm sorry about Brodie," Emilia whispered. "I should have been here."

"It's not your fault, Emilia," Oliver said. "It's mine."

Darrian waited twenty paces away. *He's changed*, the dragon said. *A darkness lives in him that wasn't there before.*

Emilia didn't know what Darrian meant, but death did funny things to people. So did guilt and rage. Maybe that was all the dragon meant.

"Did you find the Silver Towers?" Oliver asked, changing the subject.

"Yes."

"Will whatever you found save us?"

Emilia had been so sure the answer was yes, but now doubt crept in like a thief. "I don't know."

More silence.

"Darrian can breathe fire now," Emilia said.

Oliver turned to her; his eyes wide. She looked up at him and offered a smile.

"So, there's that," she teased, but her heart was only half in it. "And we met an old hermit Marauder who gave Darrian this," she said, showing him the necklace around her neck. Eventually she might find a way to affix the medallion to Darrian, but it felt good to wear his necklace right now.

"You met a Marauder and lived? Course, you do have a dragon. I suppose that would silence even the vilest enemy." He turned his eyes to the horizon. "A dragon that can breathe fire," Oliver said. "None of the dragons in our history could breathe fire. What a strange thing to be able to do. Cool, but strange."

I think he's strange too, but I keep my opinions to myself, Darrian said.

Emilia chuckled, and the corner of Oliver's mouth twitched with a half-smile. But it wasn't the same smile she was used to. He wasn't the same.

And Emilia couldn't shake the feeling that nothing

Chapter 18

from this moment on would ever be the same for either of them.

✦ ✦ ✦

Victoria and her army had marched across the desert as a brigade of black: black horses with riders outfitted in black, traveling under the cover of black nights. They spotted the mountain range on the third day and now stood at its towering base. The giant waterfall loudly beat down before them.

It seemed like a dead end.

The boy is near, just beyond where you stand. The queen had diligently led Victoria and the army after the boy, whose connection to the queen was strong with dragon's milk.

"Are you sure, my queen?" Victoria asked.

Do you question me? she snapped.

Victoria cringed. "No."

She dismounted and walked to the edge of the small lake that the waterfall fed. A bright moon helped them see, and she held a torch in her hand. A path led around the lake to the far side, right up to the waterfall itself, before vanishing.

She called for a Keeper named Swasi, who had once been a scout. He came quickly and dipped his head.

"Yes, my lady?"

"Find out what lies behind that waterfall."

"They have said the path ends there," the Keeper said.

"I'm aware. And now I'm telling you to go behind the waterfall and tell me what you see. Now!"

"Of course, my lady."

She watched carefully as the Keeper rode down the path, around the lake, and to the waterfall, where he appeared to vanish behind the wall of falling water. When he didn't emerge immediately, she knew the truth.

They had been hiding in plain sight all these years, right under the nose of the Order, within a three-day ride!

She waited as minutes passed and her patience grew unsteady. She imagined her queen's anxiousness.

Then the scout reappeared, racing around the lake toward Victoria. He was breathing heavily as he slid from his horse.

"I found them," the scout said, breathless. "The Guardians live in a village behind the waterfall and through a cave system. They've built a village that looks to be many years old."

"How many people?" Victoria asked.

"Over a hundred perhaps, but many are women

Chapter 18

and children."

The Order would crush them, Victoria thought.

"And the dragon?" she asked.

"No sight of it, but I was cautious. And it's dark."

The dragon is near. I can feel it, the queen whispered to Victoria, and her heart started to race. She dismissed the Keeper and turned to Quinn, who was standing at her side.

"We've found them," Victoria said as much to Quinn as to the dragon.

Good. Now destroy them.

Victoria smiled as a thrill rippled across her skin. "We attack at dawn. Spread the word."

"Why not now?" Quinn asked.

Victoria let out a good-humored huff. "I want them to see us coming."

"And what do we do when we find the dragon?"

"Leave the dragon to me. I have the weapon needed to destroy it." Victoria hadn't mentioned this to anyone—there had been no need—but she'd always known how to kill the dragon. The queen had assured her the weapon could kill any dragon. It was how they killed Silvers.

"As you wish," Quinn said and rode toward their desert camp.

Our time has finally come.

"Yes. In all things be diligent. In all things be true."

The queen purred in Victoria's chest.

Tomorrow morning, the golden dragon and its rider would die.

To Be Continued in

BOOK THREE

The Rise of The Firewalker

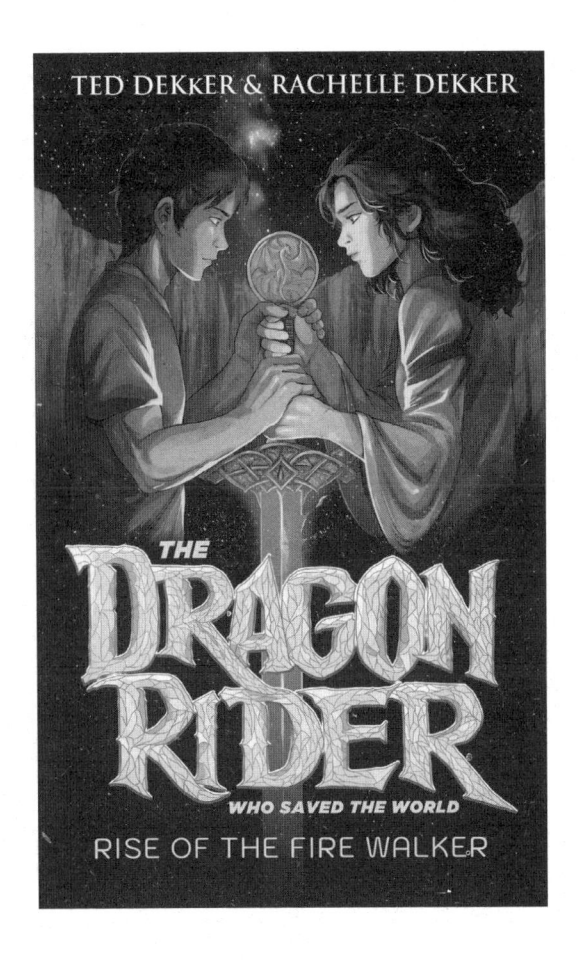

MORE ADVENTURES AWAIT

THE IMPOSSIBLE PLACES SERIES

Journey to Impossible Places

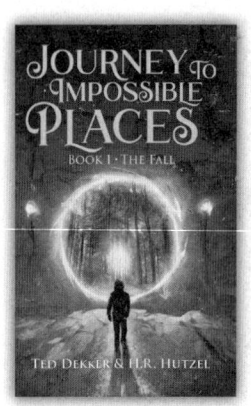

World of Impossible Things

WWW.TEDDEKKER.COM

Discover the entire
Dekker young reader universe.

THE DRAGONS SERIES

And They Found Dragons

The Dragons Among Us

WWW.TEDDEKKER.COM

THE DREAM TRAVELERS SERIES

The Dream Travelers Quest

The Dream Travelers Game

WWW.TEDDEKKER.COM

THE MILLIE MAVEN SERIES

THE DRAGON RIDER SERIES

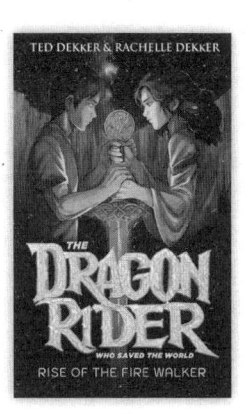

WHICH ADVENTURE WILL YOU CHOOSE?

WWW.TEDDEKKER.COM